197 — rep [?]

Theory → practice
of theory — How ede writes her text.

SITUATING COMPOSITION

p. x   Gap bet scholarship & pedagogy

P.102   Course Description re errors

P.102   Surprise to expectations

P.109   Defense of fw courses

p.82   Political motivation (Faigley)

~~p.75~~

p63   Resistance (Olson)

192 — Process — first use

75   Problem of Comp Studies. what
       ideologies → overlook.

49   Ideology = default = most powerful

Social turn — fr. 1980s (late): prior focus on
text → focus on writer + audience interaction.

Ede argues for valorization of Ts' work
+ authority

SITUATING COMPOSITION

Composition Studies and the Politics of Location

LISA EDE

SOUTHERN ILLINOIS UNIVERSITY PRESS / CARBONDALE

Library of Congress Cataloging-in-Publication Data
Ede, Lisa S., 1947–
Situating composition : composition studies and the
politics of location / Lisa Ede.
  p. cm.
Includes bibliographical references and index.
1. English language—Rhetoric—Study and teaching—
United States. 2. English language—Rhetoric—Study
and teaching—Political aspects—United States.
3. Academic writing—Study and teaching (Higher)—
United States. 4. Report writing—Study and teaching
(Higher)—United States. I. Title.

PE1405.U6E33 2004
808'.042'071073—dc22
ISBN 0-8093-2581-0 (alk. paper)
ISBN 0-8093-2582-9 (pbk. : alk. paper)   2004011168

For Andrea
And, as always, for Gregory

CONTENTS

PREFACE

Situating Composition represents my effort to make sense of the recent development of composition as an academic discipline and to inquire into the politics of composition's location in the academy. As such, *Situating Composition* is itself situated in multiple contexts. Some of these contexts will be evident to readers. Those familiar with such works as Stephen North's 1987 *The Making of Knowledge in Composition: Portrait of an Emerging Field;* Louise Phelps's 1988 *Composition as a Human Science: Contributions to the Self-Understanding of a Discipline,* Susan Miller's 1991 *Textual Carnivals: The Politics of Composition,* Lester Faigley's 1992 *Fragments of Rationality: Postmodernity and the Subject of Composition,* Sharon Crowley's 1998 *Composition in the University: Historical and Polemical Essays,* Hephzibah Roskelly and Kate Ronald's 1998 *Reason to Believe: Romanticism, Pragmatism, and the Teaching of Writing,* Bruce Horner's 2000 *Terms of Work for Composition: A Materialist Critique,* Geoffrey Sirc's 2002 *English Composition as a Happening,* and Chris Gallagher's 2002 *Radical Departures: Composition and Progressive Pedagogy* will recognize that this study participates in a long-standing scholarly conversation about the nature and status of composition as an academic discipline—and about the multiple consequences of composition's professionalization.

It is for readers of this text to determine whether *Situating Composition* represents a productive contribution to this conversation. In this preface, I want to comment on some of the ways this study is situated in my experience as a teacher and writing program administrator. Not that these connections are absent in the study itself. At various points, I bring my own experience into—rather than exclude it from—my analysis: The scenarios that open chapter 1 are an example of such an inclusion. What I want to comment on here are some subtler connections between lived experience and scholarly work, connections that help to clarify the motivation and perspective that I bring to this study. I also want, if only briefly, to call attention to the material contexts, catalysts, and collaborations that have made this study possible.

Perhaps the strongest catalyst for this study was the desire to make sense of my own experience. When I "converted" from literature to composition in the mid-1970s, the scholarly field of composition studies did not exist— at least not in any conventional sense. There were a few PhD programs in composition, though most PhD students in English departments were unaware of them. Nor were these students aware of the scholarly work on composition undertaken by such early scholars as Fred Newton Scott and Gertrude Buck or being done at the time by Edward P. J. Corbett, Janet Emig, James Kinneavy, Janice Lauer, and others. Only near the end of my graduate work did I become aware of these developments. Since that time, composition has achieved if not full disciplinarity then something remarkably close to it. Composition is recognized as a scholarly field in most PhD programs in English studies, and as a field it has developed a full complement of professional associations, journals, conferences, book series, and scholarly awards.

This is a considerable achievement—one that I value, have worked to support, and have benefited from. And yet it is an achievement that comes with costs and dilemmas. In *Situating Composition,* I attempt to inquire into the multiple consequences of composition's professionalization. As I do so, I raise a number of questions about the ethics, politics, and rhetoric of scholarly work in composition. How can scholars best understand the relationship between what I refer to in chapter 5 as "the practice of theory" and "the practice of teaching" in composition? (Chapter 5 defines my use of the term "theory," which I see as an overdetermined term.) Given our privileged position in academic and professional hierarchies of knowledge, how can scholars productively address what feminist philosopher Linda Alcoff refers to as "the problem of speaking for others" when we write about teachers and students (5)? Given the gap between the scholarly theories presented in articles and books and the pedagogical practices enacted daily in many first-year and advanced composition classrooms, how can scholars in composition best assess the impact (or the lack thereof) of our theories? What *are* scholars claiming when we claim that the field of composition studies has decisively rejected the writing process for social process and post-process theories? What, for that matter, constitutes progress in a field that is committed to pedagogical as well as scholarly action?

As my use of the pronoun "our" in the previous paragraph suggests, as I address these and related questions, I attempt to hold myself accountable for the problems and difficulties my text exposes. I attempt, in other words, to write not as someone who has already seen and understood the issues that my text uncovers but rather as someone who is implicated in—and continues to struggle with—these issues. The questions that I articulate about the scholarly work of composition are questions that I hold about my own work as well.

When I think about my preoccupation with questions such as these, I can identify a number of influences that have encouraged me to try to look hard at, rather than turn away from, these dilemmas and difficulties. I have spent my entire academic career teaching in two English departments, neither of which offers a PhD in English.[1] As a consequence, when I teach classes in composition theory to advanced undergraduate and MA students, I am always working with—and learning from—students who are new to the scholarly work of composition. These students—many of whom are teaching first-year writing as graduate teaching assistants or are in our Master of Arts in Teaching (MAT) program and are taking my class to fulfill a requirement—have proven wonderfully adept at challenging my assumptions about theory and the relationship of theory and practice in composition. Their resistance has, I believe, instructed my understanding in powerful ways and has encouraged me to attend to the material situations of *their* learning and teaching, and to the intellectual and pedagogical priorities that such situations assume and encourage.

My teaching situation is serendipitous in the sense that I did not consciously choose to teach at a university that does not offer a PhD in English, in the way that some faculty choose to teach at community colleges or small liberal arts colleges rather than at research universities. Instead, once I moved from my first tenure-line position at the State University of New York at Brockport to Oregon State University, I found that I enjoyed working with undergraduates and, later, MA students. I believe that my academic location has benefited, rather than hindered, my research—and that it has done so *because* I rarely work with students who operate comfortably within the discourse of composition studies. My students' questions and challenges have been powerful catalysts for this study, and I wish to acknowledge the critical role that they have played in my thinking and writing.

Other aspects of my material situation have also influenced my effort to both articulate and address the issues I raise in *Situating Composition*. Since arriving at Oregon State University in 1980, I have directed at least one writing program, and at times—both in my early years at OSU and more recently—I have simultaneously directed two such programs. Though I coordinated OSU's first-year writing program from 1980 to 1986 and served on two different occasions as the acting director of our Writing-Intensive-Curriculum Program, my most consistent involvement has been with the Center for Writing and Learning, which I have directed from 1980 to the present. The center has housed a number of programs over the years, but the Writing Center has always been one of its key components. (Currently the Center for Writing and Learning includes the Writing Center and the Academic Success Program, a program that offers a number of credit- and non-credit-bearing study skills courses and services.) Working with my colleagues at the center, and with the writing assistants who conference with students, has taught me that practitioners, including undergraduate writing assistants, can have quite sophisticated insights about writing, tutoring, and teaching writing—and that they can develop powerful ways of expressing and enacting these insights.

I remember in particular one Writing Center staff meeting in the early 1980s when a writing assistant, a junior majoring in history, articulated an approach to error that was almost identical to Mina Shaughnessy's approach in *Error and Expectations*. Experiences such as this one have reminded me that although writing assistants, instructors, and others who work closely with students on writing might not be able (or wish) to articulate their insights according to scholarly conventions of argument and style, that does not mean that they do not have powerful understandings about the work with which they are engaged.

In making statements such as these, I in no way intend to idealize or glorify the teaching of first-year and advanced writing classes or of such related activities as conferencing with students in writing centers. As I argue in part 3 of *Situating Composition*, the practice of theory and the practice of teaching are both *practices*. (In this section I also explain why I have found it necessary to characterize what scholars often describe as a theory-practice split as a practice-practice split and acknowledge the limitations as well as strengths of this formulation.) As such, these practices can be enacted well or poorly, thoughtfully or unthoughtfully. Moreover, the material situation in which these practices are enacted can exert a powerful influence on the assumptions that practitioners hold about "what is real, what is good," and "what is possible" —to quote from James Berlin's discussion in "Rhetoric and Ideology in the Writing Class" (492). (For an extended discussion of these differences, see chapter 5.)

My work with the Center for Writing and Learning has also reminded me that at times the material exigencies of writing program administrators' and teachers' situations can figure so prominently that it is all one can do to address (or try to address) them. During the years that I have worked at Oregon State, the Center for Writing and Learning has been on the brink of closing on multiple occasions. Though the center's financial stability has improved in recent years, I am always aware of its potential vulnerability—and I am always working to strengthen the center's situation vis-à-vis the university. As the director, I would like to be able to focus primarily on pedagogical and curricular issues, but as an administrator, I spend a good deal of my time working on budgetary and bureaucratic matters that are distant from the conferences that take place daily in the Writing Center and the classes and other activities that make up our Academic Success Program.

administrator dilemma

This is an unfortunate situation at best—and it in no way approaches the difficulties that part-time or adjunct instructors teaching multiple sections of writing classes, often at several different universities, encounter. But it is hardly an uncommon one. My awareness of the material exigencies that even someone in a privileged position, such as myself, can face has reminded me that there is an inevitable gap between that which seems real, good, and possible in the realm of scholarly research and that which seems real, good, and possible in specific situations where material constraints interact with theoretical possibilities. This recognition has not caused me to curtail my commitments to the scholarly work of composition, but it has reminded me that as a scholar, I would do well to be modest in my expectations of the direct influence that my or any other scholars' research can have on teaching, tutoring, and related practices. It is one thing to proclaim a revolution in the scholarly world of theory; it is another thing to enact that revolution in the pedagogical world of practice.

adjuncts

It is the nature of practice to elude or resist representation. Even when this or that practice results in a product, as happens when scholars write articles, chapters, and books, that product at best gestures toward the process that led to its completion. Hence the existence of prefaces, which attempt to restore some of the lived experience that led to the article or book that readers hold in their hands. As Andrea Lunsford and I have argued on numerous occasions, most notably in *Singular Texts/Plural Authors: Perspectives on Collaborative Writing,* the role that collaborations with others play in a single-authored text is particularly likely to be ignored or undervalued when that text is published. I am thus especially pleased to acknowledge several collaborations here.

Collaboration plays a key role in any endeavor, whether scholarly or pedagogical—but its significance is all the more important when a project has extended over a significant period of time, as this project has. The first table of contents for this study that I have in my files is dated August 14, 1994. By the time this book was completed in September 2003, this table of contents had gone through nineteen iterations. Chapters that I had intended to include in the book, such as a history of the founding and early years of the Conference on College Composition and Communication, fell away, while others that I had not anticipated including demanded to be written.

I'm not sure why *Situating Composition* required such a long gestation, but I can certainly point to material factors that made sustained work on this project difficult. Between 1994 and 2003, I edited one collection of essays and coedited another, while also revising three editions of my textbook, *Work in Progress: A Guide to Academic Writing.* My instincts tell me, however, that it wasn't just other projects that slowed me down. In retrospect, I believe that I needed to proceed slowly. As readers of this study will recognize, I often approach issues in composition studies analogically via research in such related areas as feminist theory, critical pedagogy, and cultural studies, and I needed time to read and digest this research. I also needed time to develop the blurred genre approach that characterizes this study. As readers will discover, I find the warrants for my argument in multiple sources—from historical data to personal experience to theoretical and textual critique. Moreover, while the style and approach of *Situating Composition* are hardly radical, I invested a good deal of effort and time in trying to write a text that—while most directly addressed to other scholars in the field—might be accessible to others engaged in the work of composition, should they find their way to it.

I mention the material conditions surrounding my work on *Situating Composition* because too often, scholarly books and articles seem to appear magically out of nowhere. Such virgin births threaten to mystify the very material processes and collaborations that enable one scholar to bring a project to completion, while another finds it difficult to do so. I know that I would never have completed this project without the support of a number of friends and colleagues.

I have dedicated this book to two of my most important collaborators. Andrea Lunsford and I have worked together for over twenty years on countless scholarly projects, and we continue to do so. As she has done since our first years together as graduate students, Andrea provided intellectual and emotional support for this project; at several key junctures she also encouraged me to put one of our collaborative projects aside to work on *Situating Composition*. This book is—like all of my books—dedicated to my husband, Gregory Pfarr, who has collaborated with me on that most important project of all, life. My life—and my work—are both richer as a result. I particularly value our conversations on the shared demands and rewards of composing visual and written texts.

Other friends and colleagues supported this project when I wondered if it ever would see the light of day. Suzanne Clark and Beth Flynn provided the best kind of encouragement by reading the manuscript, as Andrea also did, as it evolved through its various drafts. A number of other colleagues generously read sections of this study: my thanks go to Jean Ferguson Carr, Suellynn Duffey, Melissa Dunbar, Peter Elbow, Cheryl Glenn, Anita Helle, Tracy Ann Robinson, Kate Ronald, Jack Selzer, Vicki Tolar Burton, and Susan Wells. My thanks go as well to John Trimbur, who reviewed my manuscript for Southern Illinois University Press, and to the second anonymous reviewer for the press. Over the years, I have had many thought-provoking conversations with Marilyn Moller, my editor first at Bedford/St. Martin's and now at W. W. Norton. Marilyn's insights and questions have enriched this study—and Marilyn has patiently waited for me to complete it so I could turn to our next project.

As anyone who has completed a book knows, many others play a significant role in its completion. I owe a debt of gratitude to a number of students and colleagues at Oregon State University who provided support at key moments. Nghia Banh, Stevon Roberts, Sue Lee, and Melissa Weintraub helped me to check the references in the works cited. Saundra Mills, secretary at the Center for Writing and Learning, assisted in countless ways—from photocopying texts and troubleshooting word processing problems to library and Internet sleuthing. I could accomplish little in my scholarly and professional life without the support and friendship of Moira Dempsey, Assistant Director of the Center for Writing and Learning and Coordinator of the Center's Academic Success Program, and Wayne Robertson, Coordinator of the Writing Center. Particularly as this text moved toward completion, Wayne and Moira insisted repeatedly that my work on *Situating Composition* was as important as my work for the Center for Writing and Learning and encouraged me to take the time I needed to complete it, even when that meant time away from the center.

I have two academic homes at Oregon State University, and the support that I have received from faculty and staff of the English department has been equally essential to the completion of this project. English department chair Robert Schwartz has consistently supported my scholarly, professional, and pedagogical work, as have the staff in the main English department office: Linda Hoyser, Rachael Shook, Dina Stoneman, and Aurora Terhune. My work has received institutional support from Oregon State University as well. A 1996 fellowship at the Center for the Humanities provided time at a particularly opportune moment for me to work through my ideas. Grants from the Oregon State University Valley Library and Research Council enabled me to spend two weeks in the summer of 1996 researching the early years of the Conference on College Composition and Communication at the archives of the National Council of Teachers of English in Urbana, Illinois. The results of this research most directly informed my work in *On Writing Research: The Braddock Essays, 1975–1998,* but they also helped me to think in productive ways about the politics of composition's location in the academy.

Thanks go to Karl Kageff, acting editor-in-chief at Southern Illinois University Press, who graciously extended deadlines for me and whose support and interest helped keep me going. Thanks also to managing editor Carol Burns and project editor Kathleen Kageff, also at Southern Illinois University Press, for their careful work on this manuscript.

Finally, in a work that reflects on the development of composition as an academic discipline during the last thirty years, I would like to acknowledge (though I cannot name) the many faculty whose commitment to the scholarly and pedagogical work of composition has inspired me and deepened my own engagement with writing and with the teaching of writing. No discipline or field is perfect, and in *Situating Composition,* I have attempted to raise a number of difficult questions about the politics of location in composition. But if others had not inspired me with the strength of their teaching and research, I would not have wanted to embark on—much less complete—this study. The teaching of writing as it takes place in classrooms throughout North America is a vital context for this study, and one to which I hope this work contributes.

PART ONE

Composition in the Academy

Theory, Practice, Situation

INTRODUCTION
Some Opening Questions

1. What are we talking about when we talk about composition? A scholarly discipline that seeks to generate and disseminate knowledge? An interdisciplinary field that marks the site of a variety of scholarly, pedagogical, civic, and cultural projects? An area of specialization within English studies? A curricular program that provides a variety of required and elective writing and rhetoric courses? An administrative and assessment structure that responds to institutional needs to sort and evaluate students? A site of cultural production? A workplace?

2. What counts as work in composition—not in the literal sense of how faculty members earn our paychecks, but in the common sense of ideology? What possible relations obtain between work as location and work as value?

3. How would are the following situated in the work of composition? First year writing programs? Writing centers? MA and PhD programs? Writing-across-the-curriculum programs? The publication of scholarly articles and books? Of textbooks? Websites? Technical and business writing programs? English-as-a-second-language programs? Teacher research? Participation in an e-mail listserv? In professional meetings and state, regional, and national organizations? In institutional committees that address either the teaching of writing or teaching in general? Service-learning or community literacy programs? Programs designed to bring the benefits of computer and online technologies to writing classrooms? Are some of these projects more primary or central to the work of composition than others?

4. What's in a name? What differing connotations do the following terms evoke for faculty in composition? (For chairs and deans? For students or faculty in general?) Composition? Composition studies? Rhetoric? Rhetoric and

composition? Composition and cultural studies? Composition and cultural rhetoric? Rhetoric and writing? Rhetoric, composition, and pedagogy? Language, literacy, and rhetoric? The teaching of writing? Writing studies? Literacy studies?

5. Who are the subjects of composition—and how many ways can the term
"subject" be troped in this question? Who is most readily recognized as an agent,
as a creator and disseminator of knowledge? Who is likely to find his or her
authority limited to the local, to the specific and concrete? Who is subjected to
the work of composition? Students? Teachers? Writing program administrators?
What subjects does composition engage? Rhetoric? Writing? Non-fiction prose?
Cultural studies? Feminist studies? Creative writing? Academic writing? Professional writing? Literacy studies? Something else?

6. Consider the following potential starting points for a genealogy of com-
position. What do these various locations expose or repress? Fifth-century
Greece? Harvard in the 1890s? The first meeting of the Conference on College
Composition and Communication held at the Stevens Hotel in Chicago in 1950?

7. What centripetal forces give composition coherence and stability? What
centrifugal forces threaten to pull composition apart? What boundary work has
composition had to undertake in order to support its claims for status as a discipline or field?

8. What structures of desire and resistance circulate in composition? What
is the relationship, for instance, between composition's desire for professional
legitimacy and disciplinary status and its curricular positioning in the academy
as gatekeeper and certifier? Between its desire to effect broad social reform and
its identification in both popular and academic cultures with linguistic correctness and propriety?

9. What does it mean to take theory seriously? To take practice seriously?
Are there limits to theory? To practice? What might a theorized practice look
and be like? What might a situated theory look and be like?

10. What kind of a text is this list? Does it encourage productive thinking?
What are its limitations?

4

1 What Are We Talking about When We Talk about Composition?

What *are* we talking about when we talk about composition? This is a question that has concerned—if not obsessed—scholars in composition for at least the last three decades. From James Kinneavy's 1971 lament that composition "is so clearly the stepchild of the English department that it is not a legitimate area of concern in graduate studies" (1) to Louise Phelps's 1988 effort to define composition as a human science to Geoffrey Sirc's 2002 charge that a professionalized composition has failed "to exploit its most radical practices" (14), scholars in composition have attempted to define what composition has been, is, and might become. The field's professionalization seems to have increased, rather than decreased, these anxieties. It has also, at least in the eyes of some, raised questions about composition's commitment to the teaching of basic and first-year writing courses. In her 1998 *Composition in the University: Historical and Polemical Essays,* for instance, Sharon Crowley argues that "the traditional function of the required first-year course is increasingly hard to reconcile with the professionalization and specialization that now characterize the American academy" (10). For Crowley, composition's commitment to the first-year requirement limits—rather than forwards—its ability "to become a theoretical and pedagogical site wherein the sorts of institutional changes currently advocated by materialist, feminist, ethnic, and postmodern theorists could be worked out" (4).

Situating Composition represents my effort to, as Kenneth Burke might say, "put in [my] oar" and participate in the (apparently) "unending conversation" about the nature, status, and consequences of composition's professionalization (*Philosophy* 110, 111). Rather than offering one or more solutions to the "problem" of composition's professionalization or

5

developing a sustained argument about whether scholars should or should not work to abolish the required first-year writing requirement, in *Situating Composition* I attempt to raise questions about the politics of composition's location in the academy—questions that I hope can help those engaged in the work of composition better to negotiate its politics, rhetoric, and ethics.

At times, I address these questions through theoretical critique. Readers will notice that analyses of Susan Miller's *Textual Carnivals: The Politics of Composition* and Sharon Crowley's *Composition in the University: Historical and Polemical Essays*—as well as a number of other scholarly texts—are woven throughout this study. At other times, I turn to inquiries that are grounded in other kinds of documents and experiences. In chapter 4, for instance, I analyze course descriptions for every first-year and advanced composition class I have taught since coming to Oregon State University in 1980. In chapter 6, I include a reading of "Lesson 19: Grad School—Some People Never Learn" from Matt Groening's cartoon book *School Is Hell* as part of my discussion of the "disciplining" effect of all education.

Every method has its advantages and disadvantages. To quote Kenneth Burke again, any given method or "terminology is a *reflection* of reality, by its nature as a terminology it must be a *selection* of reality; and to this extent it must function also as a *deflection* of reality" ("Terministic Screens" 45).[1] In *Situating Composition,* I attempt to provide multiple perspectives on—and reflections about—composition's current scholarly and pedagogical enterprise. In part 2 of this study, for instance, I take yet another look at the writing process movement and argue paradoxically both that from one perspective nothing so unified and coherent as a writing process movement ever existed and also that despite claims that composition is post-process, signs of an ongoing commitment to process are everywhere evident. In part 3, I raise the often-discussed question of the relation of theory and practice in composition, arguing that one productive way to address this question is to recognize that, as Deborah Britzman argues, "practice makes practice" (240). In chapter 5, for instance, I consider some of the differences between the practice of theory and the practice of teaching and argue that scholars would do well to attend more carefully than we currently do to these differences—especially when we represent the work of both teachers and students.

Such an argument might seem to suggest that I view practice as a

① *Lg As Symbolic Action 1966: 44-62*

monolithic or essentialist category: one is either a scholar or a teacher, for instance, and one's practice follows accordingly. As I point out several times in this study, though I have at times found it helpful to contrast the practice of theory with the practice of teaching, I recognize that this distinction inevitably not only *reflects* but also *selects* and *deflects* the complicated mix of experience that we, for lack of a better term, refer to as reality. In "reality," I experience my life not as a monolithic or essentialist commitment to a particular constellation of practices but rather as a series of negotiations within and among the various practices that make up my life. I want to begin *Situating Composition,* then, with a series of scenarios drawn from my own experience that call attention to the contradictions, tensions, and paradoxes that are (in my experience, at least) inherent in the work of composition.[1] These scenarios—which are based on real events, as I recall them, that have occurred during the last five years—also serve, I hope, to give concreteness and specificity to the questions articulated in the introduction to this part, for they are a potent reminder of the complexity of composition's location in the academy.

SCENARIO 1

It is the first day of class, and I and the students enrolled in my graduate-level composition theory class have just seated ourselves around a seminar table. After making some remarks about our work together, I ask the students to introduce themselves and to say something about their program of study and their reasons for taking the class. All of the students are enrolled in either our disciplinary MA or an interdisciplinary master's program. (My department does not offer a PhD.) Most, though not all, of the students are teaching assistants (TAs) in my department.

The first student who speaks is majoring in the area that my department calls rhetoric and composition, so his reasons for taking the class are easily articulated. The second student is one of several fiction writing students enrolled in the course. She begins by admitting that she is taking this class solely because it fulfills the department's requirement that students take at least one "theory" class. She's afraid of this beast called "theory," she says—several other students sigh with relief as she admits this—and so she's put off taking this class until her final term. She chose this rather than other "theory" classes because she is a TA, and TAs are also required to take at least one class in rhetoric and composition. WR 512 thus allows her to fulfill both obligations with a single class. She concludes her comments by saying that though she's fearful about this class, she is also a deeply committed and engaged teacher, so she hopes she will be able to forge connections between our readings and her teaching.

SCENARIO 2

As part of a larger effort to respond to changes in assessment in K–12 public education in my state, my university is revising its entrance requirements. Instead of relying upon grades and test scores, as in the past, the university is considering basing entrance decisions on a series of outcomes-based assessments undertaken by public school teachers. In an effort to increase the reliability and validity of these assessments, the university and the state Department of Education are holding a series of (unfortunately named) "Calibration Institutes." At these institutes, faculty members from a variety of disciplines review portfolios that have already been evaluated by public school teachers and make independent judgments as to their ranking; these rankings are then calibrated with those of the public school teachers.

Shortly after the call for participants for the first local calibration institute appears, my chair e-mails me requesting that I and other faculty in composition studies attend the institute. Somewhat reluctantly, I agree. When I contact the person in charge of the institute to tell him who will represent the English department, I receive the following response: "I'm of course pleased that you and your colleagues will participate, but I hope that your department will consider sending other faculty members as well. The composition faculty always seem to be the ones who participate in activities that have to do with teaching. For our project to be successful, we need widespread involvement from faculty. I hope you can persuade your chair to ask some literature faculty to attend our institute."

SCENARIO 3

I am meeting with my dean to discuss (yet again) the budget for the Center for Writing and Learning, the unit that I have directed since I came to Oregon State University in 1980. The Center for Writing and Learning includes two programs: the Writing Center and the Academic Success Program. In the early years of the CWL, our fiscal situation was so dire that we were threatened with closure on more than one occasion. In recent years, however, the CWL has limped along with a small but relatively stable recurring budget, one that still left me scrambling for funds to cover operating expenses but that at least guaranteed the salaries of the two instructors and half-time secretary with whom I work (something that I could not always do in the CWL's early years).

Recent changes in the university's approach to retention and to study skills have created a crisis, however. The CWL used to offer a non-credit, fee-based study skills course; funds from this course were used to support work-study writing assistants in the Writing Center. Now that the university is taking retention more seriously, our study skills course has been integrated into a credit-bearing, tuition-based Academic Success Program. This is very good news from a curricular perspective. But there is a problem: in our transitional state, we have lost the funding we used to earn from our fee-based study skills course but have not received an increase in our budget to cover this loss. Only a last-minute transfer of funds from Academic Affairs provided the funds necessary to hire work-study writing assistants: had these funds not been provided, the Writing Center would have had radically to limit the availability of conferences. There is no guarantee, however, that this transfer will become permanent. Without these funds, the Writing Center would be crippled. And if the Writing Center is crippled, the entire CWL might well be threatened with closure.

My dean and I discuss various ways of dealing with this situation and agree that, as we have in the past, we'll just have to take it a day at the time and hope for the best. As I'm getting ready to leave, I talk about how discouraging it is to face yet another budget crisis. Searching for a way to boost my spirits, my dean reassures me that as dire as the CWL's situation is, central administrators would be reluctant to close our unit. "With the current focus on retention," she says, "they understand the contribution that the CWL makes. Besides, thanks to your fine scholarly record, you provide a kind of protection for the CWL. Administrators know that if you back the CWL it must be worthwhile."

SCENARIO 4

I am sitting in my English department office trying to catch up on mail, forms, and other paraphernalia of my work life. Since I have two offices on campus—an office at the CWL, where I spend most of my time, and an English department office—the latter office often suffers. Taking a quick look at the stack of materials before me, I realize that I am late in completing my department's teaching request form. I begin to move through the form, checking off classes according to the following categories: 1) would like to teach; 2) would be willing to teach; 3) would prefer not to teach.

When I come to the box for WR 121, our required first-year writing class, I pause. Should I write a note to my chair, as I sometimes have in the past, asking to be allowed to teach this class? I taught this class regularly during my first eleven years at Oregon State University. But after my department developed a master's degree and began recruiting TAs, I have most often taught advanced undergraduate and graduate level writing classes; I also regularly teach a 100-level, high enrollment introduction to fiction class.[2] I know from previous discussions that my chair is sympathetic to my desire to teach WR 121, but in the past when I have raised this issue, he has reminded me that thanks to my administrative duties I teach only half-time and am needed for other courses, especially since the composition and rhetoric faculty are down two positions. Furthermore, now that we have TAs, I'm an expensive way to staff a course that can be taught at a greatly reduced cost. Should I take the time to write yet another note?

SCENARIO 5

I am still in my English office, still sorting through mail, forms, newsletters, and so on. This time, I come across a copy of the information sheet that describes the areas of specialization within my department's MA program. On it is a post-it with a note that I scribbled several months earlier. The note reads: "Ask again to be included in the literature and culture faculty list?" I couldn't decide when I wrote the note whether the timing for such a request was good, and I find myself tempted to once again dodge this issue and move this sheet to the bottom of the pile. Why? Some context may help. The information sheet is a handout designed to inform graduate students of faculty who are qualified to teach and direct theses in the various areas of specialization within our master's program. Though I have a PhD in Victorian studies and have upon occasion taught courses in that area in our department, I have never considered asking to be listed under British literature, for I no longer see this specialization as central to my teaching and research.

In the last ten years, I have been increasingly engaged with cultural, feminist, and critical pedagogy studies. The area within our master's program that best reflects this engagement is called literature and culture, and I have thought on occasion that I would like to be recognized as engaged with this scholarly and pedagogical project. (I have thought, as well, of the difference it might make if this area title were more inclusive of composition.) After all, I regularly teach an Introduction to Literacy Studies course that is listed under the literature and culture category, and I would like graduate students majoring or minoring in literature and culture to realize that I have an interest in this area.

Several years before, I had moved from thought to action and e-mailed the graduate studies director about being added to the literature and culture list. His carefully worded response, while not specifically dismissive of my qualifications, cited a concern for the integrity of that area. Cultural studies and related projects have become so popular in recent years, he observed, that it's easy for faculty to feel an interest in and commitment to them. But is that the same thing as having a clear scholarly focus? Since my department had just come through a volatile series of meetings about hiring priorities—and since we had voted with a narrow margin to hire in rhetoric and composition rather than in literature and culture or poetry (the other two contending areas)—I decided that this was hardly the time to press for inclusion. Sitting in my office now, I wonder if the situation has changed enough to warrant another try.

As these scenarios suggest, the question of what we are talking about when we talk about composition is anything but obvious. To the fiction writing student in my graduate class, composition is an academic subject—one that she encounters under the rubric of theory. Like many others in this class, this student does not connect the daily decisions she makes as a teacher with theory, which she associates with the scholarly work of the academy. Even if I attempt, as I regularly do, to redefine theory and, more importantly, to demonstrate that theorizing about practice is one of the most powerful ways to inquire into one's teaching, certain aspects of our material and rhetorical situation (such as assumptions about theory and practice that circulate in the academy and in popular culture) speak more clearly and loudly to many students than the words that come out of my mouth.

Though composition is situated primarily as a theoretical subject in my graduate classroom, within the English department and university, composition is often aligned not only with practice but also with a whole array of related bureaucratic and curricular obligations—as the second scenario involving my university's calibration institute demonstrates.

Indeed, my colleagues in rhetoric and composition and I often find ourselves representing or embodying our department's commitment to pedagogy. The fact that three of the four faculty members in composition studies in my department currently administer writing programs further emphasizes the extent to which we are structurally and bureaucratically configured with practice. This is not to say that we are the only faculty members in our department who are identified with pedagogy. There are a number of other faculty members who have a deep and thoughtful commitment to teaching, and some of these faculty members eventually joined us at the Calibration Institute. These faculty members' commitment is generally seen as personal, however, rather than as a central part of their professional and scholarly identities; nor is it institutionalized in the way that our identification with pedagogy is.[3]

A comment made by the editors of the recently established journal *Pedagogy: Critical Approaches to Teaching Literature, Language, Composition, and Culture* emphasizes the extent to which composition is institutionally and professionally aligned with pedagogy. As its subtitle suggests, *Pedagogy* focuses not only on composition but also on literature, language, and culture. Nevertheless, as editors Jennifer Holberg and Marcy Taylor recount, "Again and again, as we developed *Pedagogy* and explained its mission, invariably the response was 'Oh, so it's a 'comp' journal'" (2).

This identification with pedagogy at times feels dangerous. For although I and my colleagues are regularly assured by our chair, dean, and others of the importance of our work, we are aware of the extent to which practice is devalued in the academy. The third scenario provides an example of that devaluing, and also of the kind of disjunction between work as use-value and work as exchange-value that can result. With the exception of the time that I spend teaching or serving on committees, the majority of my time at my university is spent in CWL-related activities. It would seem commonsensical (to anyone but an academic, that is) that this is the work that should "count" the most—be valued the most—by my colleagues. As my dean's comment suggests, however, the work that I do that is most valued on my campus is that which takes place in stolen moments on weekends or in the summer. This work—my scholarly work—has sufficient value that it can, to a certain extent at least, authorize and protect the work that I do at the CWL, work that is otherwise suspect because of its (inaccurate, but impossible to shake) association with remediation. If the norms of the academy render pedagogy suspect, then an association with remediation represents a double devaluing. My scholarly work serves to counteract this devaluing, but the cost is the metaphoric erasure of the actual work that I do day in and day out at my university.

I am caught in a different kind of double bind when in the fourth scenario I consider whether to try yet again to persuade my department chair to schedule me to teach my university's required first-year writing course. I am too valuable, I am, in effect, told, to teach this class. I am valuable because I have scholarly expertise that the norms of the academy say are best utilized in upper division or graduate classes or in literature courses that are seen as central to an English department's mission. And I am valuable in a different sense: why pay me to teach a first-year writing class that can be taught so much less expensively? For though (to turn to the fifth scenario) my department, like other departments, is very careful indeed when it considers who is qualified to teach graduate-level classes, or classes in the major, similar norms do not hold for first-year writing. I find myself with too much expertise to teach first-year writing on a regular basis but not enough expertise to be included on a list of literature and culture faculty—at least not without a possible fight. From this perspective, the apparently simple and straightforward information sheet about my department's MA program becomes fraught with significance, for it reveals the ongoing struggle within departments of English for territory and privilege.

Composition and the Return of the Repressed

When considered from a departmental perspective, this struggle often seems primarily to involve members of different areas within English. When a new position in my department opens up, faculty in a variety of areas—from American studies and British literature to film, literature and culture, creative writing, and composition—are likely to argue that their area needs additional representation. But struggle also occurs within areas. In composition, faculty engaged in the work of writing centers and of writing across the curriculum, ESL, basic writing, and professional writing programs often feel marginalized in relation to other colleagues in composition, particularly those whose work is identified with the general project of theory. In "Identity and Location: A Study of WPA Models, Memberships, and Agendas," Jeanne Gunner argues that despite some positive developments, writing program administrators are generally unable to represent their work in the most powerful and authoritative scholarly venues in composition; she finds little "cross-talk" between those whose research is published in such major journals as *College Composition and Communication (CCC)* and *College English* and those who publish in the *Writing Center Journal, Writing Program Administration,* or similar journals. In her study of issues of *CCC* from 1989 to 1999, Gunner identified only "eight articles that have a WPA-related focus: two articles on the WPA's professional situation; two on writing centers; two on WAC-related topics; and two on assessment" (48). Of these, she goes on to add, only two "specifically address the topic of program administration/administrators" (48).[4]

As Cynthia Lewiecki-Wilson and Jeff Sommers argue in "Professing at the Fault Lines: Composition at Open Admissions Institutions," writing program administrators are not the only faculty in composition to feel marginalized within the discipline. Those who teach at open admissions institutions, such as two-year colleges and general admission colleges and universities, often feel that their work is either disappeared or, worse yet, represented "as a site for the discipline of punishment, applied to both students and teachers, and legitimated through metaphors of deficit" (439). In their essay, which I will return to in later sections of this study, Lewiecki-Wilson and Sommers ask readers to consider "the teaching of writing in open admissions sites as central to the historical formation and continuing practice of composition studies" (440). They recognize, however, that to do so they must provoke "a crisis of representation" (445)—for given composition's development as an academic discipline, the forces working against such an effort are substantial.

Those who are familiar with the development of composition as an academic discipline and, especially, with the founding and early years of the Conference on College Composition and Communication (CCCC) will recognize a potential irony inherent in Lewiecki-Wilson and Sommers's assertion. At its inception, those involved with the CCCC clearly hoped that this professional organization, which played and continues to play an essential role in composition's professionalization, would unite all involved with the work of composition, rather than creating caste-like cohorts of differently valued workers. In the first issue of *CCC,* John Gerber, the association's first chair, began a statement on the CCCC's founding by invoking all who teach writing in colleges and universities and articulating a strong sense of shared needs:

Someone has estimated that there are at least nine thousand of us teaching in college courses in composition and communication. Faced with many of the same problems, concerned certainly with the same general objectives, we have for the most part gone our separate ways, experimenting here and improvising there. Occasionally we have heard that a new kind of course is working well at Upper A. & M. or that a new staff training program has been found successful at Lower T. C. But we rarely get the facts. We have had no systematic way of exchanging views and information quickly. Certainly we have had no means of developing a coordinated research program.

To meet such obvious needs the Conference on College Composition and Communication has been formed.

That such a unification has not happened, despite the efforts of many in composition, is obvious.

How *can* we best understand composition's development as a discipline? As I have already noted, this is a question that has been much asked in the last ten to fifteen years (see, for example, Crowley, *Composition;* Faigley, *Fragments;* Gallagher; Gere, "Long Revolution"; Harkin; J. Harris, "New Boss"; Horner, *Terms of Work;* R. Miller; S. Miller, *Textual Carnivals;* North, *Making of Knowledge;* Phelps, *Human Science;* Roskelly and Ronald; Royster, "When the First Voice You Hear"; Sirc; and Trimbur, "Writing Instruction"). And it is a question that I take up again in *Situating Composition.* As I do so, I upon occasion include my own experiences in my inquiry: hence the scenarios that open this chapter. I chose to begin this chapter with a series of scenarios that grow out of my experiences as a teacher, writing program administrator, and scholar because of a desire to shift from the relatively abstract problem-posing nature of the introduction to a more materially grounded analysis. As I have worked on this project, I have been haunted by a comment made not by a compositionist but by a geographer. In introducing what he believes to be "breakthrough" books on geography to readers of *Lingua Franca,* Donald Mitchell comments that the "use of spatial metaphors in current humanities and social science scholarship has ironically led to a decreased interest in actual geographical space. Only rarely do theoretical works connect spatial metaphors to existing places" (16).

I will have more to say about the role that spatial metaphors play in my analysis in the following chapter. For now, I will simply observe that as I write this book organized around the spatial metaphors of *situating* composition and developing a politics of *location,* I want to find ways to connect my analysis with "existing places." Many of these "places" will necessarily be texts. But when it's feasible, I hope to remind readers of the material situatedness of all textual practices (including my own). In so doing, I hope to give specificity and concreteness to my observations and to invite readers to relate these observations to their own experiences. I also hope, as the title of part 3 of this study, "Thinking Through Practice," suggests, to emphasize the potential heuristic value of thinking *through* practice. Such a thinking entails not only thinking *about* practice—about teaching, writing program administration, research, and so on—but also attempting to use practice as a means of thinking *through* complex scholarly and professional issues. Such a thinking through practice does not privilege practice over theory—does not, in other words, simply reverse conventional hierarchies—but rather looks for productive ways to place the two in dialogue. It looks, as well, for ways to call attention to contradictions and paradoxes that are sometimes overlooked in scholarly work.

The scenarios that appear earlier in this chapter emphasize some of the contradictions and tensions inherent in composition's location in the academy. Since references to personal experience are uncommon in scholarly work in composition, I want to make several observations about these reflections. Of these, perhaps the most important is this: I do not assume that my experience is representative of that of others. Nor do I assume—as I hope the scenarios demonstrate—that my experience holds some singular, univocal meaning. My hope, in fact, is that the scenarios' specificity, and the difficulties that they expose, will serve as a pointed reminder of the limitations inherent in singular, univocal narratives about the work of composition. For it is a central concern of this study to question the helpfulness of such narratives and to encourage more situated and self-reflexive analyses—analyses that are more open to paradox, tension, and multiplicity.

As an example of a narrative about the nature, history, and mission of composition studies that would benefit from a more situated and self-reflexive analysis, I would cite the introduction that Robert Connors, Andrea Lunsford, and I wrote for our 1984 *Essays on Classical Rhetoric and Modern Discourse.* Our introduction follows a singular master plot, one that identifies contemporary composition with the long-lived and (in some eyes at least) powerful rhetorical tradition, particularly the classical rhetorical tradition as exemplified in the works of Aristotle, Cicero, and Quintilian. There is a good deal that I still value about this introduction, but when I reread it today, I am aware of the seamlessness of the story we narrate about composition's recovery of classical rhetoric. I am aware, as well, of the extent to which we repress counternarratives and fail to acknowledge the desires for disciplinary success that motivate our effort to identify contemporary composition with the classical rhetorical tradition.

Since the mid-1980s, a number of studies have attempted, as ours did, to narrate if not *the* then *a* story of composition. Some of these studies, such as James Berlin's 1984 *Writing Instruction in Nineteenth-Century Colleges* and his 1987 *Rhetoric and Reality: Writing Instruction in American Colleges, 1900–1985,* continue our emphasis on the rhetorical tradition. Others, such as Martin Nystrand, Stuart Greene, and Jeffrey Wiemelt's 1993 "Where Did Composition Studies Come From?" point to different sources and genealogies, such as cognitive research on writing. As John Trimbur observes in "Writing Instruction and the Politics of Professionalization," however diverse these and other narratives may first appear to be, the majority—Geoffrey Sirc's recent *English Composition as a Happening* being a clear exception—share an implicit master narrative, one that "points to professionalization and discipline formation as the inevitable outcome of the plot" (134).[5] While acknowledging the gains that professionalization has brought to composition, Trimbur reminds readers of several problematic consequences of discipline formation, such as the "normalizing of intellectual work, subjugation of counterknowledges, overemphasis on specialization, [and] monopolies of expertise" (136).

In *Situating Composition,* I continue the inquiry that Trimbur and others have undertaken on the costs, as well as the benefits, of disciplinarity. I will ask, for instance, whether scholars in composition have somehow expected that we could avoid having our work "disciplined" by disciplinarity. I will also ask whether scholars in composition have been attentive enough to the rhetoric, politics, and ethics of our *own* discursive actions. My interest in so doing is not to pose dichotomous alternative futures between which scholars in composition must choose. (In "Composition History and Disciplinarity," for instance, Bob Connors paints a picture of two possible futures for composition: a "return to" an "earlier and more service-based world" [17] versus eventual "MLA-ization" [19].)

Rather, I am interested in analyzing and modeling ways of reading the work of composition that enable those committed to that work better to recognize and respond to the contradictory situations within which we operate.

I am concerned that even apparently rigorous critiques of composition—critiques that seem to resist a simple narrative of disciplinary and professional progress—nevertheless can oversimplify the complexity and difficulty of composition's location in the academy. The critique that Susan Miller makes in her 1991 *Textual Carnivals: The Politics of Composition* seems, for instance, to be as clear-eyed—and pessimistic—as a narrative could be. As readers of Miller's study are aware, Miller situates composition as the "low" partner in a "low/high" binary that poses the actual production of writing (composition) against the study of privileged aesthetic texts (literature). Teachers of writing, in Miller's narration, are "sad women in the basement" (121) who unwittingly serve as "agents of hegemonic selection" (9). As such, they inhabit "an institutionalized place for a specific but broadly constitutive social ambivalence in our cultural systems" (3). And the writing process movement—rather than being the revolution in theory and practice that many in the 1970s and 1980s claimed it to be—served in Miller's view "mainly as an affective improvement in the classroom and as a way of granting composition a qualified academic legitimacy" (108).

This is a bleak narrative, one that portrays both composition teachers and students as largely unable to resist their cultural and academic positioning. Nevertheless, Miller is not entirely pessimistic. In her closing chapter, "On Seeing Things for What They Are," Miller suggests that "composition studies has always had the process available to transform its marginalized culture into a site where cultural superstructures and their privileging results are visibly put into question. An *actually* improved status depends on openly consolidating the field's internal, existing resistance to the cultural superstructure that first defined it" (186).

Miller's depiction of composition as the "low" partner in a "low/high" binary that privileges belletristic texts is surely accurate. But notice the extent to which the preceding statement portrays composition as an agent that can—if only it can marshal the intelligence and will to see things as they really are—take charge of its destiny. As the scenarios at the start of this chapter emphasize, important as insights such as Miller's may be, they can hardly suffice to smooth out the contradictions and paradoxes inherent in composition's location in the academy. For one thing, a number of these contradictions and paradoxes are too deeply embedded in the academy, and in the culture at large, to be successfully resisted by a single academic field, however consolidated and aware its members are. Scholars in composition are hardly the only faculty members in the academy to discover that their value is determined primarily on the basis of their curriculum vitae, rather than on the work that they perform day in and day out. Nor are faculty members in English departments the only persons to engage in internal struggles over territory and privilege, or to discover that scholarly work that they hope will have broad social, cultural, and political consequences is more easily coopted or in other ways tamed than they might have imagined.[6]

More than many disciplines, however, composition is marked by a tension between its institutional location—which aligns composition not only with practice but in the minds of many with remediation—and its aspirations of achieving full disciplinarity. For disciplinarity in the academy emphasizes not practice, but theory; not remediation, but the (disinterested) advancement of knowledge; not engagement with a topic of broad social and cultural concern, such as literacy, but rather conversation among experts about a clearly defined and limited subject matter. And there are additional complications. At various moments in its history, and certainly from the 1960s to the present time, a significant number of scholars in composition, myself included, have articulated the utopian desire to challenge conventional understandings of literacy and to use such revised understandings not only to improve the teaching of writing but also as a means of effecting broad social, cultural, and political change. Nevertheless, many of these same scholars have directed (or are in other ways supporting or aligned with) writing programs that are identified primarily in the minds of other faculty members, and in the culture at large, with literacy as it has been traditionally conceived. Already troubled by hierarchies within English departments that privilege literature and such projects as feminist theory and cultural studies over composition, scholars who share a progressive or utopian vision of composition must also contend with assumptions and practices that challenge, and at times forcefully resist, our own scholarly, pedagogical, and political commitments.

How can those committed to the work of composition most productively understand and address dissonances such as these? Are there ways in which scholars in composition have yearned to escape the difficulty of our location in the academy? In what ways have these yearnings been reinforced by conventional disciplinary assumptions and practices? In considering these and related questions, I hope to encourage a rhetorical rereading of the field, one that reminds readers that, as Ann Gere observes, one of the meanings of "field" is that of a "charged space in which multiple 'sites' of interaction appear" (*Into the Field* 4).

2 Situating Myself— And My Argument

In a work that inquires into the politics of composition's location in the academy, it seems particularly important that I acknowledge my own situatedness in the work of composition, and the ways this situatedness influences my perspective. One way to characterize this situatedness is in terms of the "passionate attachments" that I bring to my work. This is a term used by Jacqueline Jones Royster in the concluding chapter of *Traces of a Stream: Literacy and Social Change among African American Women.* In this chapter, "A View from a Bridge: Afrafeminist Ideologies and Rhetorical Studies," Royster explores her own standpoint as a researcher and scholar and develops some principles to guide scholarly work. Royster argues, for instance, that "People who do intellectual work need to understand their intellectual ancestry" (265) and that they similarly "need to understand power and how they are affected by it" (268). They also need to acknowledge their "passionate attachments" (280). For such acknowledgment "reminds us that knowledge has sites and sources and that we are better informed about the nature of a given knowledge base when we take into account its sites, material contexts, and points of origin" (280). Articulating these attachments reminds us, as well, "that knowledge is produced by someone and that its producers are not formless and invisible. They are embodied and in effect have passionate attachments by means of their embodiments" (280).

I bring my own embodied knowing and passionate attachments to this study. As both a student and teacher, I have spent my adult life at state universities. Like many in composition, I feel a strong sense of commitment to public higher education. From my first teaching experience as a graduate student at Ohio State University to subsequent positions at the State University of New York at Brockport and Oregon State University,

I have taught composition courses at various levels and served as a writing program administrator. I have a passionate attachment to these programs, one that causes me (for instance) instinctively to resist calls to abolish the first-year writing requirement and to advocate for the important role that writing centers and writing-across-the-curriculum programs can and do play in students' experiences of writing.[1]

Another passionate attachment is to the field of composition itself. As someone who came to the work of composition in the early 1970s, I feel a deep sense of identification with composition's scholarly and pedagogical work. This identification is undoubtedly all the stronger because I "converted" from Victorian literature to composition soon after completing my PhD. When I was hired to direct the first-year writing program at the State University of New York at Brockport—and, later, to direct both that program and the Center for Writing and Learning at Oregon State University—I was the first person in each department who professed the teaching of writing as my scholarly work.

In the years since, I have both participated in and benefited from composition's professionalization. *Situating Composition* represents, in part, my effort to understand both the material and rhetorical interventions that enabled this professionalization and its consequences. As I do so, I endeavor to hold myself accountable for—rather than exempt myself from—the concerns that I articulate in this study. Thus when I suggest, as I do in part 2 of *Situating Composition,* that scholars in composition have been and continue to be drawn to a rhetoric of revolution—a rhetoric that enables the field's claims for scholarly progress but that disappears important material realities of teaching and writing—I am articulating a suspicion that I hold about myself and my own work. As I explain in chapter 3, I have been as drawn to this rhetoric as have other scholars, and even though I am now more aware of the way this rhetoric works in me, I cannot wholly bracket its influence. Nor would I want to. For as I note at several points in part 3 of *Situating Composition,* though scholars would do well to be more suspicious of our desire for disciplinary progress, we need to retain some notion of progress to continue to mark developments in our work.

In reconsidering composition's professionalization, my intention is neither to establish a genealogy of villains and heroes nor to delineate a utopian/dystopian vision of composition's past, present, and future. Rather, my hope is that by reflecting on the past—and on issues such as the relationship of theory and practice in composition—scholars can better assess the rhetoric, politics, and ethics of our own situations and actions. When I think back to my early years in the field, for instance, I now recognize the extent to which my awareness of my own and my profession's embattled location in the academy encouraged me to view myself as an underdog fighting the good fight. In such a situation, it becomes easy to conflate the advancement of one's own career with the advancement of one's discipline—and the advancement of one's discipline with the advancement of all teachers and students of writing. It becomes easy, as well, to turn away from such potentially unpleasant and inconvenient realities as the extent to which composition as a professional field has largely reproduced our society's hegemonic structures and relations, or the ways in which at the material level of practice it has assumed, rather than challenged, conventional understandings of the relationship between theory and practice—and theorists and practitioners—in composition. When I raise issues such as these, I write not as someone who has "always already" seen the problems that I will discuss, but who has experienced many of the same desires and needs that I now wish not so much to challenge (in an agonistic sense) as to place in view for discussion.

Notes Toward a Politics of Location

I write, as well, as a scholar situated at the intersection of several intellectual and disciplinary communities. As the subtitle of this book suggests, one of those locations is feminist theory. By the time I read Adrienne Rich's "Notes Toward a Politics of Location"—first presented at a conference in Utrecht, Holland, in 1984 and later published in her 1986 collection *Blood, Bread, and Poetry*—I had already begun to look for ways to bring my personal commitment to feminism to my scholarly work. Such feminists as Linda Alcoff, Gloria Anzaldúa, Barbara Biesecker, Susan Brown Carlton, Suzanne Clark, Jane Flax, Elizabeth Flynn, Diana Fuss, Cheryl Glenn, Jennifer Gore, Donna Haraway, Sondra Harding, Anita Helle, bell hooks, Susan Jarratt, Elspeth Probyn, Trinh T. Minh-ha, Andrea Lunsford, Patty Lather, Jacqueline Jones Royster, and Lynn Worsham have helped me to identify, and begin to act on, those ways. I include this long—and yet still incomplete—list of scholars to acknowledge my intellectual indebtedness to these and other feminists, and also to emphasize the wide-ranging influences within contemporary feminist theory. For those listed here represent diverse intellectual and disciplinary backgrounds, from philosophy, composition, political science, film studies, and rhetoric to literary, cultural studies, and educational theory.

Given this diversity, it is hardly surprising that my engagement with feminism has taken me down several pathways. One such pathway has encouraged me to reflect on the connections between, and consequences of, feminism's and composition's disciplinary projects. That there are connections seems clear. After all, as scholarly and disciplinary projects, composition and feminism took hold in the academy at roughly the same time, the mid-to-late 1970s and early 1980s.[2] Both projects grew out of and reflected cultural, political, and educational concerns of their time. Both projects hoped to work against the grain of conventional disciplinary and institutional practices. And as Susan Jarratt observes in the introduction to *Feminism and Composition Studies: In Other Words:*

> Both feminist inquiry and [what Jarratt terms] post-current-traditional composition studies . . . seek to transform styles of thinking, teaching, and learning rather than to reproduce stultifying traditions. They share a suspicion of authoritarian pedagogy, emphasizing instead collaborative or interactive learning and teaching. They resist purity of approach and the reduction of their scope by moving in and around many contemporary critical theories and disciplines. (3)

At their most utopian moments, a number of scholars in feminist and composition studies have articulated the hope that their work might have consequences beyond the academy, might serve as a catalyst for broad social, cultural, and political reform. And yet as scholars in both fields are aware, it has been easier to call for than to enact such reform. Both fields have found it difficult, as well, to resist conventional disciplinary and institutional norms. Indeed, as Jarratt notes, both fields are "caught in a bind vis-à-vis the institution: despite the desire to reconfigure disciplinary boundaries, both [composition and feminist studies] need to claim disciplinarity to achieve academic legitimacy and obtain resources" (3).

A key question for many scholars in both feminist studies and composition, then, is how they can best understand their field's development as an academic discipline—and what productive uses they might make of these understandings. This is an issue that Flax, *Thinking Fragments;* Fuss; Gore; Harding; hooks, *Talking Back;* Lather; Messer-Davidow; and others take up for feminist studies and that Berlin, *Rhetoric and Reality;* Connors, "Composition History"; Crowley, *Composition in the Univer-*

sity; Dobrin; Faigley, *Fragments;* Gallagher; Gere, "Practicing Theory"; J. Harris, *A Teaching Subject;* Helmers; Horner, *Terms of Work;* Jarratt and Worsham; Kent; S. Miller, *Textual Carnivals;* North; Ray; Schell; Sirc; and others have taken up for composition. Central to these efforts in feminist studies are questions such as these: Has academic feminism compromised its commitment to social, cultural, political, and economic change? What does it mean for the field that many academic feminists have engaged in the kind of agonistic intellectual combat that many associate with patriarchy? What indeed constitutes effective resistance to patriarchy within the academy? Does resistance expressed at the level of style (through, for example, personal criticism) represent a significant intervention in contemporary assumptions and practices?

And what about composition? Has it abandoned its traditional commitment to teaching—especially to the teaching of basic and first-year writing courses? What does it mean for composition that many scholars, myself included, seldom if ever teach the course that once provided the raison d'etre for the discipline and that the gap between those who are situated as theorists and those who are situated as practitioners has grown greater, not smaller, during composition's disciplinary ascendancy? How should we view the theory wars that have played such a prominent role in recent scholarly work? What constitutes progress in a field committed to pedagogical as well as scholarly action?

At the heart of questions such as these is the concept of accountability. This concept plays a key role in Rich's essay, which discusses ways a "politics of location" might enable Western feminists to interrogate and deconstruct white privilege as it has circulated in North American feminism. Rich is careful to emphasize the tentative and ongoing nature of her inquiry: "I come here," she observes, "with notes but without absolute conclusions. This is not a sign of loss of faith or hope. These notes are marks of a struggle to keep moving, a struggle for accountability" (211).

In scholarly work, issues of accountability are linked to issues of methodology and argument. These issues constitute a second pathway or engagement with feminist theory that has influenced the development of this project. In writing *Situating Composition,* I have been influenced by such scholars as Code, Flax, Fuss, Gore, and Haraway—feminist theorists who have raised powerful and important questions about the role of writing in contemporary theory. In *Simians, Cyborgs, and Women: The Reinvention of Nature,* for instance, Haraway emphasizes the limitations

25

of such traditional analytical strategies as taxonomizing, arguing that "Taxonomies of feminism produce epistemologies to police deviation from official woman's experience" (156). As an alternative, Haraway calls for what she terms "situated knowledges" (183)—knowledges that are "tuned to resonance, not to dichotomy" (194–95).

As these comments suggest, Haraway believes that scholars would benefit from considering alternatives to traditional textual practices. She is quick to note, however, that no practices, including her own, hold ethical or political guarantees. "All components of the desire" that motivate her work she observes, "are paradoxical and dangerous, and their combination is both contradictory and necessary" (*Simians* 187). Haraway also acknowledges the dangers that postmodern assumptions and practices pose for scholars. In reflecting on her own work and that of others participating in what she terms "the radical social constructionist programme" (185) in science studies, Haraway sees much to criticize:

> I, and others, started out wanting a strong tool for deconstructing the truth claims of hostile science by showing the radical historical specificity, and so contestability, of *every* layer of the onion of scientific and technological constructions, and we end up with a kind of epistemological electro-shock therapy, which far from ushering us into the high stakes tables of the game of contesting public truths, lays us out on the table with self-induced multiple personality disorder. . . . We unmasked the doctrines of objectivity because they threatened our budding sense of collective historical subjectivity and agency and our "embodied" accounts of the truth, and we ended up with one more excuse for not learning any post-Newtonian physics and one more reason to drop the old feminist self-help practices of repairing our own cars. They're just texts anyway, so let the boys have them back. (*Simians* 186)

In comments such as this, Haraway points to the need for greater attention to the rhetoric, politics, and ethics of scholarly writing and emphasizes that, as Gore puts it in *The Struggle for Pedagogies,* "there are no inherently liberating practices or discourses" (58).

This is as true of Rich's effort to formulate a politics of location as it is of any other work, including my own. At the time that it was published and in the years immediately thereafter, Rich's "Notes Toward a Politics of Location" made an important contribution to feminist and critical inquiry. As Caren Kaplan points out in "The Politics of Location as

Transnational Feminist Critical Practice," in the mid- and late 1980s, Rich's essay helped to deconstruct "hegemonic uses of the word 'woman' within a context of U.S. racism and elite or academic feminist practices" (138). That the concept of a politics of location met a strong need is evident by its broad circulation. As Kaplan notes, since Rich's essay was published, this term "has traveled far afield to alight in the proceedings of the Modern Language Association as well as various humanities conferences, publications, and other cultural forms of articulation" (138). But particularly from the perspective of hindsight, there is a significant limitation to Rich's formulation. For as Kaplan observes, while Rich succeeded in challenging "Western feminists to acknowledge the problematic power of mapping, naming, and establishing agendas," her analysis also tended to simply "[conflate] 'Western' and 'white,' reinscribing the centrality of white women's position within feminism" (141).[3]

In *Situating Composition,* I hope to remind scholars that the power we hold of "mapping, naming, and establishing agendas" for composition can be equally problematic. Not surprisingly, the criticism that Kaplan makes about Rich's essay is one that, potentially at least, could be made about *Situating Composition.* For in my effort to hold myself and other scholars in composition accountable, I could be viewed as attempting to reinscribe the centrality of scholarly work in composition. This is not my intention. Rather, I focus on scholarly work because I want to inquire into some of the consequences of composition's development as a discipline and to suggest some ways that scholars in the field might productively hold ourselves accountable for our work. Thus my emphasis on the politics of location.

I have been drawn to this concept because it offers, as Caren Kaplan points out in *Questions of Travel: Postmodern Discourses of Displacement,* a potential "solution to the universalizing gestures of masculinist thought" (143) and a way of avoiding "the abstract aestheticization of theoretical practices" (144). Kaplan goes on to argue—as I will do throughout *Situating Composition*—that there is nevertheless no guarantee that the concept of a politics of location, or any other concept, can necessarily resist universalization and totalizing theoretical practices. Consequently, whether the concept of a politics of location "encourages resistance to hegemonic formations, whether it becomes its own academic reification—turning into an instrument of hegemony itself—or whether it marks important shifts in discourses of location and displacement depends, not surprisingly, upon who utilizes the concept in what particular context" (Kaplan *Questions* 162–63). Although Kaplan never refers to rhetoric, this statement clearly reflects a rhetorical understanding of discourse, one that emphasizes that what writers *do* in scholarly texts—the specific decisions they make at every level as they move through their analyses—is at least as important as what they *say* at the level of theory. This understanding applies as much to *Situating Composition* as it does to any other scholarly effort.

There is a final point I need to make. A politics of location could seem to suggest a limited notion of subjectivity, one that assumes that location determines or reflects identity—as in "I was born in Ohio, but I now consider myself an Oregonian." With Kaplan, I view location instead as "discontinuous, multiply constituted, and traversed by diverse social formations" (*Questions* 182). In this sense, location is not fixed, and its interests, subjects, social formations, and purposes are sometimes in harmony, sometimes in tension, sometimes in conflict. Any location, in other words, is multiply constituted and cannot helpfully be characterized as a single place or identity. As a result, issues of power and authority are key to understanding the politics of location, and there is—as I hope the scenarios at the start of chapter 1 suggest—no "place," no location, that is without potential dangers as well as benefits.[4] I make this point to emphasize that my inquiry into the politics of location in composition is in no sense a celebration of the local. It is, instead, a rhetorically and materially grounded effort to think through some issues of scholarly practice in composition. In this sense, this text shows, in Rich's terms, the "marks of a struggle to keep moving" (211).

Though I have cast the preceding understanding in the context of Rich's "Notes Toward a Politics of Location," the insight is hardly limited to her work or to feminist theory. Earlier, I referred to Kenneth Burke's observation that "if any given terminology is a *reflection* of reality, by its very nature as a terminology it must be a *selection* of reality; and to this extent it must function also as a *deflection* of reality" ("Terministic Screens" 45). The work of Burke and other scholars grounded in the rhetorical tradition is another important intellectual and disciplinary location for me. Indeed, several of Burke's concepts play an important role in part 3 of this study. Also important have been the efforts of such diversely situated scholars as Deborah Britzman; Michelle Fine; Patty Lather; Richard Miller; Ellen Messer-Davidow, David Shumway, and David Sylvann;

Richard Miller; James Sosnoski; and Evan Watkins—all of whose work has encouraged me to step outside my commonsense understandings of academic norms and practices and to look at them—and at my own experiences within the academy—from new perspectives. And of course I would not have undertaken this project at all if I were not deeply immersed in and committed to the scholarly work of composition.

If I were to identify all the scholars in composition whose work has been important to me and explain the reasons why this has been so, this chapter would be considerably longer. There are two scholars who I do want to mention here, however: Susan Miller, author of *Textual Carnivals: The Politics of Composition,* and Sharon Crowley, author of *Composition in the University: Historical and Polemical Essays.* As I noted earlier, reflections on these studies play an important role in my analysis. In their studies, Miller and Crowley challenge basic understandings of the work of composition, and their challenges have served as a powerful stimulus to my own thinking and writing. Even when I have found myself in disagreement with them, Crowley's and Miller's work has both enriched and enabled my effort to inquire into composition's politics of location in the academy.

The Problem of Writing

My hope is that *Situating Composition* will encourage those situated in a variety of locations in composition—but especially scholars in privileged positions—to think productively about our work and its ongoing potential and difficulties. Obviously, I hope that readers experience my text in this way. I want to acknowledge, however, that as is the case with all scholarly work, there are limitations as well as advantages to my effort. I also want to acknowledge that although I have attempted to interrogate my own assumptions and practices—to implicate myself in, rather than distance myself from, that which I analyze—I can never fully succeed in doing so.

I am no more capable than any other scholar is, in other words, of escaping what I have come to think of as the problem of writing. My understanding of this problem is indebted to postmodern critiques of power and knowledge—critiques that emphasize that language is not a transparent means of expressing ideas but is instead implicated in foundational ways with the desire for individual and institutional power. I can attempt to recognize the ways these desires circulate in my writing, but I can only partly do so. Nor can I escape the limitations, as well as the strengths, of my embodied experience. The ideas I present in *Situating Composition* are inevitably contextualized by my experience as a scholar of this and not that generation, as a teacher who has taught at this but not that kind of institution, who has read these but not those other scholarly works. I want to emphasize, then, that the perspective I bring to this study is limited in significant ways; it enables me to see some things and not others.

I cannot identify all the potential limitations of my work, but I can acknowledge those that are visible to me. I have already recognized, for instance, that what I intend to serve as an invitation to accountability could be viewed as an effort to keep scholarly work at the center of composition's disciplinary focus. Other potential limitations inform this work. In *Situating Composition*, I hope to encourage scholars to consider the costs and dangers, as well as the benefits, of conventional disciplinary assumptions and practices. I will suggest, for instance, that we might do well to be suspicious of calls for broad paradigm shifts and of taxonomies that, as Haraway observes, can serve as much to police deviations from privileged narratives as to clarify differences in theory and practice. And yet the consequences of changes at the level of scholarly practice for those who are diversely situated in the work of composition are hardly clear. As I will emphasize in part 3 of *Situating Composition*, scholarly work circulates primarily among scholars; for this reason, changes in scholarly practice may hold few consequences for the majority of teachers of writing.

There are other questions I would like to raise about the effort I undertake here. Does my attempt to inquire into negative as well as positive effects of such practices as taxonomizing represent an intervention in assumptions and practices at the formative level of style and content, or is it instead an example of what Watkins in *Work Time* terms the "ideologies of 'the new' as a privileged form of value" (15) in the academy—yet another effort, in other words, to justify one's writing through the modernist strategy of "making it new."

It would be ironic indeed if a work intended at least in part to question conventional notions of disciplinary progress in composition nevertheless in some ways depends on and enacts this construct. And yet at one level, this contradiction surely exists, for to secure a contract for this book I had to convince my editor and various reviewers that this study would contribute something that was if not new then at least timely to current scholarly conversations—that it would contribute, in other words, to disciplinary progress. This is not the only potential irony inherent in my textual practices. One argument I hope to make in this work, for instance, is that what is sometimes termed a theory-practice split in composition is better understood as a practice-practice split. Nevertheless, with the exception of chapter 5, where I substitute the terms "practice of theory" and "practice of teaching" for "theory" and "practice," elsewhere I use these terms and in so doing reify the very construct that I wish to challenge.

I have done so because I could not find other terms that would communicate my intended meaning in any succinct way. I also could not identify or create terms that would avoid suggesting a fixed location, as the terms "theory" and "practice" do. As a consequence, even though I theorize location as a fluid, dynamic intersection of subjects, purposes, and interests, at the level of textual practice, I found myself forced to depend on terms that suggest otherwise. I considered placing these two terms in quotation marks to suggest my discomfort with their conventional connotations—but the thought of page after page littered with quotation marks caused me to abandon this idea. Readers should know, however, that when I use these terms, I consider them to be overdetermined, contested, and problematic—if also necessary for the development of my argument.

I was aware of another terminological problem as I worked on *Situating Composition:* the problem of pronouns, particularly the pronouns "we" and "they." Most typically, scholars use the pronoun "they" to refer to those about whom they are writing. But such pronoun use distances the writer from the issue or problem being discussed. I want to acknowledge my "thereness" in the work of composition during the last three decades: hence my intermittent use of the pronoun "we" throughout this study. I hope that readers find that this effort to claim my involvement with scholarly projects that I now wish to reexamine justifies the stylistic awkwardness of inconsistent pronouns.

There is a final terminological issue I wish to discuss, and this is my use of the term "composition." As question 3 in the introduction to part 1 of *Situating Composition* indicates, I am aware that for some, the word "composition" holds connotations they wish to resist. Hence the adoption of such terms as "rhetoric and composition," "composition studies," and "rhetoric and writing" as designators for the field. When I use the term "composition"—as I do in the title of this book and throughout my analysis—I am intentionally evoking this term's problematic genealogy (which links it with traditions of schooled literacy instruction that many deplore) and its ambiguous, overdetermined status. I do so to call attention to the tensions and contradictions inherent both to this term and to the field at large.

What We Talk about When We Talk about Composition

When I was completing final revisions of *Situating Composition,* I was surprised to discover that I had misremembered the title of the Raymond Carver story that I hoped the title of chapter 1 would evoke in the minds of readers. The short story that I remembered as "What Are We Talking about When We Talk about Love?" is actually titled "What We Talk about When We Talk about Love." I discovered, as well, that I had actually read a text titled "What Are We Talking about When We Talk about Composition?," for an article by David Foster with this title appeared in volume 8 (1988) of the then-titled *JAC: Journal of Advanced Composition.* Whether Foster meant to evoke Carver's story, originally published in 1981, I do not know. Clearly, however, the two became linked in my mind.

It seems appropriate to evoke Carver's original title here, for in this concluding chapter of part 1 of *Situating Composition,* I not only situate myself in the work of composition but also situate my argument by previewing its chapter-by-chapter development. Before doing so, however, I want to comment briefly on Foster's article, for despite its distance in time it is relevant to my own study. Foster's article is a review of three books: Richard Beach and Lillian S. Bridwell's 1984 *New Directions in Composition Research: Perspectives in Writing Research;* George Hillocks Jr.'s 1986 *Research on Written Composition: New Directions for Teaching;* and Stephen M. North's 1987 *The Making of Knowledge in Composition: Portrait of an Emerging Field.* Foster begins his review by reminding readers of the disciplinary and professional gains that composition has made in the 1970s and 1980s. He points out, however, that as an "awakening giant," composition "is only now testing its limbs and eyeing its proffered seat in the academic circle" (30). As a result, composition is in the midst of an identity crisis, one characterized by "an acutely self-reflexive mood" (30). Central to this identity crisis "is the question of composition's status as a discipline" (31).

Though Foster calls attention to composition's obsession with its own disciplinary and professional status, his main concern in the review is to argue against a narrow reliance on empirically based studies in favor of a broader "intellectual pluralism" (38). The latter is an argument that no longer needs to be made in composition; if anything, the situation is now reversed and those who favor what Davida Charney in "Empiricism Is Not a Four-Letter Word" refers to as "socially-situated studies" are on the defensive (567). Nevertheless, in many ways, when one considers what scholars talk about when we talk about composition, often the answer is this: scholars talk about our field's standing in the academy.

As chapter 3 will suggest, this was certainly the case in the 1970s and 1980s. Part 2 of *Situating Composition* takes up issues surrounding scholars' anxieties about composition's professional and disciplinary status, and it does so by undertaking yet another reading of the writing process movement. The introduction to part 2, "A Profession in the Making," argues for the importance of rereading the writing process movement. In this introduction, I point out that while I hope in this section of *Situating Composition* to provide a more historically accurate portrait of the years that saw the ascendancy of the writing process movement, my primary interest in rereading this movement is in identifying those developments in the past that are relevant to composition's contemporary situation. I emphasize, in other words, that in rereading the writing process movement, I am not arguing that this movement should somehow, phoenix-like, rise up from its ashes to claim its place at the center of theory and practice in composition. Indeed, my analysis in part 2 is meant to challenge the way initiatives such as the writing process (or social process, or post-process) movement circulate in scholarly work in the field.

In chapter 3, "Paradigms Lost: The Writing Process Movement and the Professionalization of Composition," I take a historically situated look at the writing process movement, and I do so primarily in the context of composition's professionalization. Chapter 3 opens with a review of critiques of the writing process movement and of claims that composition is now firmly post-process. Despite the fact that this position has been broadly accepted by scholars, I argue it is time to take another look at the writing process movement. To do so, I present a materially grounded history, one that draws both on generally available information about composition's development during the late 1970s and early 1980s (starting dates of journals, development of PhD programs, tables of content of notable scholarly anthologies, etc.) and on my own lived experience.

I also analyze the writing process movement in the context of research on professionalization by such scholars as Magali Sarfatti Larson and Andrew Abbott. Others, such as Susan Miller and Sharon Crowley, have also discussed the role that the writing process movement played in composition's professionalization. Indeed, both Miller and Crowley argue that the writing process movement was the primary engine of composition's professionalization. I hope to complicate arguments such as these. I hope as well to suggest that rather than being an event of the past, professionalization is an ongoing process, one that requires continual examination. I conclude chapter 3 by reflecting on the writing process movement in the context of issues surrounding the politics of location.

Chapter 4, "On Process, Social Process, and Post-Process," continues my effort to reread the writing process, but it does so from a different perspective than chapter 3. This chapter questions scholars' tendency to proclaim decontextualized theoretical revolutions, and it does so by looking concretely at the ways process, social process, and post-process assumptions and practices have (and have not) influenced my own teaching practices. While the resulting analysis is hardly generalizable, it does, I believe, remind readers that in many cases, pedagogical change occurs incrementally and partially, and is influenced as much by teachers's predilections and institutional situations as by theoretical movements.

I conduct this inquiry by analyzing course descriptions for every first-year and advanced composition class I have taught since coming to Oregon State University in 1980. While these are only artifacts of a more complex and situated teaching experience, they nevertheless suggest that while my teaching reflects developing trends in composition, elements of current-traditional, process, social process, and post-process theories can all be identified in these documents. In particular, the basic structure of my composition classes reflects an ongoing commitment to process in its emphasis on invention, collaboration, peer response, and revision. I conclude this chapter by encouraging scholars to explore ways of getting beyond "killer dichotomies" (Berthoff) and of enacting more situated, materially grounded practices.

By focusing on the writing process movement in part 2 of *Situating Composition,* I hope to accomplish several interrelated goals. I hope, first of all, to provide a materially grounded portrait of the disciplinary and professional work of composition during the 1970s and 1980s, the period of time during which many important steps toward composition's professionalization were taken. I want to remind readers of the *multiple* movements that were underway at that time and to challenge the generally accepted view that the writing process movement was the primary engine of composition's professionalization. As I have already mentioned, I wish to do so because statements such as these come dangerously close to letting contemporary scholars in composition off the hook, for they imply that composition's professionalization is an event of the past. Yet as Larson, Abbott, and others argue, professionalization is an ongoing process for which those involved must remain responsible.

I also want to raise questions about such conventional scholarly practices as the establishment of taxonomies that place scholars in opposing camps and histories of composition that rely upon a revolutionary rhetoric that chart "progress" via the enactment—and then defeat—of such theoretical and pedagogical initiatives as the writing process movement. There have been many struggles over pedagogy in composition during the past thirty years, and I hope to encourage scholars to consider whether there might not be more productive ways to enact disciplinary progress. As my summary of chapter 4 suggests, I also want to remind readers that progress often takes different forms in scholarly work and in teaching.

In part 3 of *Situating Composition*, "Thinking Through Practice," I continue to explore issues surrounding the writing process movement, but I subordinate these issues to a broader inquiry into what in chapter 5 I refer to as "the practice of theory" in composition. As the introduction to part 3, "Practice Makes Practice," suggests, I do so because I want to address a number of issues related to the politics of location in composition. In the introduction, I raise one such issue or problem—the sense on the part of many teachers of writing that, as Cynthia Lewiecki-Wilson and Jeff Sommers argue in "Professing at the Fault Lines: Composition at Open Admissions Institutions," increasingly scholarly work in the field "structure[s] perceptions so that it is very difficult to see, let alone seriously consider, any possibility of satisfying intellectual work occurring between composition teachers and their students in open admissions programs" (439)—and, I would add, in many other settings as well.

In the introduction to part 3 of *Situating Composition*, I briefly explore efforts that such scholars as Stephen North, Patricia Harkin, and Bruce Horner have made to address this problem, and I argue for the value of inquiring into the *practice* of theory. I conclude the introduction by arguing that when scholars consider issues of theory and practice in composition, it is crucial that we recognize that, as Deborah Britzman argues in *Practice Makes Practice: A Critical Study of Learning to Teach,* practice does indeed make practice. I argue as well for the value of thinking *through* practice. Such an effort entails not only thinking *about* practice—about teaching, writing program administration, research, and so on—but also attempting to use practice as a means of thinking *through* scholarly and professional issues. Hence the title of this section of *Situating Composition.*

In composition, issues of the practice of theory have generally been considered in the context of the theory/practice nexus. In chapter 5, "On Theory, Theories, and Theorizing," I acknowledge the insights that such scholars as Stephen North, Louise Wetherbee Phelps, Anne Gere, Beverly Moss, Bruce Horner, and Hephzibah Roskelly and Kate Ronald have made to considerations of theory and practice in composition. I describe my own approach to the theory/practice nexus, which as I have already mentioned is to think *through* practice. Such an approach encourages scholars to view theory as nothing more—and nothing less—than situated practice. As practice, theory can circulate in multiple ways in composition, and in the academy. In this chapter, I consider some of limitations as well as strengths of critiques of the writing progress movement—particularly critiques by Susan Miller and Sharon Crowley. I conclude the chapter by stepping back from Crowley's and Miller's studies to consider some general issues involved with theoretical critique in composition, such as differences in the ideologies that inform the practice of theory and practice of teaching. I do so not to challenge the usefulness of theoretical critique; indeed, *Situating Composition* not only draws upon but also exemplifies this scholarly methodology. Rather, I hope to encourage scholars who, like myself, are drawn to this critique to consider the disadvantages and dangers, as well as the benefits, of this scholarly practice.

In chapter 6, "Who's Disciplining Whom?" I continue my argument that scholars in composition—particularly scholars engaged in theoretical critique—would do well to attend more carefully than we sometimes do the to the politics of our location in the academy. I argue here, as I argue elsewhere in part 3 of *Situating Composition,* that the consequences of theory depend upon the ways theory is deployed and on scholars' attentiveness to the politics of our location. In this regard, I consider

Susan Miller's and Sharon Crowley's arguments that required first-year composition classes serve primarily to discipline students—and teachers—as subjects. While I acknowledge the hegemonic function of all educational practices, I suggest (via an analysis of a cartoon in Matt Groening's *School Is Hell*, "Lesson 19: Grad School—Some People Never Learn") that those who have willingly acceded to the disciplining rigors of graduate study should think twice before arguing about the consequences of one or more ten- or fifteen-week terms of required writing courses for others. In this and other ways, I hope to remind readers that no one—however politically, culturally, and ideologically aware—can escape the disciplining influence of ideology. I suggest that those who engage in theoretical critique might helpfully attempt to find ways to read against the grain of our arguments to identify the ideologies that circulate within them. Following the principle that what I advocate for others I should practice myself, I close this chapter by attempting to read against the grain of my own practice in *Situating Composition*.

In the final chapter of *Situating Composition*, I move from critique to constructive suggestions about potential ways scholars in composition might think more productively *through* practice. In so doing, I attempt to flesh out what Min-Zhan Lu in "Redefining the Literate Self: The Politics of Critical Affirmation," refers to as the practice of critical affirmation in composition. I also attempt to convey some of the ways that thinking through practice has enriched not only my scholarly work but also my teaching. Doing so has enabled me to think in more complex and helpful ways about my effort to help students experience the benefits of collaborative learning and writing, and it has also reminded me of the import role that emotion plays in learning. Thinking through practice has reminded me, in other words, that what I *do* as a teacher is at least as important to students as what I *say* at the level of explicit theory.

In the concluding pages of *Situating Composition*, I raise a number of unresolved questions that I continue to ponder as I consider composition's professionalization and the practice of theory as it has developed in composition. What, I wonder, might the turn toward politics *in theory* but the continuation of business-as-usual in the politics of location *in practice* reveal to scholars about our own impulses and desires? Why has there been so little interest in and discussion of the teaching of writing *as writing* in recent years? With these and other questions, I hope to invite readers to inquire further into the politics of composition's location in the academy.

PART TWO

Rereading the Writing Process

A Profession in the Making

Part 1 of *Situating Composition* raised a number of questions about the politics of composition's location in the academy. The introduction to part 1 presented ten sets of questions that I hope to address in various ways throughout this study. In chapter 1, I attempted to give specificity and concreteness to these questions via a number of scenarios grounded in my own experiences as a teacher, scholar, and writing program administrator. In these and other ways, I hope throughout *Situating Composition* to call attention to the helpfulness of looking beyond commonsense assumptions about what composition is and does to consider the multiple, and at times competing, activities that fall under its domain. Composition has proven to be an elastic construct that can represent both the disciplinary enterprise of composition—an enterprise that is carried out largely by tenure-line faculty whose position descriptions carry the expectation of ongoing research—as well as a multitude of related curricular, administrative, and social and political activities. These activities include, among others, teaching an array of undergraduate and graduate writing courses in a wide range of programs (from basic, first-year, and advanced writing to adult education, ESL, service-learning, and distance education programs) in diverse kinds of appointments (from part-time to full-time adjunct and tenure-line positions); participating in a variety of bureaucratic and curricular efforts that either directly or indirectly involve the work of composition (such as the Calibration Institute that I described in chapter 1); administering first-year, advanced, and graduate-level writing programs; and directing or working in writing centers, writing-across the curriculum, and service-learning programs, and community and workplace literacy centers.

Given the variability of work that occurs under the rubric of composition, it is hardly surprising that some of composition's activities are more visible— and more valued—than others. Thus a related theme in part 1 calls attention to the politics of location in composition. As someone writing about the politics of location, it seems incumbent for me to inquire into the politics of *my* location, and I attempted to do so in chapter 2. I also commented on the "passionate attachments" that I bring to this study and articulated the significance that the term "politics of location" holds for me (Royster, *Traces* 280; Rich 210). I closed chapter 2 by examining some problems of writing that I encountered in working on *Situating Composition,* for I hope in this study to demonstrate the potential heuristic value of self-reflexive, self-critical scholarly practices— practices that encourage scholars not only to interrogate the work of others but also to interrogate our own ideas and arguments.

In part 2 of this study, I shift gears from the problem-posing emphasis of part 1 to consider the nature, status, and ongoing significance of the writing process movement. Such an effort might seem decidedly passé. By the early 1990s, there was a growing consensus among scholars that composition has "moved on" from the writing process and is in one way or another "post-process." The scholarly conference that I attended at the University of New Hampshire in 1992, "The Writing Process: Retrospect and Prospect," had an alternately nostalgic, defensive, and elegiac air. By the late 1990s, composition seemed more and more to be post-process, as collections such as Thomas Kent's 1999 *Post-Process Theory: Beyond the Writing-Process Paradigm* attest.

The challenge I face in part 2 of this study is to persuade readers that the writing process movement still merits scholarly interest. In chapter 3, "Paradigms Lost: The Writing Process Movement and the Professionalization of Composition," I argue that there is indeed much that can still be learned from a reconsideration of this movement, particularly when one considers it from the perspective of composition's professionalization as an academic discipline. As Richard Ohmann observed in a 1992 conversation with John Trimbur,

> a profession in the making will seize on whatever impetus and opportunity there are. ... [P]rofessionalizing itself inevitably has to create something that looks like a body of knowledge, some sort of theory at the center. You have to acquire it to gain admittance or otherwise it isn't going to be a profession. (Trimbur, "In the Beginning" 140)

In the 1970s and 1980s, composition definitely constituted a profession in the making; chapter 3 attempts to chart a number of the activities that provided "impetus and opportunity" for that effort. In so doing, it contributes to the line of inquiry exemplified by such historical projects as Maureen Daly Goggin's *Authoring a Discipline: Scholarly Journals and the Post–World War II Emergence of Rhetoric and Composition*, Gerald Nelms's "Reassessing Janet Emig's *The Composing Processes of Twelfth Graders:* An Historical Perspective," Donna Burns Phillips, Ruth Greenberg, and Sharon Gibson's "*College Composition and Communication:* Chronicling a Discipline's Genesis," and Mary Rosner, Beth Boehm, and Debra Journet's *History, Reflection, and Narrative: The Professionalization of Composition, 1963–1983*. Studies such as these attempt to provide a materially grounded perspective on—and history of—composition's development as a discipline.

Histories are both interested and situated: however strong their reliance on materially grounded artifacts, histories are stories. In reexamining the story of the writing process movement, my primary interest is in identifying those developments in the past that have ongoing presences—especially those presences that reveal continuing tensions and contradictions in composition's location in the academy. I am also interested in providing a materially grounded history of this time period; such an analysis reveals that the writing process movement was hardly the singular engine of composition's disciplinary success and that composition's professionalization was the result of multiple forces—multiple movements, as it were.

I bring an additional interest to this effort to reread the writing process movement: I want to challenge readings of the writing process movement that present that movement as either so discredited or so clearly in the past as to be no longer relevant to the field. Such an approach, I argue, is problematic in several respects. From the perspective of pedagogical practice, activities associated with the writing process movement continue to play a role in many writing courses—including, as I demonstrate in chapter 4, my own. An equally if not more important issue involves the connection that a number of scholars have posited between the writing process movement and composition's professionalization. Such a connection, I argue, makes it too easy for scholars to view professionalization as an event of the past and thus to let ourselves off the hook vis-à-vis contemporary dilemmas and problems that grow out of composition's professionalization. As I will argue in chapter 3, professionalization is an ongoing process, so it is important that scholars hold ourselves accountable for the role we play in composition's current disciplinary and professional development.

As these comments suggest, in part 2 of *Situating Composition,* I want not only to challenge some prominent narratives about the professionalization of composition in the 1970s and 1980s but also to raise questions about the strategies scholars have drawn upon as we have told these stories. Too often, I argue, scholars narrating composition's recent history have relied on notions of disciplinary progress that are grounded in what Evan Watkins terms "ideologies of 'the new'" in the academy (15). I also comment on another common scholarly practice, which is to employ a rhetoric of crisis and revolution that depends upon the creation of opposing projects or camps—current-traditional rhetoric versus the writing process movement, for instance, or the writing process movement versus social and/ or post-process theories. These camps often circulate as decontextualized, commodified representations of pedagogical practice—and thus can be quite distant from the material practices involved in the teaching of writing.

In an effort to lessen this gap, in chapter 4, "On Process, Social Process, and Post-Process," I attempt a materially grounded examination of the ways change happens in one teacher's classroom. This examination is limited, and in multiple ways. For one thing, the classroom that I examine is my own. Furthermore, this examination is limited to such pedagogical traces of teaching as course descriptions and syllabi. Nevertheless, this analysis will, I hope, serve to remind readers that progress often takes different forms in the scholarly and pedagogical work of composition. It reminds readers, as well, of the situated, incremental nature of pedagogical change and the difficulty of generalizing broadly about teachers' practices.

Before turning to chapters 3 and 4, I would like to mention a few caveats. The first reiterates a comment I made in chapter 1, but it seems important to repeat this comment here: in writing about my own experience—as I do in different ways in both chapters—I do not assume that my experience is representative. I recognize, as well, that my perspective and insights are limited by the temporal and material situatedness of my experience. This experience enables me to see and understand some things, and not others.

I also want to emphasize that although I am attempting to encourage those in composition to think about the writing process movement in different ways, I am not arguing for some new, improved version of the writing process. Rather, I am using the writing process movement as a test case for a larger reconsideration of the development of composition as a discipline and of the nature and consequences of scholarly practice. As I hope my analysis in chapter 4 demonstrates, I have in a number of important ways "moved on" from my teaching practices in the 1970s and 1980s. In looking at the writing progress movement, I hope to encourage scholars to reconsider the ways we have tended to enact disciplinary progress and to acknowledge some of the negative, as well as positive, consequences of this enactment.

One such consequence is an increasing distance from the materially grounded scene of the classroom. Hence my decision to provide glimpses into my own teaching practices in chapter 4. I do so with some hesitation. While I take teaching very seriously indeed, I am hardly an exemplary teacher, and it felt—and still feels—uncomfortable to expose my teaching to public scrutiny. I do so in the hope that others will make a similar effort to find spaces for their teaching in scholarly work.

One final comment: in looking at the writing process movement in the context of composition's development in the 1970s and 1980s, I want to emphasize that I recognize that the story I narrate here is most assuredly not *the* story of composition but *a* story, one that highlights certain events, persons, and experiences while placing others in shadow. To the extent that this story resonates with readers—to the extent that it encourages readers to consider their own assumptions and practices—it will be heuristic. But it will not lead to some broad revolution in theory and practice in the field. Rather, it will at best lead to the asking of further questions.

Some of these questions may and should be directed toward the inevitable lacunae in my narrative. In "History in the Spaces Left: African American Presence and Narratives of Composition Studies," Jacqueline Jones Royster and Jean C. Williams comment on gaps and omissions in many histories of composition. They point out that often "the viewpoint of these narratives has not had to be articulated" (565). Even when scholars have done so, they have still often failed to "craft a space . . . for the voices of people of color," or for others whose experiences are outside the mainstream (566). Though I have attempted to articulate the viewpoint that I bring to *Situating Composition,* I have been significantly less successful in "craft[ing] a space . . . for the voices of people of color" (566). This is a failure that I regret.

In their article, Royster and Williams assert:

> those of us who write composition narratives and those of us who use them need to be critically disposed to see the negative effects of primacy, the simultaneous existence of multiple viewpoints, and the need to articulate those viewpoints and to merge them in the interest of the larger project of knowledge making in the discipline. (568)

I agree. I thus invite readers to read this section of *Situating Composition* with the following questions posed by Royster and Williams in mind: "For whom is this claim true? For whom is it not true? What else is happening? What are the operational conditions?" (581).

3 Paradigms Lost

The Writing Process Movement and the Professionalization of Composition

> I believe that composition theorists and writing teachers can learn from Thomas Kuhn if they see his theory of scientific revolutions as an analogy that can illuminate developments that are taking place in our profession. Those developments, the most prominent of which is the move to a process-centered theory of teaching writing, indicates that our profession is probably in the first stages of a paradigm shift.—*Maxine Hairston, "The Winds of Change: Thomas Kuhn and The Revolution in the Teaching of Writing"*

In the years since Maxine Hairston made the preceding proclamation, there have been many different readings of what is alternately referred to as the writing process movement or paradigm. As early as 1982—the year that Hairston's essay was published—Patricia Bizzell in "Cognition, Convention, and Certainty" challenged cognitive research on the writing process, charging that cognitivists' focus on "inner-directed" processes caused them to ignore powerful social forces at play in writing (77). "Writing," Bizzell asserts, "is always already writing for some purpose that can only be understood in its community context" (89).

Just as Hairston was praising compositions studies' "move to a process-centered theory of teaching writing," then, scholarly consensus over the nature and helpfulness of process-centered research and teaching was beginning to be challenged. In 1984, for instance, in "Exploring Options in Composing," Jack Selzer questioned the "the" in the writing process, arguing (on the basis of his research on nonacademic writers) that "good writers . . . have several composing styles, not one" (279). While generally praising the research of Linda Flower and John Hayes, Janet Emig, Sondra Perl, and others, Selzer also commented on the tendency for teachers influenced by this work to "attempt to impose a single, 'ideal' composing style on their students" (276).

Other criticisms soon followed. In his 1985 "Writing and Knowing: Toward Redefining the Writing Process," James Reither acknowledged the impact of writing process research, noting that "Composition Studies was transformed when theorists, researchers, and teachers of writing began trying to find out what actually happens when people write" (620). Reither went on to charge, however, that process-based research and teaching are limited to the extent that they focus only upon cognitive concerns:

> writing and what writers do during writing cannot be artificially separated from the social-rhetorical situations in which writing gets done, from the conditions that enable writers to do what they do, and from the motives writers have for doing what they do. (621)

Marilyn Cooper's "The Ecology of Writing," published just a year later, continues Reither's critique of the writing process movement's preoccupation with individual cognition and proposes a new ecological model of writing, one "whose fundamental tenet is that writing is an activity through which a person is continually engaged with a variety of socially constituted systems" (367).

At the time that these and other criticisms of the writing process movement were articulated, I found myself very much in agreement with them—and in many respects I still do. As a scholar and a teacher, I believe that writing needs to be understood in its "community context" (Bizzell, "Cognition" 89), that "writing cannot be artificially separated from the social-rhetorical situations in which writing gets done" (Reither 621). I am deeply sympathetic to the turn toward social constructionism that Cooper's article heralded. And I share Selzer's concern about teachers whose theoretical commitments cause them to impose a rigid and decontextualized pedagogy on their students.

Given this agreement, why entertain yet another rereading of the writing process movement? Why look back? Why not make some new point about what the field should be and do next, rather than focus yet again on where it has been? There are several reasons why I believe such a rereading is necessary. I am concerned, first of all, with the ease and rapidity with which one ostensible revolution in theory and practice was overturned in favor of another. I worry that such revolutions can only occur if research on writing is divorced in essential ways from the "community context" of the messy, impure world of teaching (Bizzell, "Cognition" 89). As I will describe more fully in the next chapter, as a teacher, my efforts to engage and enact the pedagogical implications of recent research have resulted not in revolutionary changes in my teaching but in small, incremental revisions.

I am also drawn to a rereading of the writing process movement because I believe that despite numerous and thoroughgoing critiques, scholars have not attended sufficiently to certain of the "social-rhetorical situations" that both grounded and enabled that movement, particularly those that require self-scrutiny and self-reflexivity (Reither 621). Scholars in composition, like scholars in the humanities in general, have become accomplished at the kind of critique that exposes the working of ideology in both texts and lives. But we have generally aimed our critique at others, not ourselves.

And yet no one, however attuned to the nature of ideology, is immune from its influences—for ideology works most powerfully when we are so immersed in it that we do not even recognize its existence but rather see it as natural or commonsensical—as how things are. Thus for centuries, many women acquiesced to and even embraced traditional gender stereotypes, as indeed many still do. And thus too do many scholars, particularly those privileged by conventional hierarchies of knowledge, accept as natural and commonsensical—as how things are—the ideologies of professionalization and disciplinarity that play such a central role in the academy.

One might think that composition's long-standing marginalization within the academy would encourage resistance to such ideologies, rather than acquiescence. But as John Trimbur points out in "Writing Instruction and the Politics of Professionalization," the need to professionalize and to achieve disciplinary legitimacy is central to "the master plot of the history of writing instruction" in the United States (133). In his essay, Trimbur wonders, in fact, if composition is not "in the thrall" of this master plot and urges greater attention to the multiple consequences of professionalization for composition (134).

In this chapter, I hope to contribute to an understanding of these consequences by exploring the writing process movement and its role in the professionalization of composition. I am hardly the first to address this issue. In *Textual Carnivals: The Politics of Composition,* Susan Miller notes the role that the writing process movement played in legitimating composition studies and analyzes this movement from the perspective of composition's carnivalesque relationship to literary studies and to our culture's

49

broader anxieties about literacy. Lester Faigley takes a different tack in *Fragments of Rationality: Postmodernity and the Subject of Composition*. Here Faigley looks at the process movement—which he calls "the engine of disciplinary success that gained academic respectability and institutional standing for composition studies"—against the background of political change in the United States (49). Faigley thus situates the process movement in the context of large-scale political and economic shifts that occurred in the 1960s and 1970s, and with the ways these impacted public concerns about literacy and education. Faigley also analyzes the impact of the political activism of the 1960s and 1970s on the process movement.

My focus is considerably narrower: in this chapter, I will examine the writing process movement in the context of the specific material interventions that enabled the field to—in a remarkably compressed period of time—improve its professional and disciplinary status. I wish to do so for two reasons. I believe, first of all, that the history of composition's professionalization is both interesting and significant, and I wish to contribute to ongoing research on this history. I also believe that a symptomatic reading of this history, one that is open to multiple and even paradoxical understandings of both the writing process movement and composition's professionalization, can helpfully inform not only our understandings of the writing process movement but also of contemporary scholarly practices.

As this statement suggests, in rereading the writing process movement, I am as much interested in learning about the present as about the past—am interested, in fact, in the ways in which past practices continue into the present. For I am concerned that although contemporary theorizing has shifted considerably since the 1970s and early 1980s, a number of scholarly practices have remained constant. If advocates for the writing process movement created an essentialized and totalized straw man in current-traditional rhetoric, as Susan Miller claims, to what extent have those critiquing the writing process movement relied upon a similar strategy? To what extent, in other words, have arguments in composition studies relied upon what Ralph Cintron characterizes as the "rhetorical rules of *reductio ad simplifacationem*," rules that encourage opposing theoretical camps to "push themselves forward by creating caricatures of each other" (376)? And what does it signify if, despite considerable changes in theory, underlying continuities affecting the relationship of theory and practice remain substantially unchanged?

To raise questions such as these is to challenge the conventional scholarly narratives that composition studies has relied upon to enact disciplinary progress. These narratives have most often emphasized changes
enacted at the level of theory, such as composition's rejection of current-
traditional rhetoric and adoption of a writing process approach to teaching and research, and its subsequent rejection of process for what are
often termed post-process theories. (See, for instance, Kent, *Post-Process*.)
They have focused much less on the scholarly practices that enabled various theories to gain ascendancy.

At the risk of repetition, I want to remind readers of my purpose. In
questioning conventional scholarly narratives of progress in composition,
I do not mean to write a heroes-and-villains history of the field. Rather,
I want to explore multiple understandings of composition's professionalization. I am interested as well in exploring potential tensions and contradictions between composition's sense of itself as an academic outsider
seeking to do good not only in the academy but also in the culture at large
and the reality that, as Susan Jarratt observes in her introduction to *Feminism and Composition Studies: In Other Words,* in many ways, composition (like feminism) is "caught in a bind vis-à-vis the institution: despite
the desire to reconfigure disciplinary boundaries, both [feminist and
composition studies] need to claim disciplinarity to achieve academic
legitimacy and obtain resources" (3). As I do so, I want to argue, with John
Trimbur, that those committed to the scholarly work of composition
should not in any unilateral way reject or embrace composition's professionalization. Rather, we need to attempt "to develop new ways to read
the contradictions of professional life, to grapple daily with the persis-
tent conflicts between building individual careers and popularizing expertise for broader social purposes" (Trimbur, "Writing Instruction" 145).

This chapter represents my effort to read the writing process movement from just such a perspective. In the next section, I look particularly
at the interconnections of individual career building and the effort to
establish composition's scholarly expertise in the academy in the 1970s
and early 1980s. As I do so, I include relevant experiences from my own
academic career, for I want to acknowledge my immersion in the narrative I tell. I want to emphasize, in other words, that I write not as an ob-
jective observer from nowhere, but as someone situated in a specific time
and place. Thus my narrative begins with my own engagement with composition in the 1970s.

The Stepchild of the English Department

When I think back to the 1970s, two passages from scholarly texts of that time speak with particular power to me. The first passage introduces James Kinneavy's 1971 *Theory of Discourse:*

> The present anarchy of the discipline of what is commonly categorized as "composition," both in high schools and colleges, is so evident as scarcely to require proof.
>
> Composition is so clearly the stepchild of the English department that it is not a legitimate area of concern in graduate studies, is not even recognized as a subdivision of the discipline of English in a recent manifesto put out by the major professional association (MLA) of college English teachers . . . in some universities is not a valid area of scholarship for advancement in rank, and is generally the teaching province of graduate assistants or fringe members of the department. (1)

Kinneavy goes on to bemoan the chaotic and precarious situation of composition courses in the academy and to decry these courses' lack of coherence, noting that the "agenda of freshman composition vary from nothing to everything" (1). He is not entirely pessimistic, however. Indeed, Kinneavy argues that "the field of composition . . . is a rich and fertile discipline with a worthy past which should be consulted before being consigned to oblivion" (2). Kinneavy's monumental *Theory of Discourse* is an effort to help revive that discipline.

The second passage, which also opens its text, is from the preface to Mina Shaughnessy's 1977 *Errors and Expectations.* This passage begins with a moment of reflection, as Shaughnessy recalls "the first papers I ever read by severely unprepared freshman writers," (vii) but it quickly moves from reflection to crisis to resolution:

> I keep in my files a small folder of student papers that go back ten years in my teaching career. They are the first papers I ever read by severely unprepared freshman writers and I remember clearly the day I received them. The students who wrote the papers were then enrolled in the SEEK Program at City College, a program for poverty-area youth which preceded Open Admissions at City College and served in many ways as the model for the skills programs that were to be developed under that policy.
>
> I remember sitting alone in the worn urban classroom where my students had just written their first essays and where I now began to

read them, hoping to be able to assess quickly the sort of task that lay ahead of us that semester. But the writing was so stunningly unskilled that I could not begin to define the task nor even sort out the difficulties. I could only sit there, reading and re-reading the alien papers, wondering what had gone wrong and trying to understand what I at this eleventh hour of my students' academic lives could do about it.

Looking at these papers now, I have no difficulty assessing the work to be done nor believing that it can be done. (vii)

What is it about these passages that speaks so powerfully to me? As one who entered composition in the 1970s, I can identify strongly with the sense of professional and disciplinary marginality that Kinneavy expresses—and with his desire both to name and to claim composition's intellectual tradition. I can also identify with the sense of pedagogical crisis that Shaughnessy describes so clearly in the second paragraph of her preface, for my earliest years as a writing program administrator coincided with the perceived literacy crisis heralded by (among other things) *Newsweek's* 1975 article "Why Johnny Can't Write."[1]

Taken together, these two passages provide a compelling portrait of the challenges facing those in the 1960s and 1970s who wanted to argue that, as Kinneavy puts it, composition "is a rich and fertile discipline." For if composition were ever to be anything other than the "stepchild of the English department," scholars needed not only to establish the kind of research agenda that traditionally garners respect in the academy; they also needed to persuade a variety of audiences (from colleagues in English departments to deans and provosts and state and federal officials concerned with issues of literacy and education) that they had the kind of research-based expertise that could authorize them to state with confidence that they had "no difficulty assessing the work to be done nor believing that it can be done" (Shaughnessy, *Errors* vii). There was certainly considerable scholarly work to build upon—from the rhetorically grounded work of such scholars as Wayne Booth and Edward P. J. Corbett, to Francis Christensen's work on style and D. Gordon Rohman and Albert O. Wlecke's early work on invention.

There are additional reasons why Kinneavy's and Shaughnessy's texts speak to me, for in retrospect, they mark my initial distance from—and ultimate engagement with—composition. In 1971, when Kinneavy's *A Theory of Discourse* was published, I was a PhD student at Ohio State University, taking courses that would lead to a dissertation on the Victorian nonsense literature of Edward Lear and Lewis Carroll. Although I would eventually teach composition as a graduate student, my National Defense Education Act fellowship required that I not teach during my first two years of PhD work. (I had no previous teaching experience since the English department at the University of Wisconsin, where I got my masters degree, did not allow MA students to teach.) I could not have been further away from the concerns articulated in the opening of Kinneavy's *Theory of Discourse.*

Nevertheless, by 1977, the year that Mina Shaughnessy's work appeared, I was deeply if erratically immersed in the scholarly work of composition and had a considerable personal and professional investment in the projects of Shaughnessy, Kinneavy, and others. By that time, I had embarked upon my second year as director of the State University of New York at Brockport's writing program. (Like a number of other PhDs in English, I had "converted" from literature to composition and accepted a newly created position in my department.[2]) I thus spent a good deal of energy attempting to persuade others on my campus that, like Shaughnessy, I had "no difficulty assessing the work to be done nor believing that it can be done" (*Errors* vii). Such assurances required a degree of bravado, for although I had worked closely with Susan Miller, Ohio State's director of composition, during my final years of graduate work, the only formal training I had in the teaching of writing was the practicum required of all new teaching assistants at Ohio State.

I am hardly the only faculty member trained in literature who became seriously engaged with the work of composition during the 1970s. The following scholars who completed their PhDs between 1969 and 1980 all wrote their dissertations on literary topics. By the mid 1980s most of the faculty listed here held tenure-line positions in composition—many, though by no means all, as directors of writing programs.[3]

> David Bartholomae, Charles Bazerman, Walter Beale, John Bean, Carol Berkenkotter, James Berlin, Patrick Bizzaro, Patricia Bizzell, John Brereton, Jean Ferguson Carr, Suzanne Clark, Donald Daiker, Timothy Donovan, Peter Elbow, Lester Faigley, Linda Flower, Elizabeth Flynn, Janis Forman, Toby Fulwiler, Richard Fulkerson, Anne Ruggles Gere, Diana George, Michael Halloran, Patricia Harkin, Muriel Harris, Patrick Hartwell, Bruce Herzberg, James Lee Hill, Deborah Holdstein, Harvey Kail, Paul Kameen, Erika Lindemann, Kitty Locker, Elaine Maimon, Susan McLeod, Susan Miller, Gerald Mulderig, Christina

Murphy, Neil Nakadate, Douglas Park, John Ramage, James Reither, Mary Rosner, John Ruszkiewicz, Dennis Rygiel, John Schilb, Robert Schwegler, Charles Schuster, Marie Secor, Jack Selzer, James Slevin, Nathaniel Teich, Victor Vitanza, Steve Witte.

(For a discussion of the influence of literary training on this generation of scholars see Patrick Bizzaro's "What I Learned in Grad School, or Literary Training and the Theorizing of Composition.") A number were also engaged in the effort to develop graduate programs in the teaching of writing. As Richard Lloyd-Jones observes, these programs often grew out of already-developed writing programs: "in response to conscience or public relations, deans asked research people to set up training programs and mass-management procedures to improve the quality of undergraduate teaching. Some of the in-service training programs emerged as *de facto* doctoral programs in composition" (491). The source of these deans' sudden interest in the teaching of writing was, of course, the literacy crisis of the mid 1970s. As Lester Faigley observes in *Fragments of Rationality: Postmodernity and the Subject of Composition,* the literacy crisis provided an important stimulus to the work of composition during this period:

> The literacy crisis gave an air of urgency to curricular reform. Soon provosts and deans began creating positions for writing specialists. New sources of funding became available to launch innovative undergraduate programs and support graduate students in newly formed graduate rhetoric programs. . . . In spite of the continuous skirmishes between literature and composition factions in English departments during the 1970s and 1980s, the institutional conditions at many schools favored the development of writing programs. (67)

The following statement by Walker Gibson in a 1979 article in *ADE* gives some sense of the time and its opportunities and difficulties:

> Obviously, we are all working under the constraints of the current public brouhaha about literacy, a new rage for testing, a return to the basics, and all the rest of it. Much that has been thought and said on these matters, before and after that infamous article in *Newsweek* a couple years ago, is simplistic nonsense. But there is an opportunity here, in the general political climate, to do something useful, to make the teaching of writing, both in school and college, a serious and respected activity.

If, out of the current clamor, nothing more happens except that budgets for composition get a little looser and that directors of freshman writing programs feel a bit less forlorn, these results alone will be welcome progress. (19)

Whatever else the literacy crisis of the 1970s was and did, it provided jobs in composition for newly minted PhDs in English—and it did so at a time when the job market for those graduating with doctorates in literature had bottomed out. In many cases, these positions represented new commitments on the part of English departments to their writing programs. For whether "in response to conscience or public relations," increasingly it was recognized that the common practice of viewing writing program administration as departmental service rather than an area of scholarly inquiry was no longer tenable (Lloyd-Jones 491). For those hired as writing program administrators, such as myself, gratitude for employment was mixed with an acute awareness that we were hired with the understanding that we would "do" something about our writing programs. Since many writing program administrators in the 1970s were the only tenure-line faculty members in composition studies in our departments, we also felt responsible for representing and legitimating our scholarly enterprise in the eyes of our colleagues. If, like Mina Shaughnessy, we sometimes sat in our classrooms or offices wondering what to do about our courses or programs, many of us felt the (unseen) gaze of our colleagues' multiple expectations.[4]

These were considerable responsibilities—especially for those whose formal graduate study focused on literature, rather than on composition. I and others like myself thus had a good deal of scrambling to do if we were to establish the kind of research agenda that would gain credibility for our field (and tenure and promotion for ourselves). Many took advantage of opportunities such as the two-week Summer Rhetoric Seminars that Janice Lauer offered from 1976 to 1989. In an interview with Frederic G. Gale in *Composition Forum,* Lauer had this to say about the seminar:

The two-week seminar drew writing teachers from all over the country, largely college English professors, who wanted a chance to study Comp Theory as it was emerging. The seminar was extremely intense, featured leading theorists of the time and providing an extensive reading list, a massive bibliography, and a display of journals. The seminar drew 440 people over the years, the bibliography grew ten-fold, and the journals multiplied. The seminar, then, stands for me as an index of the growth of the discipline. (Gale 3)

Lauer provides more information about the Summer Rhetoric Seminar in "Disciplinary Formation: The Summer Rhetoric Seminar." She notes, for instance, that the Rhetoric Seminar "differed from a conference: It was a graduate course, offering three to four hours of credit (or official audit)" (505).

The National Endowment for the Humanities (NEH) also funded a number of seminars and institutes devoted to composition studies, such as Edward P. J. Corbett's, Ross Winterowd's, and Richard Young's various summer- and year-long seminars for college and university teachers and the University of Iowa's Writing Institute, which in the early 1980s "received a $680,000 grant from the National Endowment for the Humanities to train freshman composition directors" (Hairston 87). With Sharon Bassett, Jim Berlin, David Fractenberg, Charles Kneupper, Bob Inkster, Victor Vitanza, Sam Watson, and Victoria Winkler, for instance, I participated in Richard Young's year-long NEH seminar in 1978–79. Out of that seminar came Jim Berlin and Robert Inkster's "Current-Traditional Rhetoric: Paradigm and Practice," the article that first presented the taxonomy that Berlin would develop in *Rhetoric and Reality: Writing Instruction in American Colleges, 1900–1985,* as well as the seeds of desire and resistance that would lead to the founding of *Pre/Text: A Journal of Rhetorical Theory.*

This is hardly a definitive list of the activities that helped a generation of scholars who "converted" from literature or related areas to composition gain knowledge and expertise. In 1979, for instance, Aviva Freedman and Ian Pringle of Carleton University coordinated an international conference on the theme "Learning to Write" that attracted 1,250 delegates; in the preface to her 1983 *The Web of Meaning: Essays on Writing, Teaching, Learning, and Thinking,* Janet Emig characterized this conference as "the single most electric professional meeting I ever participated in" (n.pag.).[5] The fact that the collection of essays that grew out of this conference—*Reinventing the Rhetorical Tradition,* edited by Aviva Freedman and Ian Pringle—was published by L and S Books of the University of Central Arkansas for the Canadian Council of Teachers of English is telling. At the time, those who wished to publish scholarly work in composition had few venues available to them. (Donald McQuade's 1979 edited collection, *Linguistics, Stylistics, and The Teaching of Composition,* for instance, was published by the English department at the University of Akron.) Hence the development of such unusual means of publishing scholarly work.

Other examples of activities that played a key role as composition transitioned from being a service course to an academic discipline include the Brooklyn College Institute on Collaborative Learning and Peer Tutoring, directed by Kenneth Bruffee in the early 1980s, and biennial conferences (often organized around a single theme) sponsored by several universities. The University of Wyoming held its first such conference in 1972; Pennsylvania State University in 1982; and the University of New Hampshire in 1984.[6] While established primarily to serve teachers in the schools, such activities as the Bay Area (and later National) Writing Project and the Conference for Teachers of Composition, directed by Erika Lindemann and held at the University of South Carolina during the summer of 1977, provided opportunities for faculty to learn from each other—as David Bartholomae, Rick Coe, Joseph Comprone, Susan Miller, and James Raymond did when they taught together for five weeks at the South Carolina Conference.

As these examples suggest, in the 1970s and early 1980s, when composition was attempting to alter its status as "the stepchild of the English department," a number of newly developed seminars, institutes, and conferences played a critical role in this process. Some of these activities, such as Janice Lauer's summer workshops, relied primarily upon individual initiative and local institutional support. Others, such as the NEH seminars, required bureaucratic, professional, and political support beyond the academy. All provided opportunities for self-education and retraining for faculty members who entered the field with PhDs in literature, not composition.

In the 1970s and early 1980s, these faculty members encountered an interrelated series of opportunities and challenges. For many, including myself, one of the most positive opportunities was, quite simply, the opportunity to have full-time, tenure-line employment. In "Getting Disciplined?" John Schilb describes the role that the job crisis played in his own engagement with composition:

> I never even heard of CCCC until late spring of 1977, when I was desperately looking for a full-time teaching position. Someone told me that there was going to be, strangely enough, a conference devoted to composition, and that job interviews would be available there. So,

along with six other graduate students, I drove nonstop in a college van to Kansas City. And at the end of the trek, I did find myself stumbling bleary-eyed through a hotel where hundreds of people chatted about—of all things—writing! For more reasons than one, I felt as if I were dreaming. (398–99)

Schilb goes on to discuss how his increasing familiarization with research in composition caused him to value the field in its own right—indeed, caused it to seem "more *exciting* than literary studies . . . more open to new questions and modes of inquiry, more willing to ignore disciplinary boundaries, more capable of addressing social needs" (399). Many faculty trained in literature discovered, like Schilb, that composition could be as intellectually exciting and pedagogically rewarding as literature. Some made this discovery in graduate school, as I did. I still remember my excitement when I realized that I could bring both the passion for learning that had brought me to graduate school *and* my equally strong commitment to teaching to this new field.

Others have described similar experiences. In "Close Reading: Accounting for My Life Teaching Writing," one of many narratives collected in Duane Roen, Stuart Brown, and Theresa Enos's *Living Rhetoric and Composition: Stories of the Discipline,* John Trimbur writes: "When I started teaching basic writing, I believed I had found a new and important context for the kind of intellectual and political work I had always wanted to do. I felt that my work teaching was part of a larger struggle for a literate and participatory democracy" (137). And there were scholarly opportunities in composition that did not always seem available in literature. In another essay in that collection, Charles Bazerman's "Looking at Writing; Writing What I See," Bazerman describes his growing recognition that

all the major scholarly and critical tasks (as of the late 1960s) seemed pretty well mined out. Even if one found a 'strangely neglected topic,' as Amis' Lucky Jim put it, becoming an acolyte to another's accomplishment, an accomplishment of another place and time, struck me as a sort of weak goal for one's life. (19)

To take full advantage of these opportunities, however, I and others who had converted from literature to composition needed to find ways to make disciplinary and professional claims for our enterprise. And we generally needed to do so while teaching demanding course loads and/

or directing writing programs of various sorts, from basic and first-year writing programs to writing centers and writing-across-the-curriculum programs. We needed to develop authority not just on one front—as scholars—but on multiple fronts. As scholars, we needed to help establish a research project that would be coherent enough to make sense to colleagues but broad and deep enough to allow for diverse questions and approaches. As teachers and writing program administrators, we needed a pedagogical project that would work not only in individual classrooms but also in the teacher training programs with which many were involved.

A Need in Search of a Discipline

The writing process movement met these needs. Before turning to a discussion of the mechanisms by which it did so, I want to emphasize that the story this chapter narrates about the writing process movement and composition's professionalization is *a,* not *the,* story of how the scholarly discipline of composition came to take its contemporary form. Other stories, told from other perspectives, both supplement and complicate my narrative. James D. Williams devotes the first half of *Visions and Re-Visions: Continuity and Change in Rhetoric and Composition* to "Reflections and Reminiscences" by Richard Lloyd-Jones, W. Ross Winterowd, Frank J. D'Angelo, and John Warnock, scholars whose entry into the field preceded my own. Together, these chapters are a potent reminder of the important work in composition that was undertaken from the 1950s to the 1970s and 1980s.

Individual narratives provide one lens into a field's development; for additional stories of various compositionists' entry into the field, see *Living Rhetoric and Composition: Stories of the Discipline* edited by Duane H. Roen, Stuart C. Brown, and Theresa Enos.[7] Those interested in learning more about the forces that have played a role in composition's professionalization may wish to consult the following historically grounded resources: James A. Berlin's *Writing Instruction in Nineteenth-Century Colleges* and *Rhetoric and Reality: Writing Instruction in American Colleges, 1900–1985,* John C. Brereton's *The Origins of Composition Studies in the American College, 1875–1925,* Robert J. Connors's *Composition-Rhetoric: Backgrounds, Theory, and Pedagogy,* Charles Paine's *The Resistant Writer: Rhetoric as Immunity, 1850 to the Present,* Lucille M. Schultz's *The Young Composers: Composition's Beginnings in Nineteenth-Century Schools,* and Robin Varnum's *Fencing with Words: A History of Writing*

Instruction at Amherst College During the Era of Theodore Baird, 1938–1966.
These studies are a powerful reminder that composition has a long and
complex history in American culture and education. Other studies that
attempt to define or evaluate composition's development as a discipline
include Janice M. Lauer's "Composition Studies: Dappled Discipline,"
Louise Wetherbee Phelps's "Composition Studies," and the essays included in *Composition in the Twenty-First Century: Crisis and Change,*
edited by Lynn Z. Bloom, Donald A. Daiker, and Edward M. White.

The forces that I consider in this chapter are primarily economic and
professional. Through a confluence of events, these forces were substantial. For as I have already indicated, as a result of increased attention to
the teaching of writing catalyzed by media attention to the literacy crisis (which made chairs and deans willing to hire tenure-line faculty in
composition) and to the job market crisis (which made new PhDs in
English happy to accept these positions), in the 1970s and 1980s, a critical mass of new tenure-line faculty joined such advocates for composition as Anne Berthoff, Richard Braddock, William Coles, Edward P. J.
Corbett, Frank D'Angelo, Vivian Davis, Marianna Davis, Janet Emig,
Robert Gorrell, William Irmscher, Richard Larson, Janice Lauer, Richard
Lloyd-Jones, James Kinneavy, Ken Macrorie, Donald Murray, Mina
Shaughnessy, Geneva Smitherman, Gary Tate, Ed White, Ross Winterowd,
Richard Young, and others. Given this new cohort of faculty members, the
time was ripe for composition to legitimate its situation in the academy—
if it could develop a strong disciplinary project. From such a perspective,
composition in the 1970s and early 1980s comprised, in effect, "a need in
search of a discipline." This was indeed the way Richard Young characterized composition's predicament when he and seven others met for
three days in 1976 at the Science Camp in the Snowy Range west of
Laramie, Wyoming, to discuss whether a new discipline might be emerging (Warnock, e-mail).[8]

Interestingly, while many recent commentators acknowledge the critical role that the writing process movement played in this emergence,
most take the reality of the writing process movement and its impact on
composition's professionalization as a given—and then quickly turn to
criticisms of that movement. In *A Teaching Subject: Composition since
1966,* for instance, Joseph Harris acknowledges that the process movement helped establish composition as a research field, but rather than
discussing how it did so, he criticizes it on a number of grounds, such as

61

researchers' "single-minded focus on technique" (64). Similarly, in *Textual Carnivals,* Susan Miller asserts that it was the "'paradigm' of process theory and practice" that "moved composition from a purely applied, practical set of ways to inculcate propriety to a field claiming equality with other academic fields" (84). Like Harris, Miller focuses primarily upon the limitations of the writing process movement, which she charges with (among other things) situating students "in an infantile and solipsistic relation to the results of writing" (100). Yet another example can be found in Sharon Crowley's *Composition in the University: Historical and Polemical Essays.* Here Crowley, like Miller and Harris, accepts the role of the writing process movement in composition's professionalization as a fact (191). But, again like Miller and Harris, her primary interest is in critiquing that movement.

Even when an author attempts to define the writing process movement, as Thomas Kent does in the introduction to *Post-Process Theory: Beyond the Writing-Process Paradigm,* there is a prevailing assumption that readers already know exactly what that movement entails. Kent begins his introduction, for instance, by observing that "I suspect that the readers of this volume already know the central tenets of the writing-process movement about as well as they know the letters of the English alphabet" (1). Kent goes on to give some examples of process-based claims, such as the claim that "writing constitutes a process of some sort and that this process is generalizable," but he clearly feels that such examples serve primarily as reminders, rather than a careful elaboration of a key term in his argument (1).

And yet the meaning of the term "writing process movement" is, I would argue, far from obvious. Does this term refer solely or primarily to a research project, one that can be traced through the work of a limited number of scholars? Or does it include larger curricular and pedagogical efforts, as embodied in writing courses, programs and textbooks, writing centers and writing across the curriculum programs, and such initiatives as the National Writing Project? Who are the agents in this movement? Researchers? Writing program administrators? Teachers? Textbook authors? And what chronology best describes the trajectory of the writing process movement's development?

The failure to ask questions such as these—the sense that of course we already know what we mean when we use the term "writing process movement"—suggests to me that this term is in fact doing important

(but generally unacknowledged) rhetorical work for scholars in composition: it functions as a "floating signifier, a term that everyone recognizes
in its contexts of use but that is hard, nonetheless, to pin down" (Olson
"Resistance" xi). This is indeed how Gary Olson describes the term "resistance" in "Resistance as Theory," his foreword to Andrea Greenbaum's
Insurrections: Approaches to Resistance in Composition Studies. In another
essay in that collection, "Resistance as Tragic Trope," John Trimbur reminds readers that it is important to "think about why and how" certain
widely used terms "become so popular." He goes on to argue that "the
circulation of ill-defined terms . . . goes beyond problems of terminological clarification," and that it is critical to consider not only what a term
signifies "but also what its significations call up in us" (4).

In this regard, it's interesting to recall that such early process researchers as Janet Emig, Sondra Perl, Nancy Sommers, and Linda Flower and John
Hayes generally do not use the term "writing process movement"; rather,
they focus on the particularities of their current research.[9] With the exception of Maxine Hairston's "Winds of Change" (which refers to the writing
process paradigm, not movement), the most frequent uses of the term
"writing process movement" appear in articles and books written by those
who wish to criticize scholars who they associate with that movement. Such
a use of the term has the effect of creating an appearance of not only
coherence but also of action: movements occur when highly motivated
people who share a goal work together to achieve a particular result. The
significations that the term "writing process movement" call up, in other
words, are highly if subtly charged. After all, if one opposes a movement
one generally feels an obligation to act on that opposition.

As I hope is clear, for those critiquing process-based research and
teaching, the term "writing process movement" functions much like the
term "current-traditional rhetoric" did for an earlier group of scholars,
for it enables scholars to pit new theories against a generalized and devalued past—one that poses a threat to current efforts. As a floating signifier, the term "writing process movement" is not without meaning.
Rather, its meaning is understood, as Olson observes, according to readers' "contexts of use" ("Resistance" xi). Such variability is strategic, for it
enables authors to make broad generalizations without specifying their
particular meaning.

In the remainder of this chapter, and in the next, I want to explore
multiple understandings of the writing process movement and its role

in composition's professionalization. As I do so, I will argue that the nature and impact of the writing process movement are anything but obvious, and that there are a multiplicity of meanings that can be attributed to it. Some of these meanings are paradoxical. I will argue, as I noted earlier, that from one perspective nothing so unified and coherent as a writing process movement ever existed, and that its nature and role in the 1970s and early 1980s were as much tropological as material. But I will also argue that, despite claims that composition is post-process, signs of an ongoing commitment to process are everywhere evident. I will argue, in other words, that depending on where and how you look, there both was and was not a writing process movement. For this reason, I will continue to use the term "movement" even as I question its meaning and significance.

I begin this analysis by focusing on a crisis—in this case a self-declared crisis—that played a critical role in establishing the writing process movement. As a number of commentators have noted, by positioning process-oriented work in stark opposition to earlier product-oriented efforts, scholars were able to posit a crisis in composition, one that would both justify and unify current research efforts by, as Susan Miller observes in *Textual Carnivals,* "explain[ing] process as a theory pitted against old *practices*" (110). (That this crisis in composition studies coincided with a nationally declared literacy crisis only added, of course, to its impact.) In his "Paradigms and Problems: Needed Research in Rhetorical Invention," Richard Young articulates such a crisis, which he attributes to composition studies' commitment to the current-traditional paradigm, a paradigm that emphasizes, among other things, "the composed product rather than the composing process" (31). If we recognize that teachers' commitment to this paradigm comprises a "crisis in our discipline," we can, Young argues, "make a kind of sense out of the recent and rapidly growing interest in the composing process and the numerous proposals for controlling it. And we can also construct a rationale for a program of research" (35).

Although others writing at the time were not as explicit as Young was in asserting the existence of a crisis in composition, many also used crisis-laden language to characterize current research efforts. Janet Emig opens *The Composing Processes of Twelfth Graders,* for instance, with the assertion that "Composing in writing is a common activity of literate persons. Yet descriptions of what occurs during this experience, not to mention attempts to explain or analyze it, are highly unsatisfactory" (1).

Donald Graves similarly introduces his 1975 "Examination of the Writing Processes of Seven-Year-Old Children" by stating:"The complexity of the writing process and the interrelationships of its components have been underestimated by researchers, teachers, and other educators" (23).

In pointing out the tendency for some researchers at the time to evoke a crisis to which their and others' research was the response, I do not mean to diminish the importance of this work—or of the exigencies that teachers and administrators faced at that time. I wish, rather, to call attention to the rhetoric of such a strategy—a rhetoric that foregrounds its subject's radical newness as unclaimed territory waiting to be mined by researchers. The image that Mina Shaughnessy evokes in the introduction to *Errors and Expectations* is telling in this regard: "The territory I am calling basic writing," she asserts, "is still very much of a frontier, unmapped, except for a scattering of impressionistic articles and a few blazed trails that individual teachers propose through their texts" (4).

In asserting a foundational crisis in composition studies and in formulating rationales for various programs of research—from rhetorical studies of invention to analyses of error and cognitive-based research on composing—scholars were clearly appealing to what Evan Watkins in *Work Time: English Departments and the Circulation of Cultural Value* refers to as "ideologies of the new." Such ideologies assume that "there's something 'new,' 'contemporary,' about *any* highly valued form of . . . study in English" (15). In so doing, these ideologies sanction waves of reform—whether in the teaching of writing or in analyses of *Paradise Lost*—that encourage essentializing, totalizing readings of that which is being rejected as "old." As work by such scholars as Connors, Horner, Paine, Schultz, and Varnum suggests, such essentializing and totalizing certainly happened in the case of composition studies. For the ascendancy of the writing process movement required a nearly wholesale rejection of previous scholarly and pedagogical efforts.

The development of rationales for research also fulfilled a basic requirement for the professionalization of composition studies. As Magali Sarfatti Larson observes in *The Rise of Professionalism: A Sociological Analysis*:

> The structure of the professionalization process binds together two elements which can, and usually did, evolve independently of each other: a body of relatively abstract knowledge, susceptible of practical application, and a market—the structure of which is determined

by economic and social development and also by the dominant ideological climate at a given time. (40)

As I have already suggested, the "dominant ideological climate" of the 1970s was such that a material reality that could have been viewed positively as a sign of the increased democratization of higher education in America—the presence of a new group of students who were the first in their family to attend college—was interpreted instead as a literacy crisis. Writing from a different perspective but drawing upon their own rhetoric of crisis, scholars in composition were positioned—if only they could articulate "a body of relatively abstract knowledge"—to argue for the legitimacy of its enterprise. Such an argument is "immensely easier," Larson notes,

> when knowledge is depersonalized by formalization, for all depersonalized knowledge tends to become objectified, if not "objective." This means that the validity of this knowledge appears to transcend the particular circumstances and subjective preferences of the groups that produce it (or reproduce it, by use or transmission). The more formalized the cognitive basis, the more the profession's language and knowledge appear to be connotation-free and "objective." Hence the superiority of a *scientific* basis for professional unification. (41)

And hence also, of course, the particularly strong appeal that cognitive research had for many in this crucial stage of composition's professionalization.

Cognitive research on the composing process—as typified by studies by Linda Flower and John Hayes, Nancy Sommers, Sondra Perl, and Janet Emig—enabled researchers and writing program administrators to draw on the language and methods of science while adapting these to the needs of both writers and teachers of writing. According to scholars who have studied the development of the professions in the United States, the objectification and depersonalization that characterize many scientific efforts play a critical role in the construction of expertise. As Andrew Abbott observes in *The System of Professions: An Essay on the Division of Expert Labor,* however, there is a fine balance to be maintained in such a process, for professionalization requires that expertise be "abstract, but not too abstract" (323). Otherwise, those who wish to professionalize their field will be unable to compete successfully in a fundamental fact of pro-

fessional life—interprofessional competition over jurisdictional boundaries and processes. As Abbott observes:

> Any occupation can obtain licensure (e.g., beauticians) or develop an
> ethics code (e.g., real estate). But only a knowledge system governed
> by abstractions can redefine its problems and tasks, defend them from
> interlopers, and seize new problems—as medicine has recently seized
> alcoholism, mental illness, hyperactivity in children, obesity, and nu-
> merous other things. Abstraction enables survival in the competitive
> system of professions. (9)

In the 1970s and 1980s, interprofessional competition over jurisdictional boundaries and processes was a particularly salient fact of life as
scholars in composition sought to "redefine" composition's "problems
and tasks, defend them from interlopers, and seize new problems"
(Abbott 9). The writing process movement played a critical role in this
effort. Just the fact that faculty were able to argue that composition was
experiencing a new "movement" or "paradigm" gave them leverage in
ongoing debates with literary colleagues who challenged their enterprise
or with deans who might—or might not—fund new initiatives. But in
my own case at least, the writing process movement met other, less conscious needs as well. When I reflect on my experiences in the late 1970s
and early 1980s, I believe that I was particularly drawn to process-based
research because it so clearly and distinctly differed from traditional literary interpretation. As a convert to composition, I wanted the differences
between my former and current field of study to be strong and clear. The
scientism that I and others subsequently critiqued process-based research
for was, I see in hindsight, one of the attributes that most drew me to it
in its formative years, for that scientism gave me confidence in composition's disciplinary agenda.

The fact that this scientism coexisted and to some extent commingled
with a more politically radical and personally engaged strand of research
on the writing process—as evidenced by the work of Ken Macrorie, Peter Elbow, Donald Murray, and others—enhanced the appeal of the writing process movement. (Elbow begins the preface of his 1973 *Writing
Without Teachers,* for instance, with this statement: "Many people are now
trying to become less helpless, both personally and politically: trying to
claim more control over their own lives. One of the ways people most
lack control over their own lives is through lacking control over words"

67

[vii].) It allowed politically engaged persons such as myself (and in the 1970s many in composition were critical of both political and educational business as usual) to feel that we were advancing composition's disciplinary agenda on several fronts, while also engaging in politically and pedagogically relevant work.

On a more pragmatic note, the writing process movement also addressed a number of pressing pedagogical and administrative needs that I and many other writing program administrators faced. A boiled-down version of research on the writing process could help a chair or dean understand why enrollment in basic or first-year writing courses needed to be limited. Better yet, it could provide the basic structure for these courses—and for the training of those teaching them. And of course, the writing process was amenable to adaptation in the textbooks that play such a powerful role in the many composition classes staffed by graduate students and instructors.

The writing process movement did not, however, resolve all of the dilemmas that new writing program administrators faced. Consider, for instance, the "problem" of students' purported illiteracy. As I have already indicated, the existence of a media-supported literacy crisis was the most specific and powerful catalyst for the creation of new tenure-line positions in composition in the 1970s. (In this sense, one could argue that increased attention to basic writing played at least as important a role in professionalizing composition as did interest in the writing process.) New writing program administrators like myself needed to address concerns about this problem on our campuses; these concerns were a major reason why we had been hired. Many of us, however, questioned media depictions of the literacy crisis. When asked by my colleagues at SUNY Brockport if I believed that such a crisis existed, I responded that in my (admittedly limited) years of teaching, I had not witnessed a precipitous decline in student literacy and added that the current focus on correctness was misplaced, since what is most critical in writing are global issues of process, form, and content. Others argued that what the media described as a problem was really an opportunity, for declines in student test scores could and many argued should be attributed to the presence of a new group of students on our campuses, many of whom were the first in their family to attend college.

Although there were certainly a number of highly public challenges to the literacy crisis of the mid 1970s—the most visible of which was the

CCCC's 1974 resolution "Students' Right to Their Own Language" and the efforts surrounding it—many newly hired faculty preferred to voice our resistance in quieter ways. (For a discussion of this resolution, see Stephen Park's *Class Politics: The Movement for the Students' Right to Their Own Language*.) We were quite literally in a bind, one that according to Magali Larson is inherent to professionalization. As Larson observes,

> at the core of the professionalization project, we find the fusion of antithetical ideological structures and a potential for permanent tensions between "civilizing function" and market orientation, between the "protection of society" and the securing of a market, between intrinsic and extrinsic values of work. (63)

In the case of composition, this tension took the form of a contradiction between faculty members' desires to see ourselves as advocates for students—a stance encouraged by both the writing process movement and the political tenor of the times—and the expectation that we would do something about the literacy crisis as it was generally understood by our colleagues, and by the general public.

However much we might resist media portrayals of declines in students' writing ability, newly hired faculty in composition *needed* the literacy crisis. As Bruce Robbins succinctly states in "Oppositional Professionals: Theory and the Narratives of Professionalization," in the case of aspiring professions: "No problem, no profession" (7). Thus, Robbins observes, professions "feed off the social miseries they are called in to remedy. Social conscience is not only in their interest, but in many cases their *sine qua non*" (7).

The contradiction that Larson and Robbins describe remains an ongoing dilemma for composition. In the 1970s and early 1980s, many newly hired writing program administrators needed to respond in immediate and direct ways to a social and educational problem that many in and out of the academy believed required urgent action. (For some, this problem was best understood as a general literacy crisis; for others, it represented an opportunity to educate a new kind of student admitted via open admissions and other increased access programs.) And we needed to draw upon a newly developed knowledge base to do so. To be fully integrated into the academy, professions that want to be granted disciplinary status must prove not only that they can address their field's basic problems (as, say, faculty members working in counseling offices on campuses do) but also that the creation of new knowledge is their primary means of doing so.

One Movement or Many?

In this regard, perhaps the greatest strength of the writing process movement was its capaciousness. Because the concept of process was in Abbott's terms "abstract, but not too abstract" (323), it could both represent and authorize a wide range of scholarly activities. In the 1970s and early 1980s, as now, there were a number of competing scholarly agendas at play in composition. Some scholars, myself included, aligned ourselves as much with the rhetorical tradition as with the writing process movement and looked to that tradition to provide a (if not the) central grounding for current efforts. Indeed, many then and now prefer to characterize their discipline as rhetoric and composition rather than composition studies or some other descriptor, for they recognize that the rhetorical tradition's focus on context and on the production of discourse enriches composition's scholarly and pedagogical project. Despite this fact, the rhetorical tradition was insufficiently elastic—and perhaps also too recondite, too "abstract"—to serve as a unifying project for the field.

Another scholarly and pedagogical project that might have unified composition in the 1970s and 1980s was basic writing. In fact, Mina Shaughnessy begins her 1976 bibliographic essay, "Basic Writing," by observing that "The teaching of writing to severely unprepared freshmen is as yet but the frontier of a profession, lacking even an agreed upon name" (137). As I noted earlier, widespread concerns both within and without the academy about students' writing skills played a key role in opening up tenure-line positions for scholars in composition. Nevertheless, work on basic writing was too closely associated with the pragmatic and concrete realities of day-to-day teaching—and with remediation— to serve as a unifying project for the field.

As a scholarly and pedagogical project, the writing process movement offered a clear research agenda that (at the time at least) seemed directly relevant to the needs of both teachers and students. But to what extent was the writing process movement a materially grounded movement rather than a unifying trope, one that expressed the desires of faculty to see themselves as engaged in a coherent, multidimensional project? At the level of scholarship, the term "movement" was certainly elastic enough to allow for what in retrospect seems to be considerable diversity. Janet Emig,

Linda Flower, Peter Elbow, Janice Lauer, Ken Macrorie, Donald Murray, Sondra Perl, Mina Shaughnessy, Nancy Sommers, Richard Young: these and other scholars all were considered to be doing "process" work during this time period, and yet the nature of their scholarly and pedagogical projects varied significantly. (For an analysis of these differences, see Faigley "Competing.")

Though there was broad support for and interest in process-based research in the 1970s and early 1980s, it is important to remember that there were many scholarly and curricular projects—many "movements"—ongoing in the composition during this time. It's certainly true that few of the scholars involved with these projects saw themselves as working in opposition to the writing process. But it is equally true that research on the writing process was not central—and in some cases not relevant—to their efforts. Consider the research published in two particularly important edited collections from this period. (Such collections provide a window into the range of research projects then underway, for they represent the editor's view of the most important current research.) The first collection is Ross Winterowd's 1975 *Contemporary Rhetoric: A Conceptual Background with Readings.* Winterowd's anthology is organized around three headings: invention, form, and style. Of these, only the first relates directly to the writing process. Another collection that played a critical role during this period was Gary Tate's 1976 *Teaching Composition: Ten Bibliographical Essays.* Tate's collection contains one chapter related to the writing process, Richard Young's "Invention: A Topographical Survey." Others go far afield—from Frank D'Angelo's "Modes of Discourse" to Ross Winterowd's "Linguistics and Composition." In fact, two chapters—Richard Larson's "Structure and Form in Non-fiction Prose" and Edward P. J. Corbett's "Approaches to the Study of Style"—focus on topics often associated with the products of writing, rather than with the processes that led to them.[10]

Collections that focused on the writing process certainly were published during this period: notable examples include Charles Cooper and Lee Odell's 1978 *Research on Composing: Points of Departure* and two collections published in 1983: Miles Myers and James Gray's *Theory and Practice in the Teaching of Composition: Processing, Distancing, and Modeling* and Janice Hays, Phillis Roth, Jon Ramsey, and Robert Foulke's *The Writer's Mind: Writing as a Mode of Thinking.* These works need to be considered, however, in the context of a number of other single-topic collections published around the same time, such as Donald McQuade's 1979 *Linguistics, Stylistics, and the Teaching of Composition,* Aviva Freedman and Ian Pringle's 1980 *Reinventing the Rhetorical Tradition,* Lawrence Kasden and Daniel Hoeber's 1980 *Basic Writing: Essays for Teachers, Researchers, Administrators,* Barry Kroll and Roberta Vann's 1981 *Exploring Speaking-Writing Relationships: Connections and Contrasts,* Toby Fulwiler and Art Young's 1982 *Language Connections: Writing and Reading Across the Curriculum,* and Muriel Harris's *Tutoring Writing: A Sourcebook for Writing Labs,* also published in 1982. (In "The Role of Edited Collections in Composition Studies," Laura Micciche discusses the crucial role that edited collections played in composition's professionalization, noting that "the number of edited collections in compositions studies began a marked ascent in 1980" [107].)

As the last two examples suggest, during the 1970s and early 1980s, not only were diverse scholarly projects underway, so too were a number of curricular initiatives, such as the development of writing centers, basic and professional writing programs, and writing across the curriculum. Many of these initiatives aligned themselves with and benefited from the writing process movement. But they were hardly identical to it. And in fact, competition among various scholarly and curricular projects was then, as it is now, a fact of life. Hence the development of specialized professional associations and journals.

Before 1970, some of the most important venues for scholarly work in composition were *College Composition and Communication (CCC), College English, Research in the Teaching of English,* and *Philosophy and Rhetoric.* Of these, only *CCC* published work solely in composition. As a consequence, scholars with diverse interests—from reader response theory to rhetoric, advanced composition, and writing program administration—competed for a place in its pages. Not surprisingly, though several of the journals that appeared in the 1970s and early 1980s accepted articles on a wide range of topics in composition, the majority represented a particular focus or constituency. Some of the most notable of these journals (and their founding dates) include:

> *Rhetoric Society Quarterly* (as a newsletter, 1968; as a journal 1976);[11] *Freshman English News* (1972);[12] *Teaching English in the Two-Year College* (1974); *Journal of Basic Writing* (1975); *Reader* (as a newsletter, 1976; as a journal, 1983); *Writing Lab Newsletter* (1977);[13] *WPA: Writing Program Administration* (1977); *Writing Center Journal* (1980); *Pre/Text*

(1980); *Journal of Advanced Composition* (1980); *Writing Instructor* (1981); *Rhetoric Review* (1982); *Rhetorica* (1983); *Computers and Com-position* (1983); *Written Communication* (1984); *Writing on the Edge* (1989).

(For a fuller discussion of the development of journals in composition, see Goggin.) Many of these constituencies also developed new organizations designed to address their particular concerns. Representative examples include the Association of Teachers of Technical Writing (1973); the Council of Writing Program Administrators (1976); the International Society for the History of Rhetoric (1977); the Association of Teachers of Advanced Composition (1979); the Conference on Basic Writing (1980); the National Network of Writing Across the Curriculum Programs (1981), and the National Writing Centers Association (1982).[14]

During this same period another important movement was underway in composition: the movement to develop PhD programs. Such programs were essential to composition's professionalization, for a field cannot professionalize until it can, as Larson observes, produce "professional producers" (50). And produce producers composition did. According to David W. Chapman and Gary Tate's 1986 "Survey of Doctoral Programs in Rhetoric and Composition," sixteen doctoral programs were established in the 1970s. In the years from 1980–82, another fourteen appeared, with more soon to follow. A similar survey conducted in 1993 by Stuart C. Brown, Paul R. Meyer, and Theresa Enos published in *Rhetoric Review* identified seventy-two such programs.

Another concrete reminder of the diverse projects underway in the 1970s and early 1980s is the proposal form that Lynn Troyka instituted for the 1980 meeting of the CCCC. (Previously, chairs had "relied on an informal system of letter exchanges between program volunteers and the program chair" [Troyka].) The categories presented on this new form in some ways named the field and established its "canon." These categories were: the composing process, rhetorical theory, invention, language, basic writing, technical writing, ethnic studies, assessment, reading/writing relationships, approaches to teaching, interdisciplinary, and other. And of course other activities that would eventually be recognized on various CCCC proposal forms—such as writing program administration, business writing, English as a second language, collaborative learning, and so on—were already underway.

These and other examples of the diverse projects underway during the 1970s and early 1980s demonstrate, I believe, that what has often been characterized as a movement or paradigm, with the coherence and singular focus that these terms suggest, is more aptly described as a group of loosely affiliated initiatives. Given the diversity of these initiatives and the looseness of their affiliation with the writing process, perhaps the movement's greatest achievement was its fulfillment of a desire on the part of those in composition studies to both perceive and argue for unity and coherence in their scholarly and pedagogical endeavor—a desire that was strong enough that it encouraged many to turn away, if only for a time, from a number of differences in assumptions and practices.[15] That these differences eventually came to the fore may have as much to do with composition's evolving professionalization as with limitations inherent to various process-oriented projects. As Brian McCrea points out in relation to the professionalization of literature, "divisions within a professional group make that group stronger not weaker" (204). Thus, criticisms of the writing process movement simultaneously challenged foundational research in composition while also expanding the opportunities for further research.

The Writing Process Movement and the Politics of Location

Why insist, as I do here, that rather than viewing the writing process movement as the "engine of disciplinary success" (Faigley, *Fragments* 49) for composition, it is both more accurate and helpful to call attention to the many diverse exigencies and activities that resulted in composition's professionalization? Why remind readers that a media-proclaimed literacy crisis in combination with the collapse of the job market for PhDs in English may have played as important a role in composition's professionalization as the articulation of a new research paradigm for the field? Why remind readers, as well, that the heroic narrative that scholars (including myself) have sometimes told about composition's professionalization—one that features the efforts of individual scholars who, against great odds, established important scholarly and pedagogical projects—can also be read as a much less valiant venture, one that shows composition reproducing in classic textbook fashion the requirements of professionalization?

I have several responses to these questions. I am concerned, as I noted at the start of this chapter, that when scholars identify the writing process movement as the primary agent in composition's professionalization, it becomes tempting to view this professionalization as an event of the past, rather than as an ongoing process. For as Abbott, Larson, and others emphasize, although professions can achieve benchmarks of status and control, the activity of building upon and defending these prerogatives is never ending. (Think, for instance, of HMO-induced changes in the professional situations of doctors in recent years.) Never ending, as well, are the ethical questions raised by professionalization. To recognize these questions, however, we have to find ways to see, rather than simply inhabit, the ideologies of disciplinarity and professionalization that play such critical roles in the academy.

We have to find ways, in other words, of asking what these ideologies encourage us to overlook. This is a question that feminist philosopher Sandra Harding asks In *Whose Science? Whose Knowledge? Thinking from Women's Lives.* In this study, Harding argues that science has found it "convenient to overlook" such realities as "the deep ties between science and warmaking" (33). In focusing on the writing process movement and the professionalization of composition, I am similarly concerned about what scholars in composition have found it convenient to overlook about our own disciplinary and professional project. I believe that it has proven to be convenient to overlook the many movements that led to composition's professionalization and to focus instead of the writing process movement as its "engine of disciplinary success." For to the extent that the writing process movement is associated with a limited number of scholars in composition (scholars whose work has been critiqued on a number of counts, including a failure adequately to attend to social and political context), such critique makes it easy for other scholars to bracket ourselves from responsibility for composition's professionalization— makes it convenient to overlook our participation in institutional and professional discourses and practices.

I am also concerned because I believe that a number of problematic practices enacted by scholars critiquing the writing process movement continue to play an important role in scholarly work in composition. I have already demonstrated that just as scholars arguing for the writing process movement established a straw man they termed current-traditional rhetoric, so too have those who have critiqued this movement, for they have reified and essentialized a loosely held affiliation of projects. They have also found it convenient to ignore the rich diversity of scholarly and pedagogical work underway in the 1970s and early 1980s, much of which focused peripherally if at all on process.

75

And what about the paradigm hope that is so evident in Maxine Hairston's article—and that was challenged by Robert Connors in his 1983 "Composition Studies and Science" as an example of scientism? While those critiquing the writing process movement would not frame their comments in Kuhnian terms, paradigm hope still circulates in composition. It is evident, for instance, in the taxonomizing that played such a powerful role in fueling composition's recent theory wars. (As an example of such a taxonomy, see Berlin's "Rhetoric and Ideology in the Writing Class.") And it is evident as well in the work of scholars whose commitment to postmodern critique would otherwise suggest skepticism of such hope. As an example, consider Sharon Crowley's discussion of the emergence of process pedagogy in *Composition in the University*. As noted earlier, Crowley's discussion focuses primarily on the limitations of the writing process movement, such as the "epistemological consistency" that it shares with current-traditional rhetoric (212). In commenting on this consistency, Crowley observes that "A truly paradigmatic alternative to current-traditionalism would question the modernism in which it is immersed and the institutional structure by means of which it is administered. Process pedagogy does neither" (212–13).

Another surprising example of paradigm hope occurs at the conclusion of Susan Miller's "Composition as a Cultural Artifact: Rethinking History as Theory." In this essay, Miller argues that "we must look at composition as a cultural practice rather than as an intellectual development," observing that "if we are to explain why the field's new histories, theories, and research have so little purchase on its continuing practice, its past requires retheorization" (21). After discussing the need for this retheorization, and some of what it would entail, Miller closes her essay with these comments:

> As literary studies critiques the origins and social results of privileging a closed canon of literary texts that perpetuates embarrassingly monolithic values, we might also reevaluate the history of composition and our own experiences of it in the light of its parallel cultural origins and parallel social results. Until we do, we will not have a genuinely new paradigm for composition that replaces its original division of good and bad writing with our new expertise in historicizing, theorizing, and teaching students to enjoy the variable relations of writers to their texts. (32)

Crowley and Miller raise important issues in their analyses, but their acceptance of the possibility of a "genuinely" or "truly" new paradigm suggests an implicit, if transitory, commitment to Enlightenment notions of reason. In making this comment, I do not mean to suggest that this commitment is a central characteristic of Miller's and Crowley's projects. These scholars have consistently advocated for—and modeled—critical methodologies that reject Enlightenment reasoning.[16] Rather, I hope to show that even such rigorously critical scholars cannot entirely free themselves from prevailing disciplinary ideologies. (Nor, it goes without saying, can I.)

I am concerned about scholars' lingering commitments to paradigm hope because I believe that such commitments make it easy to ignore the gap between theoretical text and material enactment. For paradigm hope encourages scholars to believe that, once developed, the right theory can—simply by virtue of being right—effect change at the level of practice. To the extent that this paradigm hope circulates in our field, it encourages a devaluing of practice and the distancing of scholarly work from the scene of the classroom—problems that I will discuss in part 3 of *Situating Composition*. (As such recent studies as Russell Durst's *Collision Course: Conflict, Negotiation, and Learning in College Composition* and Karen Surman Paley's *I Writing: The Politics and Practice of Teaching First-Person Writing* suggest, coherent and uniform paradigms function much more easily in the pages of articles and books than in classrooms.) It also deflects attention from the working conditions of the majority of writing teachers, conditions that surely are one of the major reasons "why the field's new histories, theories, and research have so little purchase on its continuing practice" (Miller, "Composition as Cultural Artifact" 21).

Paradigm hope—which, again, I see not as a major feature of contemporary scholarly work but rather a desire that erupts in small fissures and openings—also encourages what Paley, following Henry Giroux, calls "disciplinary terrorism," where the effort to argue for one paradigm requires the demolition of those who hold, or are seen to hold, another (19). Such terrorism certainly happened in debates over the writing process. In "Rhetoric and Ideology in the Writing Class," for instance, Jim Berlin characterizes cognitive rhetoric in terms that, given the politics of many in composition, come close to demonizing that project:

77

This entire scheme can be seen as analogous to the instrumental method of the modern corporation, the place where members of the meritocratic middle class, the twenty percent or so of the work force of certified college graduates, make a handsome living managing a capitalist economy.... Their work life is designed to turn goal-seeking and problem-solving behavior into profits. As we have seen in Flower, the rationalization of the writing process is specifically designated an extension of the rationalization of economic activity. The pursuit of self-evident and unquestioned goals in the composing process parallels the pursuit of self-evident and unquestioned profit-making goals in the corporate marketplace.... (483)

Attacks of this sort continue in more recent debates. In the foreword to Andrea Greenbaum's *Insurrections: Approaches to Resistance in Composition Studies,* for instance, Gary Olson portrays composition as being in an "increasingly hegemonic struggle" (xi) over how the field should be defined and cites "the special issue of *College Composition and Communication* on 'teaching writing creatively' (51.1, 1999) as an opening salvo in what undoubtedly will come to be known as 'the new theory wars'" (xii). This issue, Olson charges, attempts "to drag composition back to its expressivist roots" (xii). Olson goes on to characterize those associated with this and related efforts as "boss compositionists," who are "struggling desperately to set back our disciplinary clock" (xii). As this example indicates, arguments about the future of composition's intellectual project often depend upon binary-driven, agonistic arguments: thus Berlin's implicit charge that Flower is complicit with ideologies of capitalism, and Olson's charge that those who he views as expressivists are "boss compositionists."[17]

I hope to resist strategies such as these; for this reason, here, as elsewhere in this study, I have tried to acknowledge my immersion in—and complicity with—the developments I chronicle. This effort has been stimulated by several catalysts. One catalyst has been my desire to understand—and hold myself responsible for—my own experience. When Jim Berlin published his taxonomy, for instance, I embraced his categorizing of recent work in composition because it met my own need to impose order on what in fact was a dizzying array of scholarly and pedagogical projects. Only later did I see the limitations as well as the benefits of his taxonomy.

As noted earlier, another significant catalyst has been my teaching of both undergraduate and graduate courses in composition theory. In recent years I have tried hard to learn from my students' sometimes resistant reading of theory. I have tried to understand that theory—to which I am very drawn—works in multiple and sometimes contradictory ways. This experience has encouraged me to attempt to step outside of, however briefly, my conventional disciplinary assumptions and practices and to look at what in chapter 5 I refer to "the practice of theory" and "the practice of teaching" in new ways.

Another important catalyst has been recent work in feminist studies, particularly work that has attempted to imagine alternative forms of scholarly discourse and of institutional and professional life. I want to close this chapter with a quotation from a feminist theorist whose work has influenced my own. In *Thinking Fragments: Psychoanalysis, Feminism, and Postmodernism in the Contemporary West,* political scientist and psychotherapist Jane Flax attempts to place the fields highlighted in her subtitle in conversation. Most typically, these fields are positioned in competition with each other as scholars attempt to demonstrate the superiority of one of the three. Flax's goal is different: she wants to demonstrate the limitations *and* strengths of each perspective, and to determine how these often-competing fields might work in more productive ways. As part of this discussion, Flax argues for a greater recognition of the complexity of the questions that feminist theorizing is attempting to address, and for a greater tolerance for multiple approaches to these questions:

> As feminist theorizing is presently practiced, we seem to lose sight of the possibility that each of our conceptions of a practice may capture an aspect of a very complex and contradictory set of social relations. Confronted with complex and changing relations, we try to reduce these to simple, unified, and undifferentiated wholes. We search for closure or the right answer or the "motor" of the history of male domination. The complexity of our questions and the variety of the approaches to them are taken as signs of weakness or failure to meet the strictures of preexisting theories rather than as symptoms of the permeability and pervasiveness of gender relations and the need for new sorts of theorizing. (179)

Following Flax, I would like to suggest that, like gender, literacy is such a complex—and situated—phenomenon that the effort to develop a single movement or paradigm that can encompass the situated diversity of both theory and practice is misguided. I would like to suggest, as well, that as Flax states of gender, "each of our conceptions of a practice may capture an aspect of a very complex and contradictory set" of literate action. When I think about arguments in composition over process and post-process theories of writing, for instance, I believe that as a scholar and teacher I have benefited both from studies that attempt to analyze generalizable composing strategies and from studies that focus on more situated aspects of writing.

What difference might if make if scholars in composition recognized the need for and valued multiple approaches to literacy? Might such a recognition helpfully remind scholars that literacy, like gender, is deeply situated in multiple, complex, and contradictory contexts and practices—and in so doing encourage us to reconsider both our textual and our pedagogical practices in helpful ways? Questions such as these play a key role in chapter 4, and in part 3, of this study.

4 On Process, Social Process, and Post-Process

"When I was told that I was living in a paradigm shift, I didn't feel the earth move." So states Donald Gray (150) about research in composition in his 1986 "New Ideas about English and Departments of English," an article reflecting upon Gray's tenure as editor of *College English* from 1978 to 1985. Gray's wry comment raises a number of intriguing questions. What might a paradigm shift look like—and feel like—in a field such as composition? How is it possible to ascertain whether a paradigm shift in composition has occurred, and to determine its magnitude and quality? Does a paradigm shift require such coherent, uniform, and broad change that the earth in effect moves? How else might changes in the teaching of composition, such as those connected with the writing process movement, be characterized and evaluated?

One way to address these questions is, of course, to consider scholarly assessments. As the previous chapter suggests, scholarly analyses of the writing process movement generally agree that in the years since Janet Emig wrote *The Composing Processes of Twelfth Graders,* composition has very much moved on from process. Marilyn Cooper begins her 1986 "The Ecology of Writing," for instance, by observing that:

> The idea that writing is a process and that the writing process is a recursive cognitive activity involving certain universal stages (prewriting, writing, revising) seemed quite revolutionary not so many years ago. In 1982, Maxine Hairston hailed "the move to a process-centered theory of teaching writing" as the first sign of a paradigm shift in composition theory (77). But even by then "process, not product" was the slogan of numerous college textbooks, large and small, validated by enclosure within brightly-colored covers with the imprimatur of Harper & Row, Macmillan, Harcourt Brace Jovanovich, Scott, Foresman. So revolution dwindles to dogma. (364)

By the time of Joseph Harris's 1997 *A Teaching Subject,* it seemed natural to speak of the writing process using past tense, as Harris does when he assesses the impact of that movement. After noting that he doesn't "want to become entangled here in the intricacies of the arguments over process theory, and thus to prolong what seems to me an increasingly tiresome professional debate," Harris nevertheless offers a judgment, observing that "while it seems clear to me that the process movement helped establish composition as a research field, I am not nearly so sure it ever transformed the actual teaching of writing as dramatically as its advocates have claimed" (55).

Not all would agree with Harris's dismissal of the pedagogical impact of the writing process movement. In *Fragments of Rationality,* for instance, Lester Faigley presents a more positive assessment. While he agrees that scholars have become disillusioned with the writing process movement, he argues that this disillusionment had political, not pedagogical grounds. According to Faigley, "the harshest critics of the process movement pointed not so much to the classroom shortcomings of process pedagogy as to the failure of the process movement to fulfill the goal of 'empowering' students as part of a larger project of creating equality through education" (68).

While Faigley, Harris, and Cooper each cite different causes for disillusionment with process, they all present interest in the writing process as being a phenomenon of the past; they all argue that composition is—or should be—post-process. This position is continued in such subsequent publications as Thomas Kent's *Post-Process Theory,* Sydney Dobrin's *Constructing Knowledges: The Politics of Theory-Building and Pedagogy in Composition,* and Sharon Crowley's *Composition in the University: Historical and Polemical Essays.* (Not all scholars take this position. Two studies that acknowledge continuities between process and post-process theories are Amy Lee's *Composing Critical Pedagogies: Teaching Writing as Revision* and Bruce McComiskey's *Teaching Composition as a Social Process.*) In this chapter, I hope to complicate assessments such as these, and to do so primarily by thinking through my own teaching practices, for I believe that when examined from the perspective of practice, clear and finite boundaries between process and post-process become harder to maintain. In classrooms, or at least in my classroom, coherent and univocal paradigm shifts rarely happen. Rather, change occurs in fits and starts—in increments, rather than in massive transformations. When I revise a syllabus or course description or develop a new assignment, the earth doesn't move. That doesn't mean, however, that significant changes in my teaching are not occurring.

In an effort better to understand how change takes place in my teaching, I will look in this chapter at a number of pedagogical documents from courses I have taught—documents that constitute, in effect, traces of or windows into a more complex and deeply situated phenomenon. I do so not because I believe that my individual experiences as a teacher are particularly significant; nor would I claim that they are representative. They are, rather, one teacher's effort to embody a range of theoretical and pedagogical understandings. My hope is that this inquiry into practices that are embodied in such documents as course descriptions, syllabi, and assignments will provide a materially grounded—albeit in many ways limited—perspective on the ways change happens in teaching.

On the Terms "Writing Process," "Post-Process," and "Social Process"

Before turning to this inquiry, I want to clarify my use of three terms that appear throughout this chapter: "writing process," "social process," and "post-process." When I refer to the writing process and the writing process movement, I am referring, as I argued in the previous chapter, to a group of loosely affiliated initiatives that in one way or another encouraged attention to the writing process. Representative texts associated with the writing process movement include Janet Emig's 1971 *The Composing Processes of Twelfth Graders,* Sondra Perl's 1979 "The Composing Processes of Unskilled College Writers," Nancy Sommers's 1980 "Revision Strategies of Student Writers and Experienced Adult Writers," and Linda Flower and John R. Hayes's 1981 "A Cognitive Process Theory of Writing."

As I noted in the previous chapter, by the mid-1980s, a number of scholars had begun to criticize the writing process movement. Scholars such as James Reither (in his 1985 "Writing and Knowing: Toward Redefining the Writing Process") and Marilyn Cooper (in her 1986 "The Ecology of Writing") increasingly argued that the writing process movement failed to recognize the extent to which writing is inherently a social process. As a consequence, many scholars and teachers shifted their theoretical and pedagogical commitments from the writing process to writing as a *social* process.

Just as the term "writing process" functioned as a floating signifier for scholars and teachers in the 1970s and 1980s, so too did the term "social process" take on similar flexibility, for just as a commitment to the writing process proved capacious, so too did a commitment to writing as a social process. Some scholars and teachers associate writing as a social process primarily with such activities as collaborative learning and writing. For others, this term signals commitments to social constructionist epistemological tenets, such as the argument that all knowledge is socially constructed. In his 1988 "Rhetoric and Ideology in the Writing Class," for instance, James Berlin argued in favor of what he termed "social-epistemic rhetoric"—a rhetoric that recognizes that knowledge "is an historically bound social fabrication rather than an eternal and invariable phenomenon located in some uncomplicated repository" and that the self or "subject is itself a social construct that emerges through the linguistically-circumscribed interaction of the individual, the community, and the material world" (489).

As many readers are aware, the writing process and writing as a social process have often been treated as mutually exclusive projects. Although Marilyn Cooper closes "The Ecology of Writing" by acknowledging that "the image of the ecological model" as described in her article is "an ideal one," for instance, the major thrust of her essay is to draw strong distinctions between the writing process and writing as a social (or in her terms "ecological") process as theoretical and pedagogical projects (364). Similarly, in *A Teaching Subject: Composition since 1966,* Joseph Harris argues that rather than representing an advance over previous assumptions and practices, the writing process movement "simply argued for what seems to me to be a new sort of formalism—one centered no longer on textual structures but instead on various algorithms, heuristics, and guidelines for composing" (56). He argues, in other words, that the writing process movement did not represent a distinctive break from current-traditional rhetoric but rather a permutation of it and suggests that writing as a social process does represent a significant break with current-traditional rhetoric.

In recent years, a new term—and a new proposed theoretical and pedagogical project—has entered the arena: post-process theory. In his introduction to the edited collection *Post-Process Theory: Beyond the Writing-Process Paradigm,* Thomas Kent distinguishes post-process theory from process theory by arguing that process theory attempted to developed a "generalized process" that could apply to most or all writers (1). Post-process theorists, he argues, believe that such efforts to develop "a Big Theory" about writing are unhelpful and inappropriate and hold quite different understandings about writing and the teaching of writing (1). Specifically, "they hold three assumptions about the act of writing: 1) writing is public; 2) writing is interpretive; and 3) writing is situated" (1).

Despite his effort to distinguish post-process theory from research on the writing process, the nature of post-process theory and practice remains somewhat fuzzy. Kent acknowledges this lack of clarity when he notes that while "the authors appearing in these pages may disagree about the nature of the 'post' in 'post-process' theory, all of them agree that change is in the air" (5). The contributors to *Post-Process Theory* do indeed articulate different understandings of post-process theory. In their contribution to the collection, "The Ethics of Process," John Clifford and Elizabeth Ervin specify that for them a commitment to post-process theory means "conceptualizing a composing sequence from invention and drafting to revision and copy editing as secondary to our emphasis on a range of literate activities that challenge sociohistorical subjects caught in a flawed social order to enact a democratic rhetoric" (179). In "Is There Life after Process? The Role of Social Scientism in a Changing Discipline," Joseph Petraglia argues that "'post-process' signifies a rejection of the generally formulaic framework for understanding writing that process suggested" (53). What for Clifford and Ervin is a modification or re-prioritizing of preexisting assumptions and practices is for Petraglia a rejection.

As I hope this brief discussion suggests, the terms "writing process," "writing as a social process," and "post-process theory" all serve as floating signifiers; the terms suggest a specificity of meaning that is deceptive. These terms also encourage readers to view these scholarly projects as discrete and mutually exclusive, rather than as interrelated. This is not to say that there are not significant distinctions among these theoretical and pedagogical projects—for there are. Rather, in calling attention to the way these terms serve as floating signifiers, I am emphasizing the rhetorical work that these terms do. In each case, the term encourages readers to view the project at hand as clearly distinguished from—and preferable to—earlier efforts.

What I have just described is an admittedly partial history of how the terms "writing process," "writing as a social process," and "post-process" have circulated in composition in recent years. I will use these terms in the following discussion—but I want to emphasize that I see them as both overdetermined and incapable of fixed definition. These terms certainly point to changes in scholarly and pedagogical assumptions and practices, but they also have evolved to meet scholars' need to continue to enact the "new" in composition—to suggest, as Kent observes, that somehow "change is in the air" (5). As the continuing inclusion of the word "process" in each of these formulations suggests, although these terms represent efforts to distinguish new scholarly and pedagogical projects from previous efforts, they cannot entirely erase their interdependence. As readers will see, my reading of a number of pedagogical texts from over twenty years of teaching confirms this interdependence at the level of classroom practice.

Pedagogical Traces: An Analysis of Twenty Years of Course Descriptions

Before looking at course descriptions I developed for first-year and advanced writing courses I have taught at Oregon State University, I should say a few words about the two courses on which I will focus. The first course is WR 121 (English Composition), the sole composition class required of every undergraduate student at Oregon State University (OSU) and one that, as its course number suggests, students are urged to complete during their first year. The second class is WR 416 (Advanced Composition), a class that fulfills several additional writing requirements. All undergraduates at OSU are required to take two writing classes in addition to WR 121 before they graduate: WR 416 is included in a menu of course options students can use to fulfill this requirement. Since my department developed a disciplinary masters degree, WR 416 has most often been offered as WR 416/516, so in recent years the course typically enrolls both undergraduates and graduate students.[1]

In my early years at OSU, I taught both WR 121 and WR 416 frequently. I also taught a number of other undergraduate courses, but these two courses figured most prominently in my teaching assignments during these years. As I mentioned in chapter 1, after my department developed a master's degree in the late 1980s, I have not taught first-year writing, despite requests on my part to do so.[2] Instead, while continuing to teach several undergraduate courses in both writing and literature, I now also teach several newly developed upper-division classes in composition. Like many, though hardly all, tenure-line faculty members in composition, then, I no longer teach the course that from one perspective is the raison d'etre of my field.

For most of my first eleven years at OSU—the years during which I taught both first-year and advanced composition—I wrote identical course descriptions for these two composition classes. The basic structure of the syllabi for the two classes was also similar, as were the assignments.[3] And I used the same text as well; for the first six years, I assigned Edward P. J. Corbett's *Little Rhetoric and Handbook,* then I began class-testing—and, eventually, assigning—my own textbook, *Work in Progress: A Guide to Academic Writing and Revising.* Students in advanced composition wrote longer essays than first-year students, but that was the primary difference between the two courses.

I have no way of knowing if I would have continued the practice of developing identical course descriptions (and similar syllabi and assignments) for both courses had I continued to teach first-year writing. But the fact that I did so for a number of years suggests to me that I brought a basic orientation to both classes—that I had a common vision of what ought to happen in these classes and how I could best accomplish that vision. This vision did not remain static. As I will demonstrate in this chapter, changes in my teaching reflect larger changes in theory and practice that developed during this period. Grounding these changes, however, are several underlying continuities.

Before I examine specific descriptions, I want to acknowledge that any effort to examine one's own teaching is susceptible to a plethora of limitations and dangers, not the least of which is the interestedness of self-analysis. There is no way to get beyond such interestedness. I have, however, attempted to ground my analysis as much as possible in texts that others can examine and interpret. I invite readers, then, to read the following discussion with an eye toward alternate understandings of the texts that I consider: twenty-plus years of course descriptions for first-year and advanced composition courses that I have taught in my years at OSU.[4] I also want to comment on my understanding of what course descriptions do—and do not—reveal. At my university, course descriptions exist primarily to enable interested students to gain a clearer understanding of a particular class's goals and requirements. Unlike the brief generic descriptions that appear in catalogs and bulletins, course descriptions provide specific information about the goals, texts, and assignments of a particular class. As such, they provide an opportunity for teachers to characterize their classes for students, who have access to these descriptions before registration. As my inclusion of the term "interested" in an earlier sentence suggests, students may—or may not—read course descriptions. I have often found that even in graduate-level classes, students have enrolled (or so they indicate in first-day-of-class introductions) primarily because a class fulfills a requirement or meets some other scheduling exigency. Rare indeed are students who attribute their decision to enroll in a class to this or that aspect of a course description, this or that assigned text.

Despite my awareness that course descriptions do not often reach their intended readership, I take these texts seriously, for they represent my initial engagement with a course. The word "initial" is important. Many teachers have had the experience of imagining a course one way when they write a course description, only to have the actual class morph into something that—were they to stop and freeze it in a written summary—would look quite different from their original statement. Even the most carefully developed course description is, after all, a prediction. And not all course descriptions are carefully developed since course descriptions are often written under time pressure. At my university, the request to order texts and write course descriptions for the next term's classes always seems to come at just the wrong time—just when (at about the third week of the term) I'm getting grounded in the courses that I'm currently teaching. Writing a description of a class that I am teaching in (what feels like) a far distant future seems like a frustrating exercise in prognostication. I won't really grapple with the day-to-day realities of the class until I develop a syllabus, and that often happens over the break before I begin teaching a class.

Despite these and other limitations, course descriptions can be revealing documents. What instructors choose to say, or not say, can expose underlying assumptions they bring to their courses. Course descriptions are, moreover, persuasive documents with multiple audiences. In this sense, course descriptions can reveal an instructor's attempt to negotiate individual and shared understandings of what a course should be and do. When I write course descriptions, I have at least two audiences in mind: the students for whom the descriptions are intended and the colleagues who might also read my descriptions and form judgments about my teaching on that basis.

I like to think that my awareness of these two audiences played some role in the first course description that I wrote for WR 121 at OSU, for I have to admit that when I discovered almost two decades later what I had written, I was dismayed. To my current eyes, this does not look like the course description written by someone who had recently had the privilege of participating in a year-long NEH seminar with Richard Young, James Berlin, Victor Vitanza, Robert Inkster, and others. Here is that description. (I should probably add that then, as now, OSU was on the ten-week quarter system):

> This course will focus upon the fundamentals of expository prose. Although we will spend some class time reviewing basic language skills, the main emphasis will be on the more complex art of essay writing. Students will write weekly essays and will be encouraged to revise frequently. Paper topics will be based upon students' own interests and experiences.

The use of the terms "fundamentals," "basic," and "expository" clearly suggest traditional assumptions about composition: these terms evoke a course concerned with written propriety and with a fairly limited range of genres. But these references exist in tension with the "more complex art of essay writing." And of course, elements of process are there as well—both in the emphasis on revision and on students' writing on topics of their own choice.

In the context of my years of teaching composition at Oregon State, this course description is anomalous. In fact, it strikes me as possible that—given the pressures of a new position that included administrative responsibilities for two writing programs—I simply used the description written by the previous director of composition. But then perhaps I'm simply embarrassed about this description's emphasis on "the fundamentals of expository prose" and wish to let myself off the hook. Whatever the case, departmental records indicate that I was willing to have this course description be the public face that my first-year writing class presented to the world.

And what about my first course description for advanced composition? Like my first WR 121 description, it too is an odd mix of elements:

> This course provides students from all disciplines practice in writing a mature, straightforward explanatory style with special emphasis on simplicity, clarity, exactness, freshness of expression, and interest to the reader. Students will write 5–7 themes (approximately 2–4 typed pages); most students will revise each theme at least once. Paper topics will be based upon students' own interests and experience.

89

As is the case with the previous course description, this combines traditional assumptions (as in the focus on "simplicity, clarity, exactness, freshness of expression, and interest to the reader") and such process-oriented features as an emphasis on revision and on student choice in paper topics. (How I thought students could write and revise as many as seven essays in ten weeks is beyond me. The actual syllabus that I later developed for this course specified five essays.)

Beginning in spring term of 1982, I wrote a new description that I used for both my first-year and advanced composition courses:

> This course is designed to help students become more effective, efficient, and flexible writers. Students will write 5 themes (3–6 typed pages); most students will revise each theme at least once—some, many more times. Paper topics will be based upon students' own interests and experiences.

To my eyes, this course description, which I used continuously for both first-year and advanced composition from spring 1982 until winter term 1987, strikes me as more coherent and more process-oriented than the preceding descriptions, particularly in its invocation of the writerly traits of effectiveness, efficiency, and flexibility. An examination of my syllabi over these years, however, both does and does not confirm this impression. When I look at my syllabi, I see a number of teaching practices that are consistent with a focus on process. Syllabi are structured, for instance, with clear attention to—and intervention in—students' composing processes. In most cases, syllabi list due dates not only for original drafts but also for revisions, and they feature required in-class peer responses. For most of these years, I used a portfolio grading system that I hoped would increase attention to process. Rather than giving students grades on individual essays, I evaluated portfolios at midterm and at the end of the term, and I required students to include reflections on their writing process with each essay. But there are also practices that are not necessarily associated with process. A number of activities—from class discussions of the rhetorical situation and of audience to daily sentence imitations—reflect my engagement with the rhetorical tradition. The presence of several days devoted to grammar and sentence structure indicate that I had hardly abandoned a concern for "the fundamentals of expository prose."

When I look at the next several years' course descriptions, I am at first confused. Why in fall 1988 did I revise the description for advanced composition so that it read:

> This course will function as an advanced writing workshop. Students will write four or five essays (four to six pages in length). Most students will revise each essay at least once.

I'm pleased to see that I dropped the term "themes" and referred to "essays" instead. This was, I believe, the result of a conscious decision. I'm less clear on the reason why I dropped the statement that I wanted to help student become "more effective, efficient, and flexible writers." It's possible that I did so because of the presence of new graduate students in our program. Then, as now, a significant number of these students are creative writers. I may have hoped that the term "writing workshop" would appeal to these students, who might connect it with creative writing workshops—but I can't be sure of my motivation.

There are echoes of my revised WR 416 course description in the description that I wrote for the WR 121 class I offered the following spring term:

> This class will function primarily as a workshop. We'll spend some time discussing the texts for the class, but we'll also work in groups on such activities as brainstorming, troubleshooting, and responding to work in progress. Expect to write four or five essays (two to four typed pages)—and expect to revise most essays at least once.

When I review the syllabi for these courses, I realize that though the changes I made in these course descriptions seem random they could (and could is the operative word here) reflect a change in my teaching— for with these two classes, for the first time, I incorporated published, in additional to student, writing into my composition classes. The fall term advanced composition class, for instance, included not only a rhetoric but Richard Rodriguez's *Hunger of Memory*. The first-year writing class included Lex Runciman and Steven Sher's edited collection *Northwest Variety: Personal Essays by Fourteen Regional Authors*. There is no mention of these texts in the course descriptions, but their inclusion may have triggered the sense that I needed to revise the descriptions.

The decision to include published readings in my composition courses reflects my questioning of at least one of the features of much process-based teaching: a focus on student rather than on professional writing. In Donald Murray's 1972 "Teach Writing as a Process Not Product," an early argument for attention to the writing process, Murray presents a series of "implications of teaching process, not product" for the composition curriculum. The first of his ten implications is that "The text of the writing course is the student's own writing" (5). For the first seven years that I taught composition at OSU, I embraced this implication, as I did the second, which states that "The student finds his own subject" (5). While I did not give students as much freedom as Murray did—he simply required them to write a certain number of essays on whatever topic they chose—I attempted to follow the spirit of this implication. Though many of my assignments identified a genre or purpose (typical assignments included writing an argument, review, oral history, and a rhetorical and stylistic analysis of a writing sample)—I otherwise made my assignments as open-ended as possible. In most classes, the final essay assignment for both first-year and advanced composition was entirely open.

When I review not only course descriptions but also syllabi from 1989 to 1991, I see that this was a period of transition for me. In addition to making reading a more important part of my composition class, I also looked for ways to encourage students to engage writing from a more social perspective—for I had been persuaded by arguments by Reither, Cooper, Berlin, and others. Beginning in spring 1989, for instance, I began requiring students to read a diverse group of literacy narratives, as well as to write a narrative of their own, at the start of my first-year and advanced composition classes. This assignment would, I hoped, encourage students to consider not only how they write language but also how language writes them—how it is interwoven into all aspects of their lives. I can see this shift to a more social view of writing in other aspects of my teaching, such as greater attention to collaborative learning and writing.

From fall 1991 to spring 1993, I did not teach either first-year or advanced composition. In fall 1994—fresh from a year's sabbatical—I again taught advanced composition, which I have taught every other year or so in the years since. This is the description that I posted for this class:

> In this course, we'll investigate what it means to write—to be a writer—while also engaging in various activities designed to help students become more effective, efficient, and confident writers. Students will complete a variety of informal and formal writing assignments and participate in regular collaborative learning activities.

I see one sign of a shift toward a more social perspective on writing in this description—though it requires some interpretation to make it evident. This involves the inclusion of the phrase "to be a writer." This is a small addition, but I believe it represents my effort—however incomplete—to suggest that writing is not simply a skill to be learned but also involves subjectivity and agency. (I have no illusions that students read my intended meaning into such an abbreviated reference.) It was not until I taught the course again the following fall that I articulated this understanding more fully. Here is the course description for my fall 1995 Advanced Composition class; I have used this course description for subsequent sections that I have taught from 1995 to the present time:

> What does it mean to be a writer? What is the relationship between the language(s) we speak and write in our home communities and the writing we do at school or on the job? How do writers learn to function in diverse (and sometimes conflicting) communities? What does it mean to have authority as a writer—to be considered literate in a particular community—and how do writers gain (and maintain) such authority? What role do textual conventions, and the assumptions underlying them, play in this process? What options do writers have if they wish to resist these conventions?
>
> In this class we will discuss questions such as these as we work together to become more effective, self-confident, and self-conscious writers. As is the case with most composition classes, we will function as a writing workshop—talking about the writing process, working collaboratively on work in progress. But we will also inquire together about what is at stake when we write. Drawing upon literacy narratives composed by both professional and student writers, we will explore the tensions (and satisfactions) that inevitably result when we wish to express our ideas, to claim a space for ourselves, in and with communities that may or may not share our assumptions and conventions.
>
> Students will complete a variety of informal and formal writing assignments and participate in frequent collaborative learning activities.

There are a number of comments that I could make about this course description. One is that the increased length of this description is the result of my growing awareness of the need not only to theorize my teaching in explicit ways but also to share this theorizing with my students. When I review course materials from my composition classes, I notice that as time passes, I increasingly take advantage of the opportunity to include an introduction to the course in the syllabus. My winter term 1983 syllabus for advanced composition simply begins with a list of the major writing assignments for the course and a reminder that the syllabus might be revised during the term. The syllabus for my fall term 1995 advanced composition class begins with comments from the course description I have just presented, but goes on to raise additional issues. Here is the text that the syllabus presents under the heading "Course Overview." The first paragraph of this course overview is identical to the preceding course description, the second paragraph revises it slightly, and the remaining paragraphs raise new issues. The text that follows begins with the second paragraph of the course overview:

> In this class we will discuss questions such as these as we work together to become more effective, self-confident, and self-conscious writers. As is the case with most composition classes, we will function as a writing workshop—talking about the writing process, working collaboratively on work in progress. But we will also inquire together about what is at stake when we write: we will explore, in other words, the tensions that inevitably result when we wish to express our ideas, to claim a space for ourselves, in and with communities that may or may not share our assumptions and conventions. And we will consider the implications of these explorations for such rhetorical concepts as voice and *ethos*.
>
> As we do so, we will work both with and against the approach taken in *Work in Progress (WIP);* we will explore, in other words, the limitations as well as the strengths of *WIP*'s rhetorical, process-oriented approach to writing. Like most composition textbooks, for instance, *WIP* emphasizes the positive role that writing can play as a means of self-expression and communication. Writing, in this view, is a primary means of gaining membership in new communities, of achieving success. But as a number of the literacy narratives we will read this term emphasize, such success sometimes comes at considerable personal cost. Writing, these narratives reveal, can be a place of struggle as well as of success. Writers also often bring quite different conceptions (and experiences) of writing to bear as they work. As you'll see when you read their literacy narratives, poet Jimmy Santiago Baca and newspaper columnist Jim Fitzgerald understand—and approach—writing in quite diverse ways.

In this class, we will draw upon all the resources available to us—our textbook, published and unpublished literacy narratives, interviews with others, and our own experiences as writers—to develop the fullest possible understanding of what it means to inhabit both the written word and the written world. The informal and formal writing assignments in this class will encourage you to reflect on your own experiences with language and literacy; they will also help you achieve an expanded awareness of various communities' assumptions and conventions and to consider the implications of this understanding for your own writing. Issues of authority and of power—of the extent to which you may wish (and may or may not be able) to resist or challenge a particular community's assumptions and conventions—will also be discussed.

I am sure that there are ways that this course overview could be improved, but I believe that it does at least an adequate job of articulating what it might mean for an advanced composition class to explore writing as a social process. The overview resists, for instance, a central feature of much process-oriented research and teaching: the emphasis on individual control and success, and it does so in part by challenging the approach taken by many composition textbooks, including my own. The course overview explicitly acknowledges that issues of power and authority are critical whenever one writes, and it promises to address ways students "may (or may not) be able to resist a particular community's assumptions and conventions." It recognizes, in other words, that "writing can be a place of struggle as well as of success." The references to literacy and to literacy narratives also emphasize the social. Whereas the course description that I used for my first-year and advanced composition classes from 1982 to 1987 alludes only to schooled writing—to the writing of "themes"—this course description situates writing in the context of "communities that may or may not share our assumptions and conventions."

Pedagogical Traces Reconsidered: Complicating the Story

From one perspective, the course descriptions that I have just presented chart if not revolutionary changes in my teaching then a clear evolution from process to social process theories and practices. Such an evolution did, I believe, occur—but the result can hardly be described a paradigm shift. For as readers have no doubt already observed, engagement with the writing process is hardly absent from my most recent course description and overview for my Advanced Composition class. Rather, these texts build on and extend, rather than reject, a process view of writing. The second paragraph of the description, for instance, observes that students will "work together to become more effective, self-confident, and self-conscious writers," and that the class will "function as a writing work-shop" by "talking about the writing process" and undertaking such activities as peer response. While the course overview calls students' attention to "the limitations as well as the strengths" of *Work in Progress*, it characterizes this textbook as having a "rhetorical, process-oriented approach to writing."

What about possible post-process features of my teaching? Ironically, according to Thomas Kent's criteria for post-process theory, my teaching was post-process quite some time before Kent articulated his project, for I have long assumed that "1) writing is public; 2) writing is interpretive; and 3) writing is situated" (Kent 1). An emphasis on the rhetorical situation has been central to my teaching, research, and scholarship for at least the past twenty years; it also provides the theoretical grounding for my textbook, *Work in Progress: A Guide to Academic Writing and Revising*. I do not see the rhetorical tradition's emphasis on the situatedness of all communication and the writing process movement's emphasis on recurring features of the writing process as incommensurate. Rather, I view them as providing alternate but related traditions upon which writers can draw. Both traditions, for instance, emphasize invention and audience. Both also, I believe, acknowledge that—as Kent observes—the "act of making sense of the world never ceases; it goes all the way down" (2).[5]

Both traditions also see writing as public. The classical rhetorical tradition arose as a result of disputes over land and was enacted in the agora. The preface to Peter Elbow's 1973 *Writing Without Teachers*—a work often cited as an early example of writing process theory and practice—begins with these words: "Many people are now trying to become less helpless, both personally and politically: trying to claim more control over their own lives. One of the ways people most lack control over their own lives is through lacking control over words" (vii). Though Elbow's work has been criticized as expressivist, his first book in its very title announces the desire to reach a broad and diverse range of readers.

I make these points not to launch another salvo in our field's recent theory wars but rather to remind readers that the world of both theory and practice in composition is more complex—and more situated—than most taxonomies can allow for. Scholars need terms and taxonomies to help organize our thinking, but we would do well to develop some healthy suspicions of them, particularly when they are used primarily to establish hierarchies and to create opposing theoretical camps that suggest that teachers can and should enact "purified" theoretical positions.

An examination of my syllabi provides additional evidence that, rather than rejecting a process approach to writing, my teaching integrates activities associated with both process and social process theories and practices. As I have already noted, from my first WR 121 syllabus in spring 1981 to my most recent syllabus for advanced composition, all of my syllabi are structured to encourage (indeed, to require) attention to students' writing processes. Central to all the composition courses I have taught at OSU is a sequence that goes something like this.

- present writing assignment to students;
- discuss relevant readings (often a mix of texts written by published and by student writers);
- engage students in formal or informal invention activities;
- facilitate peer response of drafts;
- read and respond to drafts;
- discuss revision issues with students in whole-class and individual conversations;
- read and respond to revisions.

As I read my own syllabi, this sequence is at the heart of my teaching of writing, for it is repeated throughout—and provides the essential structure for—both my first-year and advanced composition courses. This isn't to say that I enact each step in this sequence in identical ways every time I teach. Some of the assignments I give, for instance, include specific invention activities; others assume that students will rely upon such general inventional strategies as brainstorming, freewriting, and research. Often, I provide in-class time for peer response—but not always, especially as the term lurches toward its conclusion and students are working on multiple projects. Sometimes I require groups to follow a prescribed method of peer response; sometimes I allow them to agree upon their group's preferred method.

Some readers may be surprised by my insistence on identifying the sequence I have just described with a process-oriented approach to writing, for this sequence has become so commonplace that it is no longer viewed by many as connected to process theory and practice.[6] We no longer see, in other words, the process that exists in social process, for we notice the new and take the familiar for granted. To demonstrate what I mean by this, I would like to consider John Trimbur's recent textbook *The Call to Write*. I have chosen Trimbur's textbook for analysis because, more than many textbooks, *The Call to Write* attempts to enact a social view of writing. In the preface, Trimbur notes that *The Call to Write* takes as its starting point the view that "writing is much more than a school subject" (xxv). Given this statement, it is hardly surprising that part 2 of *The Call to Write*, "Writing Projects," includes not only such traditional genres as memoirs and profiles but also such forms as public documents, proposals, and reviews.

An examination of the activities included in part 2 indicates, however, that although a concern for process is backgrounded in *The Call to Write*—especially in comparison with such textbooks as Donald Murray's *Write to Learn* or Linda Flower's *Problem-Solving Strategies for Writing*—process still plays a critical role. All the writing projects included in part 2, for instance, include assignments that are structured around the following sequence of activities: working together, call to write, invention, planning, working draft, peer commentary, revising. Here, collaboration and a socially oriented exploration of the "call to write" precede traditional process-oriented activities—but they do not replace them. The assignments in part 2 of *The Call to Write* provide, in effect, the basic structure and curriculum for courses that use this text—just as the writing activities do for Axelrod and Cooper's *The St. Martin's Guide to Writing*—so the centrality of process-based activities here is important.

As both my analysis of my own teaching and of Trimbur's textbook suggest, though scholarly work has in many ways moved on from process, elements of writing process theory and practice have hardly disappeared from composition but rather are—as Victor Villanueva suggests in the title of the first section of *Cross-Talk in Comp Theory: A Reader*—"The 'Given' in our Conversations" (1). In calling attention to the "givenness" of process in composition, I am not attempting to make a broad argument in favor of process-based theory and practice as it existed in the 1970s and early 1980s: I am not trying to turn the clock back. I am pointing out that despite widespread agreement on the part of scholars that composition is in important ways post-process, engagement with process still manifests itself in both our classrooms and in the textbooks that can play such a critical role in teaching. Sometimes that engagement is enacted well; sometimes poorly. Many forces, after all—from an individual teacher's predilections to such material elements as teaching load and other institutional constraints—encourage or discourage pedagogical effectiveness.

Given the situatedness of teaching and the diverse locations where the pedagogical work of composition is enacted—from adult education courses in community and workplace literacy centers to community college, college, and university classrooms—it strikes me as naive to expect that any theoretical and pedagogical project would ever "make the earth move" (Gray 150). This is particularly true in the case of writing programs, where decisions about curricula for multisection courses are necessarily the result of compromise. In *1977: The Cultural Moment in Composition*, Brent Henze, Jack Selzer, and Wendy Sharer provide a rare—and telling—glimpse into the history of one writing program, that at Pennsylvania State University in University Park. In their study, Henze, Selzer, and Sharer look at how the strands of national conversations about composition in 1977 were being played out at Penn State during this time period. They chart the ways a budget crisis at the university interacted with local, state, and regional concerns about literacy and developments in research in composition to influence local efforts to develop a revitalized writing program. Because the authors were able to conduct interviews with many involved in these developments, and to gain access to memos and reports written about curricular and programmatic issues, they are able to provide a particularly detailed picture of how change in a writing program happens, one that includes such seldom discussed factors as department and university politics and the influences of particular individuals involved with the writing program. After two years of very hard work—and much negotiation and compromise—the faculty at Penn State did revise the second course in their required first-year writing sequence so that it reflected a strong engagement with research on the writing process. This course, they observe, though modified over the years "in many respects still prevails today at Penn State" (90).

Anyone who has ever directed a writing program is aware of the role that negotiation and compromise play in the development of curricula. But even teachers who have the freedom to choose texts and assignments for their classes must engage in a process of negotiation and compromise. This is certainly true in the case of my own teaching. Factors as diverse as constraints imposed by the official description of a class in university catalogs to departmental conversations about course expectations and my own predilections as a teacher influence the decisions I make in planning and teaching courses.

When I review the course descriptions and syllabi I have developed at OSU, and when I think further back to my teaching at the State University of New York at Brockport, I realize that some aspects of my teaching are more amenable to change than others and that I bring certain predilections to my teaching. From the start of my teaching to the present time, for instance, I have preferred to give students as much choice as possible in writing assignments. This preference predated my engagement with the writing process movement, and it continues in my current teaching, which as I hope to have demonstrated evidences a serious commitment to writing as a social process.[7]

Another predilection involves the role that reading plays in my composition classes. In spite of my literary training, as a writing teacher I have—despite my admiration of such curricular projects as Bartholomae and Petrosky's *Ways of Reading*—tended to deemphasize reading in comparison to writing and to prefer working with student rather than with professional or literary texts. For many years, as I noted earlier, I relied solely on student texts in my first-year and advanced writing classes. Gradually, I have come to assign a greater variety of readings—but their role has in many ways remained secondary. In my spring 1999 advanced composition class, for instance, readings played an important role only for the first half of the term.[8]

Other aspects of my teaching are more open to change—though sometime these changes might seem contradictory. As recent course descriptions and overviews suggest, I have given more explicit attention to issues of power and authority in my writing classes, particularly as they impinge on writers' interests in accommodating or resisting various discourse communities' expectations, than I have in the past.[9] But I have also paid more attention to craft issues as well. In the mid-1990s, I became concerned that my "turn" to social process had taken me too far away from the nitty-gritty of writing, from attention to style, sentence structure, and diction. So beginning with my fall 1996 advanced composition syllabus, I scheduled regular days devoted to "tools of the trade," where we discussed (and practiced) such elements of style as emphasis and concision.

These "tools of the trade" discussions are in some ways traditional—and in some ways not—for they include both activities that encourage attention to traditional craft issues and those that address larger issues of the politics of style. Such politics are, after all, a major site where issues of power and authority in writing are played out. In recent advanced composition classes, some students have chosen to resist the conventions of academic prose—to write personal essays or to experiment with alternative discourses, such as multivoiced writing or writing that experiments with elements of visual and well as textual form. In this sense, greater attention to power and authority in my writing class has brought both increased attention to ideological critique *and* to elements of play and pleasure in writing—elements that are associated by some with expressivism.

My interest in issues of power and authority has also caused me to rethink my approach to error, and to do so in multiple ways. As a result of this rethinking, for instance, I find myself regularly talking with students about the social nature of error.[10] "Why," I regularly ask students in composition classes, "does Joan Didion get to have comma splices in her writing, but you don't?" "Why are some forms of dialect acceptable in published prose, and others not acceptable?" (Questions like these can lead to fruitful discussions of such related issues as the relative flexibility or rigidity of genres in business, industry, and the professions.) I also give students the option of using nonstandard English in their essays—though they need to be prepared to show that this use is intentional and that it is appropriate given their rhetorical situation.

At the same time, however, I have found myself taking a stronger position on unintentional errors (whether of performance or competence) than I have in the past. The longer I have thought about issues of power and authority in writing, teaching, and learning, the more hypocritical it has seemed not to be clear about my expectations about error. This is manifested in changes in my course syllabi. There is no mention of error in any first-year or advanced composition syllabi from the 1980s. Instead, I dealt with error largely in ad hoc way through comments on students' essays and individual conferences. This still represents an important way I work with students on error, but beginning with my 1996 advanced composition syllabus, this statement now appears:

> As its title indicates, Advanced Composition is an *advanced* writing course. Students entering the class should thus have mastered the

Course
Descr

conventions of standard written English (SWE). As a consequence, I expect all drafts submitted for evaluation—as opposed to in-class or other informal writing—to be relatively free of major errors. I'm aware that even good writers can benefit from reviewing the conventions of SWE, so I've devoted a class to this topic. I'll also be happy to work with you individually on grammar, punctuation, and usage—and of course you can meet with a writing assistant at the Writing Center as well. By the end of the term, students who wish to do well in this course should be submitting essays that are free of significant errors.

This statement reflects both my understanding of power/knowledge issues and my effort to draw on years of teaching experience. For I had gradually (and largely intuitively) realized that, as Mike Rose puts it in *Lives on the Boundary,* "students will float to the mark you set" (26)—and in terms of my expectations about error, I believe that I had been setting the mark too low.

Readers may find these efforts to enact a more social view of error contradictory, or in other ways problematic. Indeed, there is much about my teaching that I feel sure is open to criticism. I have not intended my analysis of my own teaching to suggest that my teaching is exemplary; rather, I have endeavored to demonstrate through an admittedly limited and incomplete analysis of various pedagogical texts how I as a teacher have enacted pedagogical change. By extending this analysis to Trimbur's *The Call to Write* and to the history of the Penn State writing program as narrated in *1977: The Cultural Moment in Composition,* I have attempted to suggest that my experience is hardly unique.

Beyond Killer Dichotomies

As I have already indicated, my analysis suggests that in many instances, pedagogical change occurs not in revolutionary paradigm shifts but rather in smaller, incremental, and sometimes inconsistent and even contradictory efforts.[11] And yet many scholarly discourses seem to assume otherwise, for often they reify and decontextualize deeply situated practices. I have already discussed the role that taxonomies have played in recent debates in composition. Taxonomies by their nature rely on the establishment of dichotomies (such as that of process and social and/or post-process), which are often constituted as mutually exclusive categories. There is no room in the rhetorical taxonomy that James Berlin presents in "Rhetoric and Ideology in the Writing Class," for instance, for blurred or mixed rhetorics. A rhetoric must be categorized as cognitive, expressionistic, or social-epistemic.

As Anne Berthoff points out in "Killer Dichotomies: Reading In/Reading Out," the fact that dichotomies require the establishment of mutually exclusive categories is not in itself problematic. Rather, dichotomies are problematic—or in her terms "dangerous"—"because the categories they establish can so easily be confused with reality" (13). When the latter happens, Berthoff argues, dichotomies "forestall critical analysis" and "become Killer Dichotomies, hazardous to both our theory and practice as writing teachers" (13). Berthoff's discussion of killer dichotomies is a potent reminder of the need to distinguish between a logical construction, such as Berlin's taxonomy of rhetorics, and material reality. For as Berthoff observes:

> There are no dichotomies in reality: dichotomizing is an act of mind, not of Nature. We may say "as different as night and day" and know what we mean, but that dichotomy is tenuous in the real world.... But what about sea and land? Surely one is really, actually wet and the other is really, actually dry. Well, yes, wet and dry constitute a dichotomy and so do sea and land, as abstract—or mythical—categories, but where does one end and the other begin, at the shore? There is no line in nature that establishes that difference. The fact is, rather, that sea and land constitute a dialectic, which is now happily called The Coastal Zone. (13–14)

As Berthoff's example suggests, dichotomies often function as simplifications of or code words for more complex realities. Most of us have no need, after all, to make fine distinctions between sea and land—unless, Berthoff observes, we have something important at stake in such a distinction, as those living in coastal areas may have.

> In the British Isles, which have quite a lot of coast line, there is an intricate dichotomy—a trichotomy, really—that legally establishes ownership: that which lies between low-water mark and high tide belongs to the monarch (a beached whale is a Royal fish, as Melville says); whatever has lodged above high tide belongs to the property owner, to the laird; and whatever is in the sea belongs to whoever can catch it, within whatever limit has been set to protect local fishermen. (14)

Berthoff goes on to emphasize that even these distinctions are as much invented as real, for "All these lines are inventions, averaged out from local data. The twenty-mile limit is not a line in the ocean; it's on the charts, measured from some arbitrarily designated point on shore" (14).

I have belabored the importance of distinguishing between logical constructions and material reality because I believe that in scholarly work in composition, this distinction is at times overlooked. As an example, consider the extent to which James Berlin's discussion of expressionist rhetoric in "Rhetoric and Ideology in the Writing Class" blurs the distinction between expressionist rhetoric (as defined by Berlin's taxonomy), features of which can be identified in the texts published by a number of scholars, and the human beings whose texts he analyzes. Such a blurring was hardly inevitable. In the introduction to this essay, Berlin recognizes that "ideology is always pluralistic, a given historical moment displaying a variety of competing ideologies and a given individual reflecting one or another permutation of these conflicts" (479). This statement clearly acknowledges that any given individual or scholar—Peter Elbow, let's say, or Linda Flower, or Berlin himself—might enact or display "a variety of competing ideologies." Nevertheless, in his discussion of expressionist rhetoric, Berlin blurs the distinction between characteristics of a particular rhetoric that can be observed in the writing of specific scholars and those scholars themselves, who are labeled as members of "the expressionist camp" (485). Moreover, he does not take advantage of the opportunity to identify aspects of various scholars' texts that might suggest a possible resistance to the rhetoric with which they are identified. In the case of Peter Elbow, his longstanding advocacy of group work is an example of such a potential resistance.

As I have noted earlier, in pointing out a danger inherent in taxonomies, I do not mean in any unilateral way to challenge their helpfulness. (In *Singular Texts/Plural Authors: Perspectives on Collaborative Writing*, Andrea Lunsford and I rely on a taxonomy that distinguishes dialogical and hierarchical collaboration, for instance.) Generalization, abstraction, and categorization are essential to scholarly work, for they help scholars to step back from an immersion in a mass of details to see a larger picture. As a result, they can be helpful—and at times essential—to the development of scholarly ideas. Can scholars find ways to resist the tendency for taxonomies to totalize and to sever the connection between scholarly texts and materially embodied experiences? What if it were a common scholarly practice to read against the grain of—as well as with—taxonomies?

In asking questions such as these, I am not calling for a revolutionary change in scholarly work but for greater recognition that more can be at stake in logical constructions such as taxonomies than logic. The creation of a taxonomy can fulfill the very human need to establish camps of insiders and outsiders and in this sense can pose "killer" choices for individuals—choices that seem to offer no option but acceptance or rejection. In *A Teaching Subject: Composition since 1966*, for instance, Joseph Harris observes that in the early 1980s, it seemed to him that "so far as teaching went there were really only 'process people' and 'current-traditionalists,' and no one wanted to be counted among the latter" (55). Now, of course, a prevailing dichotomy is between process and social and/or post-process. These labels serve as much to demonstrate who is—and is not—"with it" theoretically as they do to clarify pedagogically useful distinctions in theories and practices of writing.

Are there ways that scholars in composition can develop our arguments and make necessary distinctions among different theoretical and pedagogical positions without reifying these arguments and positions into opposing camps that circulate as killer dichotomies? Can we find ways to acknowledge that our theories, no matter how helpful, can never be imported wholesale into any teacher's classrooms—that teaching is inevitably (and, I would argue, also productively) eclectic? These are some of the questions that I will consider in part 3 of *Situating Composition*.

On the Continuing Status of Process

As I did in the previous chapter, I want to conclude this chapter by looking at the issues that I have raised from the perspective of recent work in feminist theory. I do so because, as I noted in chapter 2, in many respects, composition and feminism are similarly situated—and face similar opportunities and difficulties—in the academy. I have also found that considering the scholarly work of composition via analogous issues and debates within feminism stimulates helpful ideas and encourages me to recognize options that I might not otherwise see.

In the previous chapter, I discussed Jane Flax's effort to articulate an understanding of theory that would encourage the acceptance of multiple approaches to such complex topics as gender and suggested that literacy is a similarly complex phenomenon. In concluding this reconsideration of the writing process movement, I want to look at Susan Gubar's reflections on developments within academic feminism during the previous thirty years. Gubar addresses this issue in the concluding chapter of *Critical Condition: Feminism at the Turn of the Century,* where she considers the future of feminism in the academy and the relationship of academic feminism to larger cultural, political, and economic projects. She wonders, for instance, what the next major tasks for feminism will be and poses "gendered approaches to the complex consequences of rapidly expanding scientific technologies and the globalization of culture in the twenty-first century" as two possibilities (155). At the heart of her analysis, however, is the question of how best to understand—and move productively on from—the sometimes fierce debates that have taken place within feminism over identity politics and poststructuralism—theoretical positions that, like process and social and/or post process, have often been figured as dichotomies.

The work of Gubar and her frequent coauthor Sandra Gilbert has been at the center of these debates, so Gubar is hardly a distanced bystander. Despite feeling battered by some of these criticisms, Gubar nevertheless hopes to find a way to acknowledge—and credit—the changes that have transformed feminist study in the academy. In particular, Gubar wants to get beyond the current impasse, where "The activist agenda of identity politics brackets poststructuralist claims, whereas poststructuralism's critique of a unified subject subverts activist agendas" (155).

In her effort to negotiate this impasse, Gubar suggests turning away from the metaphors of illness and even death that have informed some recent analyses of academic feminism and calling instead on the metaphor of the supernova. What if, she asks, feminists turned to the metaphor of the supernova to explain recent challenges to earlier concepts of gender:

> Should we think of gender as the thermonuclear fuel that propelled the establishment of feminist criticism, it might be said that its usefulness as a single, investigative category (usually applied in a Western national context) was quickly consumed by the astonishingly rapid production of scholarship and teaching during the seventies and early eighties. Brilliant and combustible, the collapse of a core—a commonly agreed upon center for feminism in the academy—released spin-off fields, area studies that provoked lively scholarly activity. (159)

Gubar sees great potential in this metaphor, noting that "the supernova as one alternative metaphor suggests that feminist studies have begun to fuel dispersed discoveries where none had been apparent before" (160).

I like Gubar's metaphor, for it acknowledges the extraordinary changes that have taken place in feminist theory while avoiding the agonism inherent in many interpretations. I believe that the metaphor of the supernova can helpfully illuminate the status of process in composition as well. When we think of process from the perspective of a supernova, we can acknowledge the "spin-off fields" that it released. These spin-offs have influenced not only various areas of research in composition, but also such curricular developments as writing centers, writing-across-the-curriculum programs, and the National Writing Project. The metaphor of the supernova suggests as well that rather than engaging in agonistic debates that pit process against social and/or post-process, we can see these projects as participating in what Gubar terms a "galactic ecology" that works not to reject but rather to reform elements of process for future use.

Lest the metaphor of a supernova seem both too grandiose and too optimistic, I would remind readers—as Gubar reminds readers of *Critical Condition*—that there is danger and even the potential for disaster in supernovas. In considering the critical condition of feminism at the turn of the century, Gubar wonders whether its supernova-like transformation might signal "a dispersal or diaspora, the danger of a dissipating 'feminist core' in academia" (160). Gubar expresses other concerns as well. She worries that "certain deployments of identity politics and post-structuralism have threatened to produce feminist knowledge purchased at the price of power" (156–57) and that "the fragmentation that specialization signifies" makes it difficult to keep criticism "teachable," especially to undergraduate students (157). Gubar is also concerned about feminism's pedagogical project. After mailing what she describes as "a hastily conceived questionnaire . . . to an unscientifically selected cohort group" (153), Gubar discovered that a number of her respondents expressed "growing anxiety . . . about the six hundred programs in Women's Studies and Gender Studies that have developed since the seventies" (157)—an anxiety also expressed in such publications as a fall 1997 special issue of *Differences* devoted to women's studies programs *(Women's Studies on the Edge)*. In her contribution to the special issue, Wendy Brown argued for abandoning women's studies as a site of pedagogical action entirely. Another contributor, Biddy Martin, expressed concerns about the ability of women's studies programs to undertake compelling interdisciplinary work.

Many of the concerns that Gubar raises for feminism are concerns that I hold for composition. It seems clear, for instance, that—as Gubar suggests of feminism—the knowledge that research has generated in composition has come with a cost. The making of this knowledge has catalyzed debates that have made some wonder whether progress in composition requires the metaphorical murder of scholarly foremothers and forefathers and the establishment of "camps" of scholars who depend on agonistic arguments to "demolish" their opponents. Another cost grows out of the professionalization of scholarly work in the field. This professionalization has had many positive benefits; it has, for instance, deeply enriched scholars' understanding of both writing and the teaching of writing, and it has improved the professional status of a small—very small—number of teachers of writing.

It has also, however, weakened the commitment that many scholars in preprofessional, predisciplinary times had to the actual *teaching* of composition. Currently, as David Bartholomae points out in "What Is Composition and (If You Know What That Is) Why Do We Teach It?" it is "increasingly common to find a specialist whose professional identity keeps him or her from the scene of instruction that defines his or her specialty" (23). This has certainly been true of my own career. As I have already noted, in my early years of teaching, both at SUNY Brockport and, later, at Oregon State University, I taught first-year composition regularly. In recent years, my teaching of writing has been limited to such courses as Advanced Composition and Critical Reviewing, another writing course that I regularly teach.

Professionalization has also caused some scholars, such as Sharon Crowley, to question composition's traditional commitment to the required first-year writing requirement. Indeed, in *Composition in the University*, Crowley argues that "The traditional function of the required first-year course is increasingly hard to reconcile with the professionalization and specialization that now characterize the American academy" (10). This limitation is hardly the primary reason why Crowley calls for abandoning the required first-year writing requirement. Crowley is much more concerned with the failure of the writing process movement to constitute itself as "a truly paradigmatic alternative to current-traditionalism" (212) and with the "disciplining function" (10) that the first-year requirement exerts on students.

I will look more carefully at Crowley's arguments against the first-year writing requirement in part 3 of *Situating Composition*. I will do so not to develop an extended argument for or against abolishing this requirement. I do hold views on this subject, however. I believe, for instance, that the question of whether first-year writing should be required is not one that can finally be resolved at the level of theory but rather requires a more situated analysis, one undertaken by those whose thinking is informed both by engagement with contemporary theoretical and pedagogical debates and by their own local knowledge of their institutions. (For an excellent example of such a discussion, see Francis Sullivan, Arabella Lyon, Dennis Lebofsky, Susan Wells, and Eli Goldblatt's "Student Needs and Strong Composition: The Dialectics of Writing Program Reform.")

Having said this, it seems only fair for me to acknowledge that I generally find myself in agreement with scholars such as Bruce Horner, who argues in "Resisting Academics" that "abolitionist arguments make the functionalist mistake of taking the historical effects of, or official purposes assigned to, first-year composition programs for their inevitable and complete functions" (177). I agree as well with the position taken by Keith Gilyard in "Basic Writing, Cost Effectiveness, and Ideology." In this article, Gilyard acknowledges the power of arguments such as Crowley's but argues that they fail to recognize the potential that these courses hold: "Sure required writing courses reproduce dominant ideologies, serve regulatory ends, and stifle creativity, but that is not all they do. The possibility for challenge and change, which could mean sustained access and opportunity for many students, is undeniably present" (41).

The question of whether scholars in composition should work to eliminate the required first-year writing requirement is certainly an important one. As Robert Connors observes in "The Abolition Debate in Composition: A Short History," this is a question that those in composition have considered several times since the first writing courses were required at Harvard. While I recognize the importance of this issue, in *Situating Composition* I want to take a broader look at the work of composition. In part 3, for instance, I will inquire into the interconnections and differences between the practice of theory and the practice of teaching; I will also consider some potential problems for those engaged in the former activity. In this and other ways, I hope to encourage scholars to attend more carefully than we sometimes do to the costs and well as the benefits of professionalization, and to the role that such assumptions as paradigm hope and practices as killer dichotomies play in this equation. One cost that I have not yet discussed—and that I will explore more fully in part 3 of this study—involves scholars' relationship with (and representation of the work of) teachers of writing. As Bartholomae observes in his essay, the claims that scholars in composition have made both *for* and *in* our work have—intentionally or not—challenged the knowledge and skills of those teachers of writing who do not meet the academic and professional norms the academy requires of scholars. In this sense, the professionalization of composition in the academy has, to echo Gubar, "threatened to produce . . . knowledge at the price of power"—for surely the most immediate and direct power that teachers of writing have is enacted daily in classrooms across the country (Gubar 156–57).

In noting these and other problematic consequences of composition's professionalization, I am not calling for a return to a preprofessional past or for the achievement of a postprofessional future. I see no easy resolutions to the problems that I articulate, for even the most brilliant proposal regarding future theory and practice would have to be enacted in the messy, constrained, problematic world of material reality. I am calling instead for scholars to attend more carefully to the politics of our location in the academy and to the discursive practices that enact these politics. These are issues that I address in part 3 of this study.

Thinking Through Practice

INTRODUCTION
Practice Makes Practice

Earlier in this study, I referred to Cynthia Lewiecki-Wilson and Jeff Sommers's "Professing at the Fault Lines: Composition at Open Admissions Institutions," an article published in one of two anniversary issues of *College Composition and Communication*—"A Usable Past: *CCC* at 50." I would like to return to their article now, and to an assertion the authors make that is relevant to my discussion of the writing process movement. This assertion is that "Teachers at open access institutions have not given up process approaches. In fact, they still struggle to get their colleagues to see the benefits of teaching process, including peer workshopping, revisions, and portfolios" (454). I want to consider this assertion in the context of the larger point of Lewiecki-Wilson and Sommers's article, which asks readers to consider the extent to which professional and disciplinary gains for the field have marginalized those teaching at open admissions institutions. Recent narratives of professionalization, they argue, "structure perceptions so that it is very difficult to see, let alone seriously consider, any possibility of satisfying intellectual work occurring between composition teachers and their students in open admissions programs" (439). Instead, to the extent that teaching at open access institutions is represented at all, it is figured as "a site for the discipline of punishment, applied to both students and teachers, and legitimated through metaphors of deficit" (439).

In what they describe as the "brief space" of their article, Lewiecki-Wilson and Sommers ask readers to shift perspectives and to

> consider the teaching of writing in open admissions sites as central to the historical formation and continuing practice of composition studies [and to]

reflect on how such a shift of thinking might change views of the profession and redirect attention to work compositionists need to do for the future. ...(440)

The authors hope that such a reversal will provoke a "crisis of representation" that will encourage readers to reconsider conventional disciplinary assumptions and practices. Their first step in provoking this crisis "is to describe us, the Others of composition" (440). To do so, Lewiecki-Wilson and Sommers rely both upon their own experiences teaching at the University of Miami, Middleton, and on interviews with "nine compositionists who have taught or currently teach at two- or four-year open admissions institutions" (440).[1] The sites at which those interviewed teach are diverse, as are their individual areas of expertise, such as basic writing and ESL. Whatever the site and expertise, Lewiecki-Wilson and Sommers argue, their interviewees' "teaching can often remain invisible when academic maps and disciplinary boundaries are usually drawn" (441).

"Professing at the Fault Lines" is an effort to make this teaching visible. (Though the authors focus on teachers and students at open admissions institutions, I believe that their observations extend beyond these borders to many other sites of post-secondary education.) To do so, the authors paint rich portraits of the teachers they interviewed. One recurrent feature of these portraits is the need to respond to local histories and conditions. In reflecting on her experience teaching at the City College of New York, Mary Soliday comments that some of the changes she charts "have resulted from institutional pressures that a responsible teacher can not ignore and that theory never fully accounts for" (452). In her case, Soliday observes that "institutional reaction and harsh penalties against students have probably pushed me towards a deeper concern about students' errors," and also toward more explicit attention to rhetorical form (452).

Lewiecki-Wilson and Sommers emphasize the evolutionary nature of the pedagogical changes that their interviewees describe. As the quotation that begins this chapter attests, most of the teachers they interviewed have maintained a commitment to process.[2] In several cases, those interviewed observed that this commitment deepened after they completed their PhDs in rhetoric and composition and began full-time teaching. Here, for instance, is the authors' summary of the experience of Rhonda Grego, who teaches at historically black Benedict College:

Rhonda Grego recalled that when she first started teaching composition as a graduate student in a Rhetoric and Comp PhD program in the early 80s, "process" didn't really get much respect. She and others in the program paid lip-service to process approaches; they used student workshopping of papers, for instance. But the grad students nevertheless felt "there was a kind of message about people who did process work that it was a little soft, that there wasn't as much academic valuing of the process approach as there was the more intellectual history of rhetoric or argumentation." (447)

Gradually, her teaching experience caused Grego to see a need for more interactive and process-oriented instruction. Hence, according to the authors, "She now does more responding to early stage writing, helping to articulate implicit pathways of development and alternative strategies" (447).

The portraits that Lewiecki-Wilson and Sommers paint—and it is good to remember that they *are* portraits—are not of teachers who are mindlessly relying on outdated practices but rather of teachers who consciously "put student acts of reading and writing at the center of their disciplinary practice" (455). In so doing, these teachers draw upon multiple sources. Lewiecki-Wilson, for instance, draws upon both process and post-process theories in her teaching. Like Grego, Lewiecki-Wilson "used the term 'process' in graduate school as a TA, but did not actually teach much process then" since (among other reasons) the program was driven by a required exit exam (448). As the authors observe,

> only when [Lewiecki-Wilson] moved to her present position at a two-year regional campus did she really develop a pedagogy emphasizing multiple and creative revising and portfolio assessment. She also started applying theory to the writing classroom, asking students to analyze the social forces that shape writing and writers. In part, her teaching evolved out of necessity. The students she now teaches have such differing levels of preparation that they need creative process and revision strategies. Their economic and social precariousness constantly threatens to overwhelm them and calls for critical analysis. In part, local conditions (no exit exams) freed her to develop. She has also become more personal in the classroom, asking students to speak out about their lives in their writing, to connect their experiences to cultural and social critique, to undertake community-based writing projects. (448)

I have quoted this reflection on Lewiecki-Wilson's development as a teacher at such length because it is a particularly powerful example of a teacher who has not just maintained but actually strengthened a commitment to process while also engaging more recent developments in composition.

In the context of the nine teachers interviewed for "Professing at the Fault Lines," Lewiecki-Wilson's experience is hardly unique. When asked to characterize the influences on her teaching, Helon Raines of Armstrong Atlantic State University shared the following list:

> The shift from current-traditional rhetoric to process writing; new approaches in grading, evaluating, and assessing writing; the emergence of comp as a professional discipline with conferences, journals, and graduate training; writing center and writing across the curriculum advances; expanded notions of literacy; the development of national and regional Writing Projects; and the validation of multiple kinds of research and scholarship in writing. (447)

In a similar vein, Nancy Thompson, who teaches at the University of South Carolina, told the authors that "film studies and feminism influenced her approaches to teaching writing and that she practiced an early form of cultural studies" (446). Given the multiplicity of these influences and practices, it is thus hardly surprising that while Lewiecki-Wilson and Sommers point to these teachers' continuing commitment to process, they also emphasize that they "have incorporated process into courses that focus on critical thinking, cultural studies, ethnography, and/or literacy" (454).

How can we best assess these teachers' practices? Is it possible to characterize these teachers' classrooms as an "intellectually productive and transformative site of disciplinary practice," as Lewiecki-Wilson and Sommers argue that we should (459)? From one perspective—that of recent scholarship—the answer would seem to be no. How can these teachers' practices be viewed as contributing to disciplinary knowledge when they maintain a commitment to process, a scholarly and pedagogical project that scholars such as Harris, Crowley, Miller, and others have argued is deeply flawed, and that scholars in general view as a movement of the past? Given their eclecticism, these teachers' practices are likely to be viewed by many scholars as lore, as teaching that in critical ways remains inadequately theorized.

There have been a number of efforts to address the questions I have just raised. Both Stephen North and Patricia Harkin, for instance, have attempted to retheorize lore so that teachers' situated knowledge can be seen and valued as part of composition's disciplinary project. But as Bruce Horner points out in "Traditions and Professionalization: Reconceiving Work in Composition," in these and related efforts, "the discourse of academic professionalism has dominated conceptions of our work" (367).[3] Horner thus calls on scholars to "relinquish the quest for academic professionalism in defining the work of Composition and to construct a sense of tradition in Composition as an active and activating force central to its work" (367). At stake for Horner is nothing less than composition's ability to "accomplish politically liberatory work" (377). As an example of such work accomplished during a time characterized in most accounts as current-traditional, Horner discusses the teaching of English 1–2 course at Amherst College from 1938–66.

There is much that I value in Horner's analysis. Horner's discussion of the nature—and value—of teachers' "working knowledge" is particularly powerful, as is his effort to reverse "the derogatory connotations of tradition in Composition" (371; 367). I have reservations, however, about the stark alternative that Horner poses in regard to composition's professionalization: "Efforts to define Composition in terms of its disciplinarity are either doomed to failure, given Composition's identity with teaching, or they will transform Composition into something unrecognizable, a discipline in which teaching is peripheral, not central" (380). Horner doesn't discuss the poles of this binary at length, but he does make it clear that he believes composition should give up its effort to achieve disciplinary status. He maintains, for instance,

> That compositionists should continue to pursue professional academic disciplinary status—despite the history of its failure to improve their working conditions and despite the dilemmas to which it leads—attests both to the hegemonic force of professionalism and to the apparent paucity of alternatives to embracing it. (380)

As my discussion of composition's professionalization in chapter 3 indicates, I believe that it is important to explore the multiple consequences of composition's professionalization, both negative and positive. But I want to resist or recast the dichotomized choice that Horner offers. There is, first of all, much about composition's professionalization that I value. I believe that composition is stronger and richer because of the development of MA and PhD programs, for instance. I also believe that given the politics of composition's location in the academy, it is important to be realistic about what composition can and cannot accomplish. The forces that maintain conventional disciplinary and professional ideologies in the academy are substantial. Moreover, as I discussed in chapter 1, many of these forces are beyond the control of those in composition. Though scholars in composition have in general accepted, rather than rejected, the hierarchies of knowledge that characterize traditional research universities, even a broad and deep rejection would leave many of these hierarchies in place. I believe, then, that we have to work *within* the ideologies of professionalism and disciplinarity. There is no pure space within which to continue the work of composition.

Though I disagree with Horner's binary-driven rejection of disciplinarity, I believe that his work represents a positive and helpful effort to reimagine the work of composition. I agree with Horner that too often, teachers are envisioned in scholarly writing as lacking agency or in other ways being the dupes of ideology. Such occurs when scholars assume that teachers who avow a commitment to writing process theories and practices are in effect dominated or "produced" by these practices. Any evaluation of the teaching of those interviewed by Lewiecki-Wilson and Sommers, for instance, would have to take a deeply situated look at their practices. Only then would it be possible to determine whether these practices are effective or ineffective, whether they represent a contribution to the discipline.

As Horner observes, the forces that promote professionalization do not encourage this kind of situated evaluation, for as Horner notes, "one's class status as a 'professional' is maintained through denying the materiality of one's work" ("Traditions" 376). If scholars working within the ideologies of professionalization and disciplinarity hope to value teaching as an "intellectually productive and transformative site of disciplinary practice," we will need to find better—and more frequent—ways of making that work visible in our own writing. Having said this, I want to remind readers (as I have before) that there is no guarantee that these efforts will have significant consequences for some of the most important—and intractable—material realities that those in composition face, such as the employment of contingent faculty. They could, however, help composition better negotiate its current impasse, where scholars often represent teachers as lacking in theoretical sophistication and teachers often represent scholars as separated from the "real world" concerns of day-to-day teaching. These efforts could, as well, encourage those whose work is most privileged in disciplinary hierarchies of knowledge to take greater care in our representations of the work that *others* do. And they could remind scholars that scholarly writing is, after all, nothing more or less than a practice, just as teaching is.

In *Rhetorical Power,* Steven Mailloux makes just this point: "Theory," he observes, "is a kind of practice, sometimes a peculiar kind when it claims to escape practice" (159). In *Situating Composition,* I hope to constitute a view of theory that exposes, rather than represses, theory's status as a material practice. For this reason, I have titled this introduction to part 3 "Practice Makes Practice," in the hope that this title will call attention to the need for greater attention to the *practice* of scholarly writing. As a practice, scholarly work produces and authorizes situated forms of knowledge and identities. As a practice, scholarly work necessarily participates in, rather than is exempt from, prevailing ideologies—including ideologies of professionalism and disciplinarity.[4]

As some readers may be aware, the title "practice makes practice" invokes Deborah Britzman's study of student teachers, *Practice Makes Practice: A Critical Study of Learning to Teach.* Britzman is a critical ethnographer and teacher educator. In *Practice Makes Practice,* Britzman examines the lived experiences of student teachers. She employs her dual investments in ethnography and in poststructuralism to complicate readers' understanding "of both the discourses that affect the lived experiences of those in teacher education and the ways in which lived experience is studied" (xiii). For Britzman, "the idea that practice makes practice is an argument for understanding the complex dialogue between practice and theory, biography and social structure, knowledge and experience, and difference and commonalities" (240).

The idea that practice makes practice also encourages an attention to the interactions between the local and the global—to "the everyday world of the university and the school" and "the social forces that organize, surround, and summon its institutions"—and to a recognition that the consequences of these actions can never be determined in advance (Britzman 240). Just as teachers may or may not be "intellectually productive and transformative," the same can be said for those primarily engaged in the writing of articles and books and the training of graduate students. In order to determine whether a practice is progressive or regressive, that practice must be considered in the context of a complex mix of factors—from the personal to the institutional, economic, and political. Applying the "correct" theory—whether done in the privacy of a study by a researcher or in the public space of the classroom by a teacher—can guarantee neither that theory's efficacy nor its ethics.

The idea that practice makes practice also reminds us of the extent to which practice participates in the social construction of reality. It reminds us, in other words, that those who view themselves primarily as scholars and those who view themselves primarily as teachers are likely to have somewhat different professional identities and intellectual commitments. The ideologies that most powerfully influence their practices may also differ in important ways. (In stating this, I do not mean to suggest that either scholars or teachers are always already constructed by these identities, commitments, and ideologies, and I surely do not mean to suggest that these identities are seamless. Scholars are, after all, also teachers. And as Lewiecki-Wilson and Sommers demonstrate, teachers are if not always publishing scholars then producers of significant knowledge. Moreover, both scholars and teachers are "hailed" by a variety of forces.) As I mentioned in part 1 of this study, scholars in English studies exhibit powerful commitments to what Evan Watkins refers to as "ideologies of the new." As Bruce Horner observers, teachers often find ideologies of tradition to be more powerful. Counterhegemonic work—work that contributes to composition's disciplinary mission—can, as Horner insists, occur within the traditional, as it can occur within "the new."

How can those differently situated in the work of composition better understand, value, and represent the contributions that others make to the discipline? One practice that I have found useful in this regard is—as I mentioned in chapter 1—that of thinking *through* practice. As I suggested there, such an effort entails not only thinking *about* practice—about teaching, writing program administration, research, and so on—but also attempting to use practice as a means of thinking *through* complex scholarly and professional issues. Thinking through practice does not privilege practice over theory—does not, in other words, simply reverse conventional hierarchies—but rather looks for productive ways to place the two in dialogue. It looks, as well, for ways to call attention to contradictions and paradoxes that are sometimes overlooked in scholarly work.

In the three chapters that comprise this final section of *Situating Composition*, I attempt to demonstrate how scholars might begin to think *through* practice about our work. Such an analysis raises fruitful questions, I believe, about the politics of location in composition studies. Chapter 5, "On Theory, Theories, and Theorizing" and chapter 6, "Who's Disciplining Whom?" might best and most broadly be described as critiques of current scholarly practices. In chapter 7, "Situated Knowledges: Toward a Politics of Location in Composition," I attempt to turn from critique to offer constructive suggestions that scholars might consider as we engage in our work. To these chapters I now turn.

5 On Theory, Theories, and Theorizing

What significance should scholars draw from the portrait of composition that Lewiecki-Wilson and Sommers paint in "Professing at the Fault Lines"? If the authors are right that scholarly work often figures teachers as the Others of composition and represents their classrooms as "site[s] for the discipline of punishment" (439), what consequences does this hold for the field? How troubled should we be that a field that has devoted so much scholarly attention to issues of representation and difference has replicated the academy's conventional, and deeply conservative, hierarchies of value—hierarchies that privilege theory over practice and thus challenge the commitment to practice that has played a central, though be no means singular, role in composition?[1]

These are questions that have drawn a good deal of attention in recent years, as scholars have attempted to redefine conventional understandings of theory and practice in composition. A partial genealogy of such efforts would certainly include the following, organized by year of publication:

> 1987: Stephen North, *The Making of Knowledge in Composition: Portrait of an Emerging Field*
>
> 1988: Louise Phelps, *Composition as a Human Science: Contributions to the Self-Understanding of a Discipline*
>
> 1991: Anne Ruggles Gere, "Practicing Theory/Theorizing Practice"; Victor Vitanza, "Three Countertheses: Or, A Critical In(ter)vention into Composition Theories and Pedagogies"; Patricia Harkin, "The Postdisciplinary Politics of Lore"; Susan Miller, *Textual Carnivals: The Politics of Composition*
>
> 1992: Susan Miller, "Writing Theory: : Theory Writing"; Charles Bazerman, "Theories That Help Us Read and Write Better"
>
> 1993: Ruth Ray, *The Practice of Theory: Teacher Research in Composition;* Linda Flower, *The Construction of Negotiated Meaning: A Social Cognitive Theory of Writing*

1994: Beverly Moss, "Theory, Theories, Politics, and Journeys"; Beth Daniell, "Theory, Theory Talk, and Composition"; Joseph Harris, "The Rhetoric of Theory"

1996: John Schilb, *Between the Lines: Relating Composition Theory and Literary Theory*

1997: Thomas Kent, "The Consequences of Theory for the Practice of Writing"; Sidney Dobrin, *Constructing Knowledges: The Politics of Theory-Building and Pedagogy in Composition*

1998: Hephzibah Roskelly and Kate Ronald, *Reason to Believe: Romanticism, Pragmatism, and the Teaching of Writing*; Christine Farris and Chris M. Anson, *Under Construction: Working at the Intersections of Composition Theory, Research, and Practice*

2000: Bruce Horner, *Terms of Work for Composition: A Materialist Critique*

2002: Geoffrey Sirc, *English Composition as a Happening*; Chris Gallagher, *Radical Departures: Composition and Progressive Pedagogy*

This is a lengthy—and yet still incomplete—compilation of research on theory and practice in composition. Though these studies vary in approach and argument, all call attention to the ethical, political, rhetorical, cultural, and epistemological issues at stake in the relationship of theory and practice—and theorists and practitioners—in the field. A number of these studies recognize that the hegemony of theory leads to the suppression of difference as it is manifested in practice and propose if not solutions then reformulations that might help those in composition better negotiate our differing situations.

In her 1988 study, for instance, Louise Phelps points out that in failing "to confront as arguable the questions teachers raise about relevance, validity, applicability, and the privileging of theory, composition has failed to address one of the constitutive problems of a practical-moral field" (207). Current assumptions and practices in the field seem to offer, Phelps argues, little choice between "oppressive theory and unreflective practice" (238). As an alternative, Phelps articulates an understanding of their relationship in which "[t]heory and praxis mutually discipline each other and ... each has its own sphere of action not to be dominated by the other" (238).

Phelps's project is grounded in such fields as philosophy, educational theory, cognitive science, and hermeneutics; not surprisingly, her analysis remains at a fairly high level of abstraction. In "Practicing Theory/Theorizing Practice," Anne Gere takes a more materially grounded look at theory and practice in composition; she does so by focusing on

123

composition's increasing professionalization. Gere points out that this professionalization "divides practice and theory because it operates on principles of exclusion and separation" (114) that draw strong distinctions between experts and non-experts. According to Gere, teacher research offers one way to breach this division—particularly when those conducting teacher research embrace a social constructionist philosophy. Gere concludes her article by asserting that "if we conceive of composition programs as centers of teacher research, research based on a socially constructed epistemology and freed from the hierarchies of professionalism, we can transform the theory-practice division into theorizing about practice and practicing theory" (121).

Gere's formulation of a revitalized theory/practice relationship is both elegant and persuasive. But when I think about issues of theory and practice from the perspective of my years of experience as a writing program administrator, I am reminded that theoretical articulations of this relationship, no matter how sophisticated, may have limited consequences for practice. In order to enact Gere's conception of a composition program, a writing program administrator would have to negotiate the messy, constrained, and often contradictory world of material reality—the world I attempted to invoke via the scenarios in the first chapter of *Situating Composition*. What would it take in material terms to establish and run a writing program where the majority of teachers had the time to engage in teacher research? What concrete steps might a WPA take to foster a workplace that successfully resists "the hierarchies of professionalism"?

Another potentially thorny issues involves the question of just what constitutes "teacher . . . research based on a socially constructed epistemology" (Gere, "Practicing Theory" 121). How explicit and extensive would teachers' knowledge of a socially constructed epistemology need to be? Who would determine what constitutes teacher research as opposed to teachers' ongoing efforts to analyze and improve their teaching? What steps would all involved in a writing program need in order to establish communally derived norms for teacher research grounded in a socially constructed epistemology?

As these questions suggest, the material world can prove remarkably intractable, particularly in an age of corporate universities and of decreasing tenure-line and increasing part-time and adjunct positions. It is humbling to recognize how little an insightful analysis of theory and practice in composition can matter to an instructor teaching five classes a term at three post-secondary institutions. For many in composition, the failure of the Wyoming Conference Resolution to effect significant change in the working conditions of the majority of teachers of writing has turned that sense of humility into something deeper and darker.[2] Indeed, as Hephzibah Roskelly and Kate Ronald observe in *Reason to Believe,* many scholars in composition have in recent years experienced "a sense of diminished hope and a retreat from action, a sense of how to name problems but no vocabulary for naming solutions as constructed within contexts that are at once philosophical, historical, and local" (13).

Roskelly and Ronald see signs of this diminished hope in such articles as Susan Miller's "The Death of the Teacher." In this article, Miller argues both that the "Teacher, erstwhile Author of class(es), has expired" (42) and that "we have no stable way . . . to imagine a purpose for teaching" (49). They cite as well Stephen North's "Revisiting 'The Idea of a Writing Center,'" where North reconsiders his influential 1984 "The Idea of a Writing Center." In his later article, North argues that his earlier formulation represents "a romantic idealization" (9) and observes that such romanticization "may actually mask its complicity in what Elspeth Stuckey has called the violence of literacy" (15). Though North emphasizes that he is not attempting to argue for a specific model of writing center work, he spends considerable time discussing recent changes in his center's mission. In the past, SUNY Albany's writing center served students across the curriculum. According to North, its services are now tied "directly to [SUNY Albany's] Writing Sequence through the English major," so that center consultations are limited to the "approximately 10 faculty members, the 20 graduate students, and the 250 or so undergraduates that," according to North, the center "can actually, sanely, responsibly bring together" (17). In his later essay, North in effect abandons his earlier vision of writing centers as transformative agents across the curriculum and proposes instead a professionalized writing center that works with a limited group of students selected for their explicit commitment to writing.

I could cite other scholarly efforts that support Roskelly and Ronald's pessimistic vision of the current state of affairs in composition. In the same article of the *Writing Center Journal* in which North's "Revisiting" appeared, for instance, Terrance Riley presents "The Unpromising Future of Writing Centers," a dystopian vision of the challenges facing those engaged in this work. In his essay, Riley looks at writing centers through the theoretical and historical lenses of disciplinary legitimation and professionalization and argues that to the extent that writing centers follow the path that composition has generally taken, "our pursuit of success and stability, as conventionally measured, may be our undoing" (20). For Riley, the only way that writing centers can sustain their "liberatory and contrarian" philosophy (29) is to refuse to participate in composition's professionalization.

North's and Riley's essays present a striking contrast, for North's essay implicitly argues that writing centers should professionalize, while Riley's explicitly argues that they should not. I have responded to North's and Riley's essays elsewhere ("Writing Centers and the Politics of Location"). At present I would simply like to note the binary-driven logic that underlies both of their arguments, and the impasse that this logic creates. Though their articles take different positions in terms of composition's professionalization, each suggests that one must choose between professionalized theory or unprofessionalized practice.

Variations of this impasse appear in other recent studies in composition, such as Horner's "Traditions and Professionalization: Reconceiving Work in Composition," which I discussed in the introduction to part 3. The assumption that professionalization must either be wholly embraced or wholly rejected also permeates Geoffrey Sirc's *English Composition as a Happening*. In this study, Sirc characterizes himself as having "a nostalgia for the pre-professional, the pre-disciplinary" (265) and argues that "It is difficult to think of Composition of the last 30 years as anything other than a retreat" (173). For Sirc, teachers of writing have two—and only two—choices: "we can allow students the seduction of texts in a carnival classroom, or we can train them to create writing that can be used in the production and marketing of bombs" (225).

There are no easy resolutions to impasses such as these, for these impasses are grounded in material conditions of work as well as in ideologies of professionalism and disciplinarity that circulate broadly in the academy, and in the culture. Efforts to retheorize theory and practice can help us better understand this impasse, but because the impasse is so deeply embedded in our institutions, the consequences of any such effort, including my own, are necessarily limited. In making this claim, I do not mean to devalue the work of scholars such as Phelps, Gere, Ray, Horner, and others. Rather, I want to remind readers of the obvious fact that interventions at the level of theory (including the intervention that

Situating Composition represents) circulate primarily among theorists. Such interventions can envision a revitalized theory-practice relationship in composition, but they cannot on their own effect the kind of changes that will bring this revitalized relationship to fruition.

There is one realm in which scholars can effect change—should change seem helpful or necessary—and that is in our own scholarly practices. In this final section of *Situating Composition,* I want to suggest that if we want to take the idea that "practice makes practice" seriously, then at the very least, scholars should be willing to subject our own practices to the same kind of scrutiny to which we subject others. For in terms of hierarchies of knowledge in the academy, our practices are privileged and may circulate in unintended ways. (There are other contexts, of course, is which theory is hardly hegemonic. One might well argue, for instance, that many teachers draw upon and value the knowledge that is presented in textbooks more highly than the knowledge presented in scholarly texts.) Such is surely the case when scholarly work that hopes to empower both teachers and students, and to encourage broad social and political change, nevertheless "structure[s] perceptions so that it is very difficult to see, let alone seriously consider, any possibility of satisfying intellectual work occurring between composition teachers and their students" (Lewiecki-Wilson and Sommers 439).

Although I will briefly sketch my own understanding of the nature of theory and its relationship to practice, in the remainder of this chapter, I will look primarily at the *practice* of theory in composition. In so doing, I am certainly engaging in "theory work." My goal is not to develop a new and improved articulation of theory and practice, however, but rather to raise questions about some of the textual strategies upon which scholars in composition have at times relied. In raising these questions, I do not intend to call for yet another revolution in composition, and I acknowledge that my questions are more relevant for some kinds of research than for others. My hope is that my efforts to raise questions about scholarly practice will help both myself and other scholars to move forward with more critical awareness of the choices we make. This is a modest—but, I believe, important—goal.

Theory as Situated Practice

How can we best understand the interconnections of theory, theories, and theorizing? That this subject is complicated is an understatement. What is the relationship, for instance, between a particular school of thought—postmodern, feminist, or social cognitive theory, let's say—and theory as a mode of inquiry? (Posed in this way, this question calls attention to differences between what I sometimes think of as Theory with a capital "T" and theory with a small "t," between theory as a noun and theory as a verb.) To what extent is theory a content, something to be mastered, or at least interrogated? To what extent is theory a practice—an action? How does theory function discursively? Is it best to think of theory through the lens of epistemology as the production of knowledge? Or is a more pragmatic understanding of theory—an understanding that emphasizes theory's material situatedness and its imbrication with the ideological, cultural, political, and ethical as well as with the epistemological—more productive?

My engagement with the rhetorical tradition—and with a number of contemporary studies in feminism, cultural studies, critical pedagogy, and other areas—inclines me toward the latter view, one that calls attention to theory as situated practice.[3] With Jane Flax, I would argue that the best understanding of theory "is a pragmatic one. Theorizing comprises a variety of practices, and no one mode can meet all our needs. Theorizing includes contextual puzzle solving as well as metalevel thinking about thinking" (*Disputed Subjects* 4). For me, theory (like all discursive acts, from teaching or writing an e-mail to participating in a department meeting or arguing a legal brief) is a mode of communicative action. This emphasis on theory as situated practice does not deny that theories can and do circulate as bodies of knowledge. There are theories about gender relations, theories about the origin of the novel, theories about the nature of human emotion and understanding—and theories about the nature of theory (such as arguments in English studies that we are now in an age of post-theory). A rhetorical view of theory would argue that these theories are useful when they function as what Charles Bazerman refers to as "heuristics for action" ("Theories" 103). As Bazerman observes:

> Theories at their best help us manage the manifold and inchoate realities we move among. They give a shape to our experiences and desires; they allow us to project our actions into a universe to which we have attributed some order. They allow us to make our actions reflective rather than reliant only on the impulses of spontaneity, habit, and

the unconscious. They also allow us to recognize and give proper influence to the processes of spontaneity, habit, and the unconscious, which we otherwise might wish to deny or obliterate with narrowly rational choices or hyperconscious mechanisms that make the simple difficult. (103)

Bazerman's qualifying "at their best" is a potent reminder that theories don't always function in the way that he describes. Theories can oppress as well as enlighten. They can circulate as regimes of knowledge that deny individuals' situated knowledge and embodied experience. In cases such as these, resistance to theory is not only justified; it may be necessary to survival. In "Theory, Theories, Politics, and Journeys," Beverly Moss has this to say about theory:

> I usually talk theory only when I have to. More to the point, I concern myself with theory only when it's useful for me. This attitude may stem from my membership in communities that have long been victimized and oppressed by Theories. As an African American woman from the South whose parents don't have college degrees, I would believe, if I trusted theory, that I'm genetically inferior to Caucasians, culturally deprived, culturally disadvantaged, educationally disadvantaged, cognitively deficient, and from a primarily oral culture. I would have to accept many other labels attached by theories that were or are meant to explain and exclude people like me. In short, I would be unqualified to write this response. Ideas like these constituted my introduction to Theory. (341–42)

In graduate school, Moss goes on to add, she gradually recognized that not all theorizing ignores context and experience while striving for universal explanations—but it is clear that Moss's early experiences with theory continue to resonate for her.

As Bazerman's and Moss's comments suggest, "theory" is an overdetermined term, one whose meaning and consequences vary for different persons and in different situations.[4] In this sense, understandings of theory are unstable and are up for grabs: one person's theory is another person's (threatening, boring—or irrelevant) abstraction or overgeneralization, and yet another person's hunch. Because theory is nothing more—and nothing less—than situated practice, its nature, efficacy, and consequences are always open to question.

Politically Enlightened Theory/Pedagogically Wrong Practice

When viewed as situated practice, theory becomes just another human activity, like parenting, practicing medicine, preaching, or teaching. Like other human activities, theory can be done well or poorly, ethically or unethically. As is the case with any human activity, we can engage in theory intending to achieve one effect but bring about quite a different one. Even when we entertain the best of intentions, our immersion in ideological, political, cultural, and other systems means that the possibility for contradiction in our actions always exists.

As humans, we cannot avoid self-contradiction. Parents who once engaged in the kind of risky behaviors that they warn their children against represent one example of such a contradiction. Another occurs when teachers tell students that they value students' ideas and want to encourage independent thinking but evaluate their efforts according to criteria that reward conformity and memorization. And yet another occurs when scholars avow a politically and ideologically enlightened agenda but rely upon textual strategies that challenge, resist, or in other ways thwart that agenda's goals.

Some self-contradictions are easy to identify. A parent telling a child to "just say no" to drugs may recall her own experimentation with marijuana and wince internally. Other contradictions can be harder to recognize. As postmodern and poststructural theorists have reminded us, the more deeply held the ideological belief, the harder it can be to see, much less challenge, its power. It is no accident that at its strongest and most powerful moments, patriarchy has seemed most natural and commonsensical. For many in the academy, ideologies of disciplinarity and professionalism function at this level. This is true, as Jennifer Gore, Henry Giroux, and others argue, even when scholars regularly engage in ideological critique and work consciously to resist the modernist ideologies with which disciplinarity and professionalism are implicated.

How can scholars gain a better, more distanced and critical perspective on our own scholarly practices, and on their possible imbrication with ideologies of professionalism and disciplinarity? Both Jennifer Gore and Henry Giroux argue that an expanded notion of pedagogy can play a helpful role in this process. In her *The Struggle for Pedagogies: Critical and Feminist Discourses as Regimes of Truth,* Gore argues for an expanded understanding of pedagogy as a "process of knowledge production" (4), one that focuses primarily on "how and in whose interests knowledge is produced and reproduced" (5). This notion of pedagogy plays a key role in Gore's study, which addresses ongoing power struggles between those committed to feminist and critical pedagogies and argues that despite their emancipatory discourses, much scholarly work in both areas has dominating effects.

Gore believes that scholars in both fields have focused too narrowly on arguments for and against their pedagogical positions, while failing to attend adequately to what Gore terms "the pedagogy of the argument (the process of knowledge production evident in the argument itself)" (5). The result is a "rhetoric of solutions and announcements" (xv) that, Gore argues, ironically transforms work that scholars intend to be critical into "a kind of norm or law" (11)—one that the teachers in whose interests the scholars believe they are working often resist.

In *The Struggle for Pedagogies,* Gore points out the extent to which the discourses of critical and feminist pedagogy reveal a will to truth/power that discourages reflexivity and self-critique and argues that despite scholars' explicit criticisms of modernism, their discourses nevertheless reveal "modernist concerns for universal explanations and for progress" (xii). Henry Giroux makes a related point in "Who Writes in a Cultural Studies Class? Or, Where Is the Pedagogy?" In this article, Giroux laments the fact that despite its progressive agenda, cultural studies has generally not taken pedagogy seriously; he argues that this failure suggests that cultural studies remains "rigidly tied to the modernist, academic disciplinary structures that it often criticizes" (6). Giroux goes on to charge that scholars in cultural studies fail to "critically address a major prop of disciplinarity, which is the notion of pedagogy as an unproblematic vehicle for transmitting knowledge" (6).

Like Gore, Giroux argues for a specific understanding of pedagogy, one that calls attention to issues of knowledge, power, and authority. While acknowledging the range of meanings that pedagogy can hold, Giroux argues that pedagogy can most helpfully be viewed as "an act of cultural production" (8)—a definition that echoes Gore's characterization of pedagogy as "a process of knowledge production" (5). He adds that "In this context, pedagogy deepens and extends the study of culture and power by addressing not only how culture is shaped, produced, circulated, and transformed, but also how it is *actually taken up by human beings within specific settings and circumstances*" (8, my emphasis).

In his article, Giroux not only critiques cultural studies for its devaluation of pedagogy but analyzes his own teaching, pointing out contradictions between theory and practice that contradict his explicit commitment to a progressive educational agenda. Giroux's analysis of such classroom practices as the making and evaluating of assignments enabled him to recognize that certain elements of his pedagogy contradicted his theoretical goals for his class, for they confirmed rather than decentered his authority and "undermined" his "efforts both to provide students with the opportunity to speak in a safe space and to appropriate power in the class" (10). In these and other ways, Giroux acknowledges, he "reproduced the binarism of being politically enlightened in my theorizing and pedagogically wrong in my organization of concrete class relations" (11).

In this section of *Situating Composition*, I want to explore the possibility that at least some scholarly work in composition manifests similar contradictions or in other ways works against the goals that scholars bring to our work. Like Gore and Giroux, I want to remind readers that even those who consciously work to resist conventional disciplinary and professional ideologies can never free themselves entirely from them. Indeed, complete freedom from these ideologies is impossible, for these ideologies are too pervasive and too multiply and deeply situated to be contained.

Theory and the Pedagogy of Critique

This discussion of theory and the pedagogy of critique builds on my earlier analysis of the writing process movement. In part 2, "Rereading the Writing Process," I questioned several strategies upon which scholars in composition have at times relied. I did so not to unilaterally reject these strategies but rather to point out that their effects can be variable. Taxonomies can help organize and clarify a confusing mass of details, for instance, but they can also oversimplify, decontextualize, and distort the very practices they are designed to study.

I want to extend the analysis of the scholarly practice of theory begun in earlier chapters by considering some of the problems, as well as the advantages, that theoretical critique has played in recent scholarly efforts. In writing about theoretical critique, I am particularly referring to analyses that attempt to raise or uncover epistemological, political, cultural, and ideological issues about a particular subject—for I am aware that other forms of critique (such as Lacanian analysis) exist. James Berlin's "Rhetoric and Ideology in the Writing Class" is an example of theoretical critique, as are Miller's and Crowley's analyses of the writing process movement and my analysis here.

Theoretical critique has played a prominent role in recent scholarly debates, especially those debates that have attempted to distinguish among various "camps" of theorists and/or to establish the ascendancy of social process and post-process theories. These critiques have served many positive functions in composition, for they have called attention to the fact that, as James Berlin observes, "a way of teaching is never innocent. Every pedagogy is imbricated in ideology, in a set of tacit assumptions about what is real, what is good, what is possible, and how power ought to be distributed" ("Rhetoric and Ideology" 492).

In my view, scholarly work in composition has been invigorated by its engagement with such projects as feminist, poststructural, critical, cultural, post-colonial, and queer studies. My research, both individual and coauthored, certainly reflects this engagement; in fact, *Situating Composition* both depends on and enacts theoretical critique. Nevertheless, I wonder if at times scholars engaged in theoretical critique in composition have deployed what Gore characterizes as a "rhetoric of solutions and announcements" (xv), while failing adequately to consider "how and in whose interest knowledge is produced" in scholarly texts (5). I also wonder if scholars, myself included, might do more to inquire into the ways our research is, as Giroux says, "actually taken up by human beings within specific settings and circumstances" (8). I wonder, in other words, if we might do more to inquire into the pedagogy of our own arguments. (For a powerful example of such an effort see Min-Zhan Lu's "Redefining the Literate Self: The Politics of Critical Affirmation.") After all, what Berlin says of teaching is also true of scholarly practice, itself considered a pedagogy or process of knowledge/culture production—and yet scholars seldom critique our own pedagogical practices.

In focusing on theoretical critique, my purpose is not to challenge its usefulness but rather to encourage scholars to recognize that there are limitations and dangers as well as advantages with any critical method. Consider the case of new criticism. New criticism provided a powerful method for analyzing the formal structure of literary texts, especially that of poems. New criticism was also adaptable to the need of both scholars and students. As readers are aware, however, one of the most salient limitations of new criticism was its narrow focus on the aesthetic and its relative lack of interest in theoretical critique.

The historical tables have turned, and theoretical critique is currently one of the most valorized forms of scholarly work in the humanities.

133

What is true of the humanities in general is also true of composition. Though there are of course diverse scholarly projects in composition, not all of which emphasize critique, some of the most highly regarded work in the field—such as that of David Bartholomae, James Berlin, Patricia Bizzell, Sharon Crowley, Lester Faigley, Bruce Horner, Min-Zhan Lu, Susan Miller, and John Trimbur—draws on theoretical critique.

In order to better understand the strengths and limitations of theoretical critique, I return to the work of two scholars whose work I discussed briefly in chapter 3: Susan Miller and Sharon Crowley. I have chosen to focus on these two scholars because each has written forceful—and influential—theoretical critiques of the writing process movement and the teaching of writing.[5] I will begin with Miller's *Textual Carnivals*, which was published in 1991. *Textual Carnivals* is a powerful, thought-provoking study that considers the status of composition in both English studies and in the general culture. Miller's study raises a number of foundational issues about both writing and the teaching of writing, from the role that language plays in culture—Miller argues that "language *learning* is the crucial locus for power, or for disenfranchisement, in any culture"—to composition's recent development as a discipline (7). Discussions of the writing process movement play a key role in her analysis.

As readers of *Textual Carnivals* are aware, Miller is critical of the writing process movement. Though she discusses the writing process movement throughout her book, Miller focuses most specifically on it in her chapter entitled "The Subject of Composition." Here, Miller attempts "to clarify the sort of subject composition has become by virtue of choosing" the process paradigm; she does so by asking "whether a paradigm shift has actually occurred, what its quality is, and how it has, or has not, created an intellectual subjectivity/subject of composition that has specific consequences for the field's intellectual politics" (106). Miller's response is unequivocal: "A realistic history of writing suggests that 'process' is serviceable mainly as an affective improvement in the classroom and as a way of granting composition a qualified academic legitimacy" (108).

Although Miller's specific focus in this chapter is the writing process movement or, in Miller's terms, the "process paradigm" (121), she also looks at the writing process movement in the larger context of the nature and purpose of first-year writing. Miller is critical of the traditional aims of this course, noting that it represents "an almost entirely formalistic and intransitive vision of writing" (97). As a result, Miller argues, the process paradigm places students "in an infantile and solipsistic relation to the results of writing" (100).

Many who argued against the writing process movement did so as part of a larger argument in favor of social or post-process theories. Miller's approach, however, is different—for she is ambivalent about certain aspects of social process theory. She approves of the extent to which "The social process theorists have . . . accepted post-structuralist views that written words are socially construed, not fixed in their meanings, and that texts negotiate within specific textual communities" (112). She is troubled, however, by the fact that "this acceptance does not give significance either to student writing or to community processes as sites for struggle against these textual worlds that actually produce ideas" (112). Instead, Miller argues for greater attention to "interpretive theory in composition, an approach that might permit the field to answer some important political questions and to gain support from the peers it wishes to persuade of its value" (119–20).

Crowley's *Composition in the University* was published in 1998, seven years after Miller's study. Though Crowley's and Miller's analyses differ in certain respects, they share a number of similarities. Crowley follows Miller, for instance, in attributing composition's professionalization to the writing process movement (which she most often refers to as "process pedagogy" [190]). Crowley notes not only that the writing process movement "professionalized the teaching of first-year composition" but also that it reconceptualized "composition teachers as disciplined professionals" (191). Crowley also observes that this pedagogy "stimulated a reconceptualization of students as people who write rather than as people whose grammar and usage needs to be policed" (191).

Like Miller, Crowley also calls attention to the positive affective consequences of the writing process movement for teachers and students. While Miller's reference to the affective benefits of process pedagogy is relatively brief, Crowley elaborates on its significance. She begins her discussion by observing that "the advent of process pedagogy made composition a lot more fun to teach" (191). Crowley goes on to observe that thanks to the writing process movement "the classroom truly was a more interesting place to be" and that it "was also much more interesting to think about than it had been prior to the advent of process, because composition teachers now gave themselves permission to think of their students as writers and themselves as people who had something to teach" (190).

Nevertheless, these accomplishments clearly do not outweigh the major disadvantage that Crowley cites, which is that rather than serving as a rejection of current-traditional pedagogy, process and current-traditional pedagogies share complementary epistemologies. Crowley cites a number of reasons why she believes these two movements' epistemologies are complementary. She points out, for instance, that many descriptions of first-year writing courses in college and university catalogs mix features of current-traditional and process pedagogy. Crowley also notes the ease with which traditional textbooks incorporated elements of process pedagogy, such as the use of heuristics. Crowley argues that

> The easy accommodation of process-oriented strategies to current-traditionalism suggests that process and product have more in common than is generally acknowledged in professional literature about composition, where the habit of contrasting them conceals the fact of their epistemological consistency. A truly paradigmatic alternative to current-traditionalism would question the modernism in which it is immersed and the institutional structures by means of which it is administered. Process pedagogy does neither. It retains the modernist composing subject of current-traditionalism—the subject who is sufficiently discrete from the composing context to stand apart from it, observing it from above and commenting on it. . . . Nor did process pedagogy change the institutional situation of composition: the introductory courses are still required, and composition teachers are still overworked and underpaid, just as they were prior to 1971. (212–13)

Clearly, for Crowley, the case is closed. Because process pedagogy does not constitute a "truly paradigmatic alternative to current-traditionalism," it represents a deeply flawed effort.

Elsewhere in *Composition in the University,* Crowley extends her critique of process pedagogy to consider required first-year writing courses in general. As was the case with Miller, Crowley is critical of these courses and challenges the viability of the required first-year writing course, arguing that "the required introductory course, considered as an institutional practice, has no content aside from its disciplining function" (10). This function, Crowley observes, is to produce "an ethical technology of subjectivity that creates in students a healthy respect for the authority of the academy" and thus renders them "docile students" (217). This ethical technology is so powerful, Crowley adds, that it "supersedes anything

136

that specific composition teachers operating in local spaces may want to do for their students in the way of helping them to become writers; it gets in between teachers and their students, in between students' writing and their teachers' reading" (217). As a result, Crowley argues that scholars in composition should urge colleges and universities to drop the universal first-year writing requirement and offer a "vertical elective curriculum in composing" instead (262).

These two examples from Miller's and Crowley's work share a number of strengths. In both cases, the authors raise important epistemological, cultural, political, and ideological questions about the writing process movement. Because their arguments challenge commonsense understandings about the writing process movement—and about the general pedagogical project of first-year writing—Miller's and Crowley's analyses invite readers to look at their subjects in new and thought-provoking ways. Their arguments have the incisiveness and element of surprise—of the overturning of the commonsensical—that characterize particularly powerful critique.

Both authors attempt to provide balanced assessments of the writing process movement, detailing positive as well as negative evaluations of its consequences. Neither author uses her critique of the writing process movement as a jumping off point for an argument in favor of a "new and improved" pedagogy. In fact, Crowley and Miller avoid the kind of negative critique of other scholarly work in the field and the establishment of opposing camps that has been relatively common in recent years. Instead, both raise incisive questions about the politics of composition's location in the academy. Miller's and Crowley's work shares another strength, for they take particular care in articulating the criteria that ground their analyses. In this regard, the care that Miller and Crowley take to make their own ideological and epistemological commitments clear to readers demonstrates a laudable attention to the pedagogy of their arguments.

Both Miller and Crowley offer alternative visions for writing courses. Crowley, in particular, takes care to consider her proposed alternative to required first-year writing courses—a vertical sequence of elective writing courses—from a materially grounded perspective. Recognizing that faculty who wish to implement her proposal would need to address many pragmatic factors, Crowley discusses such issues as implications for program administration, departmental budgets, staffing, etc. Interestingly, in the chapter in which she reflects on the universal first-year writing course and presents her alternative, "A Personal Essay on Freshman English," Crowley modifies her earlier argument that the ethical technology of first-year writing classes is so hegemonic that it makes it impossible for productive work to occur in these classes and concedes "that, in theory, somewhere in America, some students who sit through a one- or two-semester required course in Freshman English master 'correct' English, especially if these hypothetical students harbor a burning desire to succeed at the project" (231).[6] She also points out that she is "not denying that reading and writing empower some people in some places at some times" (234). These comments add a helpful level of specificity to her comments on the disciplining function of first-year writing—even as they stand in tension with them.

The strengths I have just described are, I am sure readers realize, considerable. (I should point out that in each of their books, Miller and Crowley discuss a number of issues in addition to the writing process movement and first-year writing; my criticisms are not intended to be totalizing critiques of either work but rather analyses of several elements in what are in each case larger and more complex arguments.) I nevertheless have reservations about certain aspects of the pedagogy of Miller's and Crowley's arguments about the writing process movement and first-year writing classes. In the remainder of this chapter, I want to detail some problems that I see in these particular examples of scholarly practice and to suggest some ways these problems might have been avoided.

The Problem of Speaking for Others

As a way into this analysis, I would like briefly to discuss Linda Alcoff's "The Problem of Speaking for Others." In this article, Alcoff—a philosopher who has contributed to recent work on feminist epistemologies—argues that it is important for scholars to acknowledge the authority that they have to speak for others and to recognize the responsibility that comes with this authority. In order to do so, Alcoff argues, scholars first need to consider if the practice of speaking for others is ever valid, and if it is, what the criteria for validity are. She also argues that it is important for scholars—or for anyone who speaks for others—to ask themselves if it is "valid to speak for others who are unlike me or who are less privileged than me" (7). In her article, Alcoff is particularly concerned with situations that involve differences of race, gender, and sexual preference, but I believe that the issues that she raises are broadly relevant for scholars in composition, for scholars in composition often assume or are asked to take on the responsibility for speaking for both teachers and students.

In her article, Alcoff (who does not refer to Adrienne Rich but is clearly writing in the tradition of Rich's "Politics of Location") argues that "the problematic of speaking for others has at its center a concern with accountability and responsibility" (16). Some feminists have attempted to address this problematic via what Alcoff terms the "retreat response" of identity politics. Alcoff argues, however, that while this response is motivated by a laudable desire to recognize difference, it "undercuts the possibility of political effectivity" (17). There are times, Alcoff argues, when "the practice of speaking for others remains the best possibility in some existing situations" (24).

I agree with Alcoff and believe that it is not possible for scholars in composition to avoid speaking for others—whether those others are teachers or students. With Alcoff, however, I believe that when scholars do speak for others, we need to exercise considerable care. In that regard, Alcoff suggests that those who wish or need to speak for others should first undertake a "concrete analysis of the particular power relations and discursive effects involved" (24). She argues as well that "In order to evaluate attempts to speak for others in particular instances, we need to analyze the probable or actual effects of the words on the discursive and material context" (26).

Those speaking for others also, I would add, need to attend carefully to issues of power and authority. In this regard, as readers are aware, in composition—as in the academy in general—conventional hierarchies of knowledge position scholars as experts and teachers as practitioners. As a consequence, scholars have access to means of representation that teachers often do not have. Along with access to means of representation come both the time to engage in sustained inquiry and a good deal of power in the form of scholarly authority. Scholars have the authority to abstract and generalize, to distinguish between what *seems* to be the case and what is *really* true. This authority is often denied to teachers, who are authorized primarily to speak about their own students and classrooms. Even here, teachers' authority may be limited by institutional and curricular constraints; such occurs, for instance, when teachers are assessed solely via the scores their students receive on standardized teaching evaluations. In situations where teachers and scholars disagree, scholars' views are likely to be privileged—at least in those locations where their authority is most strongly held.[7] Often, in situations such as these, teachers' only recourse is the resistant act of assuming or declaring scholarly work to be irrelevant to their local concerns.

Given the differences I have just described, scholars in composition who choose to speak for teachers have an obligation both to take these differences into account when they write and to "analyze the probable or actual effects of the words on the discursive and material context" (Alcoff 26). In this regard, I believe that Miller's and Crowley's texts could indeed demonstrate greater rhetorical sensitivity vis-à-vis the problematic of speaking for others. I believe, as well, that doing so would strengthen the "political effectivity" of their arguments.

In her argument about required first-year writing courses, for example, Crowley implicitly dismisses the local knowledge that teachers have about their students, classes, writing programs, and institutions and thus positions those teachers who believe that they can and should teach required composition courses as the dupes of ideology. I do not believe that Crowley set out to do this. Rather, this negative positioning of those who believe in the mission of required first-year writing courses is a consequence of Crowley's theoretical argument about the disciplining effects of the first-year writing requirement. This is an argument that raises important questions that those engaged in the work of composition benefit from addressing—for surely one of the purposes not only of first-year writing courses but of education in general is to produce "an ethical technology of subjectivity that creates in students a healthy respect for the authority of the academy"—a goal that Crowley identifies with required first-year writing courses (217). Greater attentiveness to the problematic of speaking for others might have caused Crowley to modify, clarify, or exemplify the strikingly general assertion that the

> ethical technology that is the requirement ... supersedes *anything* that specific composition teachers operating in local spaces may want to do for their students in the way of helping them to become writers; it gets in between teachers and their students, in between students' writing and their teachers' reading. (217, my emphasis)

(In titling her chapter on images of composition teaching "The Sad Women in the Basement: Images of Composition Teaching," Miller similarly represents teachers as individuals lacking in agency who are inevitably—whatever their own understanding of their experience—dominated, marginalized, and feminized by virtue of their professional identity [121].) This is surely the kind of statement that Lewiecki-Wilson and Sommers have in mind when they argue that scholarly work in composition figures the classrooms of teachers at open admissions universities and elsewhere as "site(s) for the discipline of punishment" (439).

It is also for all its boldness a somewhat vague statement. In what ways does the ethical technology get between teachers and students? Why is its power totalizing? (Many engaged in ideological critique, such as James Berlin, argue that rather than being totalizing, "ideology is always pluralistic, a given historical moment displaying a variety of competing ideologies and a given individual reflecting one or another permutation of these conflicts" ["Rhetoric and Ideology" 479]).[8] If the ethical technology supersedes everything else that goes on in a required writing class, does this mean that in those instances where first-year writing is required, it is useless to attempt to distinguish between better and worse practices? Since all education in an important sense disciplines both teachers and students, what is the particular nature of the first-year requirement's disciplining function?

Crowley might also have clarified why offering first-year and other writing courses but not requiring them would make such a significant difference in teachers' and students' experiences. Is any composition class that is not required automatically more productive—and less influenced by the disciplining effects of education—than any composition class that *is* required? Surely Crowley does not mean to suggest that the only factor determining a course's productivity is whether it is required or not—but how would she rank additional factors that come into play? When asked questions such as these, Crowley would undoubtedly identify elements such as class size, teacher preparation, and teaching load as playing key roles in enabling or disabling a course. Yet her statement about the disciplining effects of the "ethical technology that is the requirement" not only does not take factors such as these into consideration but also suggests that they are irrelevant.

Crowley might have avoided problems such as these if she had attempted more carefully to integrate her theoretical claims with discussions grounded in the pragmatics of teaching. Moreover, if Crowley had related her theoretical critique to her own experiences as a writing program

critique of Crowley

141

administrator and teacher, she might have avoided positioning herself as an authority who is comfortable speaking for—and dismissing the knowledge and experience of—others. Crowley has considerable experience teaching first-year writing. Did Crowley once believe that the first-year writing requirement made sense? Articulating the factors that caused her to change her mind and talking about them at the level of her own experiences as a teacher might have helped readers to build enthymematic bridges between her experience and their own. It also might have encouraged Crowley to contextualize or in other ways rethink or clarify some of her strongest generalizations about the disciplining function of the required first-year writing requirement.

In *Composition in the University,* Crowley does in fact provide some personal and professional context for her argument. She notes, for instance, that her involvement with the Wyoming Resolution played a role in changing her views on the first-year writing requirement. Crowley also mentions a recent experience teaching a required first-year writing course, one that according to her description was frustrating and unproductive. Crowley does not argue that this experience confirms her larger theoretical argument about the disciplining effects of the first-year writing requirement, but she clearly intends it to stand as a supportive example. Crowley does not attempt to clarify, however, which problems in this difficult course were the result of its being required and which had other causes. The one problem that she does cite—student resistance to "What they took to be" her "feminism"—is a problem that occurs in many composition and literature courses, not only in required writing classes (255).

I want to emphasize again that the problems I identify in Crowley's argument are best understood as unintended consequences of her theoretical critique. Elsewhere in *Composition in the University,* for instance, Crowley specifically addresses the problem of speaking for others, noting that an important lesson that she learned from working on the Wyoming Resolution was "do not presume to speak for others who do not enjoy your privileges" (239). That Crowley recognizes the problematic of speaking for others so clearly in her professional life yet nevertheless speaks for others while engaged in theoretical critique is a demonstration of the powerful impulses that such critique encourages. Indeed, at other moments in her argument—moments more grounded in material and pedagogical contexts—Crowley not only acknowledges but also calls attention to materially situated elements and the role they play in teaching. At one point, for instance, she bemoans that fact that "In composition research and lore, composition teachers speak of 'the classroom' as though this space is similarly constructed at Yale and at San Jose Community College" (221). And yet Crowley at other times not only speaks of the classroom in this way but specifically argues that situated differences are insignificant in the face of larger hegemonic forces.

I will have more to say later about the reasons why scholars are so drawn to theoretical critique—and the problems such critique can entail. I would now like to turn to Susan Miller's *Textual Carnivals*. Readers will hardly be surprised to discover that I believe that, as was the case with Crowley, Miller's analysis might also have benefited from a similar gesture toward her experiences as a teacher and an occasional shift from abstract and general assertions to clarifications and exemplifications. Like Crowley, Miller makes a number of strong generalizations about both the teaching of writing and the writing process movement. Moreover, as was the case with Crowley, the absence of any significant discussion of the role that such situated factors as differences in institutions and student populations might play in teaching positions Miller as an expert whose insights take precedence over teachers' more local, embodied knowledge.

There are ways that Miller might helpfully have both contextualized her argument and addressed the potential concerns of teachers who feel their experience is being misrepresented. In her discussion of the writing process movement, for instance, Miller argues both that the process paradigm represents an "affective improvement in the classroom" (108) and that it places students "in an infantile and solipsistic relation to the results of writing" (100). This second statement implicitly positions teachers as the agents of students' forced infantilization—so teachers might reasonably wish for a more nuanced discussion of this issue. Are there some pedagogical assumptions and practices that play a particularly strong role in encouraging this infantilization? And does this infantilization entirely outweigh the "affective improvement" that Miller acknowledges?

How, for that matter, does this infantilization differ from the general hegemony that is inherent to education? This is an issue that Miller addresses when she compares required first-year composition classes with classes in other disciplines. In composition classes, Miller argues, "The composition student is expected to experience processes, activities, strategies, multiple perspectives, peer groups, and evaluations that have no

143

articulated relations to actual results from a piece of writing" (100). Miller contrasts this with courses in other disciplines where students are "expected to compete, to master material, and even to solve problems whose answers may be either correct or incorrect" (104). Given these comments, it is hardly surprising that Miller has reservations about required first-year writing. Miller does, however, describe her vision of an effective first-year course, noting that: "A universally 'important' writing course (if one course were to serve at all) to prepare students generally to 'be' writers in these other settings and afterward could acknowledge and analyze these demands and their implications for the writing student" (104).

Here Miller helpfully clarifies her vision of a productive, non-infantilizing composition course—though her clarification raises additional questions. Don't many classes in other disciplines also require students to "experience processes, activities, strategies, multiple perspectives, peer groups, and evaluations that have no articulated relations to actual results" of their work (Miller 100)? Isn't what Miller represents as a binary something more like a continuum, with courses like first-year writing, history, interpersonal and group communication, and women's studies at one way end of the continuum and, say, a capstone engineering course, where students undertake real projects for real clients, at the other end? In what specific ways would Miller's preferred first-year writing class, one that "prepare[s] students generally to 'be' writers in . . . other [academic] settings and afterward" differ from other composition courses, especially from traditional courses that assume that first-year writing is a "service" course designed to prepare students for their subsequent academic work (104)?

I want to be clear about the point of my analysis. While I believe that Crowley's and Miller's studies would have been strengthened if these authors had attended more carefully to the politics of their location vis-à-vis the teachers and students about whom they write, the problems I discuss are typical of much theoretical critique. There are deeply situated reasons why scholars in composition find it difficult to write texts that speak to—rather than for or about—teachers. These problems are not easily resolved and represent, I believe, an ongoing challenge for scholars in the field, myself included.

If Miller and Crowley were to address the kinds of issues I have just raised about their critique of the writing process movement, for instance, they would have had to write longer—and different—books than they

wrote. In recent years, scholarly presses have demonstrated a strong preference for brief and highly focused texts. Scholars who attempt to resist
this preference could find it difficult to publish their work. They might
also meet resistance from peers, for theoretical critiques typically do not
include reflections on personal experience or interrogations of the assumptions grounding the critique. The strong reception of their studies
indicates that Miller and Crowley were writing with—not against—privileged disciplinary norms and conventions. It will not be easy to challenge
these norms and conventions, even if scholars see the merit of doing so.
Those interested in addressing these problems could, of course, turn to
other scholarly genres. Though different in many ways, both qualitative
research and personally grounded criticism encourage a more situated
analysis. These studies often result in conclusions that appear less forceful and generalizable than those generated via theoretical critique, however. As a consequence, they often do not circulate as broadly and powerfully in the field as does theoretical critique.

In this regard, the strength of theoretical critique in composition may
also be a potential weakness. Whatever the topic and discipline, a good
deal of the power of theoretical critique derives from scholars' careful
reading of other texts (rather than of teachers' materially situated practices) and their formulation of elegant, incisive arguments that make
strong generalizations. These arguments often have great power and elo-
quence, as Crowley's and Miller's studies attest. But depending on their
situation and purpose, they can raise difficulties and have unintended
consequences as well. Composition scholars cannot resolve the problem
of speaking for others by refusing to speak for and represent teachers and
students. Is it possible to revise our practices so that composition scholars retain the power of theoretical critique but are more attentive to the
politics of location in composition?

As a way into the issues that I have just raised, I would like to consider
some general—and, I believe significant—differences between the practice of theory and the practice of teaching; I believe these differences hold
potential implications for the scholarly practice of theory. In calling attention to these difference, I do not mean to obviate efforts to place
theory and teaching in the kind of fruitful dialogue that Phelps, Gere, and
others argue for. Rather, I want to call attention to the fact that, as
Britzman argues, "practices makes practice" (240). We cannot place the
practices of theory and teaching in fruitful dialogue until we recognize

that their situations, and the ideologies that inform these situations, differ in potentially significant ways.

As an example of these differences, I would like to return to Miller's and Crowley's texts. In terms of the practice of theory, Miller's and Crowley's work demonstrates, I believe, the characteristics most privileged in theoretical critique, and in much other academic research: consistency, coherence, parsimony, elegance, and originality. (And, yes, even scholars who have embraced critiques of originality and its engagement with ideologies of individualism and modernism nevertheless find some works more "original" than others.) Their work is less successful, however, in addressing difficulties associated with the problematic of speaking for others. Greater attention to differences in the practice of theory and the practice of teaching might help address these difficulties.

Consider, in this regard, the zero-sum nature of Crowley's argument about current-traditional rhetoric's and process pedagogy's shared epistemology. In Crowley's analysis, either process pedagogy represents a paradigmatic alternative to current-traditionalism or it does not. Although Crowley acknowledges the benefits of process pedagogy, including the affective benefit of making the classroom a more interesting place for both teachers and students, her privileging of epistemological and ideological critique render these benefits irrelevant to her larger argument. Crowley makes another zero-sum argument when she insists that the ethical technology of required first-year writing is so powerful that it "supersedes anything that specific composition teachers operating in local spaces may want to do for their students in the way of helping them to become writers" (*Composition* 217).

Zero-sum arguments have the consistency, coherence, and parsimony that are valued within the practice of theory. When these arguments also are stylistically and conceptually elegant and strike readers as original, as I believe is the case with Crowley's work, their effect is all the more powerful—at least for readers whose own values are consistent with the practice of theory. But what about those whose lived experience immerses them in a different network of assumptions and practices, such as teachers?

Teaching is not a zero-sum activity. As my analysis of pedagogical texts from my own teaching demonstrate, even teachers who hold strong, consciously developed philosophies are highly unlikely to achieve the kind of epistemological and ideological purity that Crowley calls for. Change in teaching is messy, impure, and proceeds through a slow process of accretion and deletion, a process that can never be made entirely explicit and is inherently evanescent. Think, for instance, of how much of my teaching—the most important part, really—is absent from my analysis in chapter 4.

In the remainder of this chapter, I want to suggest some additional ways that the practice of theory and the practice of teaching differ—and I want to do so by drawing upon James Berlin's previously quoted statement about pedagogy: "Every pedagogy," Berlin argues, "is imbricated in ideology, in a set of tacit assumptions about what is real, what is good, what is possible, and how power ought to be distributed" ("Rhetoric and Ideology" 492). In this statement, Berlin is referring to various pedagogies within composition studies. As I have done throughout this chapter, drawing on Gore and Giroux, I use the term "pedagogy" to refer more broadly to the process of knowledge/culture production.

On the Real, the Good, and the Possible

I undertake this analysis recognizing that I cannot avoid overgeneralizing and in some senses misrepresenting both the practice of theory and the practice of teaching. As I noted earlier, "theory" is an overdetermined term whose precise meaning cannot be legislated; different persons inevitably hold different understandings of what theory is and does. And the same, of course, is true of teaching. My analysis holds other limitations, for in placing these two in a dichotomous relationship, I call attention to certain features of these practices while ignoring or disappearing others and thus risk creating a "killer" dichotomy. As I noted earlier, although I am aware that many faculty members experience their identities as scholars and teachers as mutually reinforcing, my analysis deemphasizes this fact. This is surely the most significant limitation of my analysis—but I could not find a way to avoid it. I can only hope that the advantages of my inquiry compensate for its disadvantages. Whatever its limitations—and there are sure to be many—I hope that this discussion will encourage others to develop more finely grained, situated analyses of the practice of theory and the practice of teaching.[9]

What constitutes "the real" for those engaged in the practice of teaching? The answer to this question is, I believe, easy for anyone who has taught to determine: teachers experience "the real" in such activities as leading class discussions, conferencing with students, talking with colleagues, and responding to student writing. In this regard, "the real" in teaching has an in-your-face immediacy that is simultaneously both powerful and hard to capture. In making this statement, I do not intend to privilege teachers' material experiences of the real over that of scholars or to suggest that teachers' material experiences are somehow separate from and prior to language and ideology. Rather, I want to call attention to the fact that every moment—whether they are teaching a class, responding to student writing, or planning a new assignment—teachers are constantly making decisions about what to do and say, and that these decisions are grounded in the exigencies of their immediate experience.

Affect is, I would argue, another central component of the real for those engaged in the practice of teaching. When I leave a class at the end of the period or finish responding to a set of student essays, I have a strong gut feeling about what has just transpired—and that feeling matters deeply to me. Though I bring different goals to different classes, one constant is the desire for both myself and my students to experience our interactions as productive—as both intrinsically and extrinsically rewarding. This concern for affect is, I believe, much less critical to the practice of theory, which values intellect over emotion. In fact, as readers may recall, both Miller and Crowley dismiss the importance of affect in their analyses of the writing process movement, subordinating it in clear ways to such other factors as the writing process movement's epistemological and ideological assumptions.

It is hardly surprising that affect should be more central to the practice of teaching than of theory. As I noted earlier, for teachers "the real" takes place in face-to-face interactions with students, colleagues, and others involved in education. These interactions can be and are reflected upon by teachers—but they cannot be revised in the way that a scholarly article or book chapter can. Because teachers must often make many immediate, unrevisable choices, they necessarily rely upon instinct at the moment of decision. Such instinctive judgments are grounded not only in teachers' previous experiences but also in reading, discussion, research, and reflection. But at the moment of decision, teachers can hardly sift through all of the knowledge and experience they bring to teaching. They must act—and they do.

Scholars also draw on instincts—and scholars certainly act as they put word next to word, sentence next to sentence, paragraph next to paragraph. But when scholars compose articles, book chapters, and books—which for the practice of theory certainly constitutes the heart of "the real"—they have the opportunity to revise. Given the preference in the academy for single authorship, when scholars compose texts they most often work alone. And though these texts' ultimate publication involves multiple collaborations, these are typically disappeared in the academy. So if the paradigmatic scene of action—of the real—for teachers is a classroom in the midst of Henry James's "blooming and buzzing" confusion, the paradigmatic scene of action for scholars is the office or study, where a scholar sits silently reading or writing. If the students and colleagues with whom teachers interact are particularly central to the practice of teaching, then the texts with whom scholars interact serve a similar function in the practice of theory. Indeed, since these texts are one of the primary means by which scholars communicate and a source of considerable potential cultural capital, they constitute an important, though hardly singular, component of "the real" for the practice of theory.

Given these differences in what constitutes "the real" in the practice of theory and the practice of teaching, it is hardly surprising that these two practices differ in their understanding of "the good." What I'm about to say may seem obvious, but I note it nevertheless: the production and circulation of written texts is a particularly valued form of "the good" in the practice of theory. If these texts evidence such traits as consistency, coherence, parsimony, elegance, and originality, so much the better. (Depending upon their projects and methodological commitments, scholars might both enact and value these characteristics in diverse ways. A feminist interested in "writing the body" in her scholarly work might have a different understanding of, say, consistency, than a traditional literary historian might.) While teachers certainly value written communication and often share their knowledge via traditional print and other texts, I believe that for teachers, "the good" resides more in their interactions with students and with colleagues.

In the practice of theory, then, "the good" resides primarily in textual objects; in the practice of teaching, "the good" resides primarily in interpersonal relationships and in moments of learning for both teachers and students. This contrast helps explain related differences between these two practices in understandings of "the possible." As is natural for scholars who spend a great deal of time reading and writing texts, and whose professional success is evaluated primarily on their ability to produce the latter, scholars emphasize the power of the written word, for they believe these words hold the potential for changes in understandings, situations, or actions.

When scholars engage in theoretical critique, they see themselves as intervening in an important issue or problem. In this regard, in the practice of theory, the possibilities for agency and action are primarily textual. In the practice of teaching, agency and action are experienced in the moment-to-moment, day-to-day experience of teaching. Many of these moments are also of course textual, but they are as likely to take the form of oral as written communications.

Other forms of "the possible" also circulate in the practice of theory. Those trained in the practice of theory quickly learn, for instance, that for a scholarly argument to be valued it needs to follow the conventions appropriate for scholars working in a particular area; these conventions play an important role in both enabling and constraining scholarly texts. For many scholars, for instance, an analysis that is consistent and coherent develops either a single argument or a thread of related arguments. (This is true, I would argue, even though scholarly writing in the humanities in 2003 looks quite different from scholarly writing in, say, 1965.) In this sense, ideologies of "the possible" in the practice of theory are more likely to sanction logical consistency, which itself encourages either/or rather than both/and argument. Scholarly texts do of course examine opposing arguments and alternative lines of reasoning, but they typically do so for the larger purpose of supporting the text's major argument.

This preference for coherent, consistent arguments surfaces in a particularly clear way in a series of written exchanges between David Bartholomae and Peter Elbow that appeared in the February 1995 issue of *College Composition and Communication*. I will not summarize that exchange here. (Readers interested in following this conversation should see Bartholomae, "Writing with Teachers"; Elbow, "Being a Writer vs. Being an Academic"; Bartholomae, "Response"; and Elbow, "Response.") Rather, I want to point to what for my present purpose is a key moment in their exchange, a moment when Elbow says to Bartholomae: "There is a crucial matter of theory here. You say in passing that I can't have it both ways, that I can't stick up for both perspectives on the human condition. But you never give any reason for this theoretical position. I insist that I *can* have it both ways" ("Response" 88).

I believe that Elbow is correct in pointing out that an assumption that Bartholomae takes for granted and mentions only in passing is in fact nothing more or less than as assumption—one that is grounded in ideologies of "the possible." For Bartholomae, and for many scholars, in matters of argument, one "can't have it both ways" (Elbow, "Response" 88). Elbow argues that he can have it both ways—and I believe that many teachers would agree with him. Teaching is, I suggest, nothing if not an exercise in trying to have it both ways. After all, teachers must somehow function both as coach and judge. They must attempt to encourage students to develop an intrinsic interest in the subject they are teaching, while also imparting extrinsic information to them. They must at the same time negotiate their commitment to their discipline and their commitment to their students, just as they must negotiate the local politics of their particular classrooms while also interacting with larger and more powerful curricular and institutional structures.

In matters of "the possible," teachers implicitly embrace paradox and live and work within it—at least, I would argue, successful teachers do. While the practice of theory can certainly accommodate paradox, as I noted earlier, scholars seem more drawn to either/or rather than both/and thinking. These varying preferences may account for differences in the way Elbow's work has been received by scholars in composition and by teachers. Within composition, Elbow's work, while clearly influential, has been marked by controversy. Most scholars would agree, I believe, that Elbow's work has been received more enthusiastically by teachers, particularly teachers in the schools. Over the years, many teachers—and also many students—have told me that they find Elbow's work particularly relevant to their concerns. Many have mentioned as well that they appreciate the extent to which Elbow grounds his scholarly work in his experiences as a writer and teacher.

These comments lead me to the final item in Berlin's list of tacit ideological assumptions, the question of "how power ought to be distributed" ("Rhetoric" 494), for I believe that when teachers make comments like the preceding about Elbow's work, they are implicitly suggesting that when they read Elbow, they find that he is, in effect, "talking their talk." While this might appear to represent a superficial judgment that should not concern scholars, I do not believe that this is the case. In "Rhetoric and Ideology," the article in which Berlin's statement appears, Berlin notes that when he discusses power, it not only refers to "political force but covers as well social forces in everyday contacts." Berlin goes on to add that "Power is an intrinsic part of ideology, defined and reinforced by it, determining . . . who can act and what can be accomplished. These power relationships," he adds, "are inscribed in the discursive practices of daily experience—in the ways we use language and are used (interpellated) by it in ordinary parlance" (479).

Berlin's observation calls attention to the fact that differences between the ideological assumptions that inform the practices of theory and of teaching are hardly trivial and are enacted as much at the level of "the discursive practices of daily experience" as in more explicitly political acts of repression and control. That there is a substantial power imbalance between these two practices goes without saying. No one needs to tell experienced teachers who have returned to the university to take one or more courses so that they can maintain or upgrade their teaching certificate that their knowledge is valued less highly than that of the professor teaching their class, for as long as they are required to return to the university periodically to upgrade their training while their professor is not required to spend time in the schools, the simple presence of the requirement informs these students of their status and relative lack of authority.

At this point, readers may wonder what conclusion I have written my way to. Am I going to argue that scholars should write more like Peter Elbow? Or that scholars should work to change the institutional and cultural structures that privilege theory and accord less value to teaching? My conclusion is both more limited and more modest. I simply want to argue here—as I have elsewhere in *Situating Composition*—that scholars would do well to attend more carefully than we sometimes have to the differences that I have just described. We should do so because current hierarchies of knowledge in the academy valorize the practice of theory over the practice of teaching in ways that benefit scholars. We should do so, as well, if we want fairly to represent the work of and speak for—much less to—teachers.

Attention to these differences will benefit scholarly work in another respect, for it may helpfully remind scholars that while we have been engaged in vigorous epistemological, political, cultural, and ideological critiques of others, we have been less aware of the ideologies that inevitably inform and circulate through our practices. As my analysis of Crowley's and Miller's work suggests, even highly sophisticated theoretical critiques can demonstrate surprising contradictions. Crowley's posing of zero-sum arguments and her insistence that to be of value, process pedagogy must represent a "truly paradigmatic alternative to current-traditionalism" reveal a commitment to Enlightenment notions of reason and of argument (212), which require universal, totalizing explanations. This is not a commitment that Crowley consciously avows; throughout *Composition in the University,* she explicitly rejects Enlightenment and modernist assumptions and practices, and her analysis often reflects this stance. In this regard, it is important to note that the problems I have identified in Crowley's analysis of process pedagogy are not characteristic of her overall project but rather represent instances where her scholarly practice works against or resists her consciously held beliefs. This is also the case with Miller's analysis, which raises many helpful and pointed questions.

It will never be possible for scholars to become fully aware of the ideologies that inform our practices. I am sure that readers can pinpoint ways my own practices in *Situating Composition* demonstrate some of the problems that I have identified in Crowley's and Miller's work. I do believe, however, that scholars might focus more than we have in the past on these and related issues. In the next chapter, I will discuss the extent to which scholarly work in composition has generally not examined its commitment to ideologies of professionalization and disciplinarity. I want to close this chapter with a few more comments on what might be at stake for scholars in differences in the ideological assumptions that inform the practice of theory and the practice of teaching.

One thing at stake, I believe, is the relevance and credibility of our arguments for those who teach the majority of composition classes. When scholars dismiss the role of affect in teaching or establish zero-sum criteria for evaluating pedagogical theories and practices, we in effect tell teachers that we do not value their knowledge and experience. Can we find ways to raise issues of ideology, politics, culture, and epistemology— for these are certainly critical issues that we need to continue to discuss— that do not position scholars in this way? And can we be more realistic about the powers and limitations of any pedagogical project? Does it make sense to expect, for instance, that process pedagogy could ever have "change[d] the institutional situation of composition" vis-à-vis the first-year writing requirement and the working conditions of teachers (Crowley, *Composition* 213)?

Also at stake is our ability to enact a model of disciplinary progress that does not require the continual disvaluing of previous theories and practices. In *Terms of Work for Composition: A Materialist Critique,* Bruce Horner argues that scholars in composition need to gain a critical perspective on our tendency to equate the traditional with "those theories and practices against which compositionists must define themselves if they are to reclaim pedagogy as a site for Composition theory and research" (165). In order to do so, Horner asserts, scholars must contest

> a dominant ideology within Composition that conflates knowledge with writing, both understood in terms of disciplinary writing practices. This conflation denies or denigrates the validity and utility of actors' practical consciousness and nondiscursive knowledge, which are lumped under the category of the traditional. (166)

I agree with Horner that scholars need to rethink the category of the traditional in composition. I agree as well with Jean Ferguson Carr, who in a response to Anne Ruggles Gere's "Kitchen Tables and Rented Rooms: The Extracurriculum of Composition" observes that scholars need not only to examine the kinds of extracurricular writing activities Gere discusses in her article but also to return to "texts we have dismissed as simple. . . . We need to rethink the notion that influence and tradition are produced in straight lines, that theories are uttered and then get 'implemented' somehow and the influence spreads down until it is diffused in the hinterlands" (97). We need to remember as well, I would argue, that no action's political effectivity is guaranteed. Both the practice of theory and the practice of teaching can work for progressive ends—but to determine whether this is happening, we have to look not only at the pedagogy that is argued for (whether in the pages of a book or in a classroom) but also at the pedagogy of the argument.

As we do so, we would do well to recognize the key role that deeply situated material contexts play in the production and reception of both scholarly and pedagogical work. This is an issue that Susan Wall discusses in "'Where Your Treasure Is': Accounting for Differences in Our Talk about Teaching." In this book chapter, written for the University of New Hampshire's 1992 Conference, "The Writing Process: Retrospect and Prospect," Wall tries to "account for some of the often-contested differences in how we talk about what it is that we do" (239). Although Wall focuses on recent scholarly arguments about the nature and consequences of expressivism, I believe that her analysis applies more broadly to recent controversies in composition, including those regarding the nature and status of the writing process movement.

Wall positions herself with care in relation to recent debates around expressivism, noting that while in many respects she has found critiques

of expressivism by Berlin and others cogent and helpful, she nevertheless is concerned about the extent to which these critiques seem to claim
"that expressivism is somehow a 'naive' theory that our profession has
'outgrown'" (241). Wall argues that "Accounting for differences in our talk
about teaching seems to be more complicated than such a history of ideas
can account for, more located in the specific politics and material consequences of the contexts in which we teach" (241). She argues, as well,
that scholars debating expressivism would benefit by taking a more historically and materially grounded approach, one that would encourage
them "to ask for whom" expressivism "remains a popular approach, and
why" (241). Such an analysis would be, Wall argues,

> actually *more* social-epistemic than many of the theoretical critiques
> that we've seen so far since it would take seriously the claim that we
> cannot understand the terms of expressivism (or any pedagogy for that
> matter) without locating them (as Berlin suggests) in the "linguisti-
> cally circumscribed situation[s]" in which they arose, looking for the
> "historically specific conceptions" that shaped their metaphors, "es-
> pecially ideological conceptions about economic, political, and social
> arrangements." (242)[10]

Wall's analysis is an excellent example of an effort to distinguish between
the pedagogy argued for and the pedagogy of the argument. Wall makes
it clear that while she finds much of value in the pedagogy that Berlin
and others argue for—social-epistemic rhetoric—she is concerned about
the pedagogy of the arguments they employ to do so.

It is quite a leap from Wall's discussion of recent critiques of expressivism to Rich's "Notes Toward a Politics of Location"—and yet Wall's
analysis calls to mind a passage from that essay. Like Wall, Rich is concerned with the ease with which theoretical arguments can become detached from their material situations and can circulate to regulate rather
than to enlighten:

> Theory—the seeing of patterns, showing the forest as well as the trees—
> theory can be a dew that rises from the earth and collects in the rain
> cloud and returns to earth over and over. But if it doesn't smell of the
> earth, it isn't good for the earth.
>
> I wrote a sentence just now and x'd it out. In it I said that women
> have always understood the struggle against free-floating abstraction
> even when they were intimidated by abstract ideas. I don't want to

write that kind of sentence now, the sentence that begins "Women have always. . ." We started by rejecting the sentences that began "Women have always had an instinct for mothering" or "Women have always and everywhere been in subjugation to men." If we have learned anything in these years of late twentieth-century feminism, it's that *"always" blots out what we really need to know: When, where, and under what conditions has the statement been true?* (213–14, my emphasis)

As readers have doubtless already observed, the question that ends Rich's reflection is a profoundly rhetorical question. Why have scholars in composition, many of whom are grounded in the rhetorical tradition, not done a better job of asking this question about our own theoretical arguments? How can we rethink our scholarly practices so that in the future we are more likely to do so?

6 Who's Disciplining Whom?

In the previous chapter, I attempted to inquire into the rhetoric, politics, and ethics of the practice of theoretical critique in composition, and to do so in the context of arguments surrounding the writing process movement. I did so not to challenge the validity and helpfulness of theoretical critique, which I value and which plays a key role in this study, but rather to raise questions about it. How can scholars engage in epistemological, political, cultural, and ideological critiques of theories and practices in composition that honor the knowledge that teachers have of their own material and pedagogical situations? How can we avoid the kind of zero-sum arguments that cause at least some teachers of writing to question the relevance of scholarly work and that lead to pronouncements of revolutionary changes in theory that may not reflect the complexity and situatedness of practice? How can we best negotiate what Alcoff refers to as "the problematic of speaking for others" (16)? What benefits might we see if scholars attended as carefully to the pedagogy of our own arguments as to the pedagogy that we argue for?

Scholars who find these questions compelling and want to follow up on them may find it helpful to retheorize certain terms and constructs that I have not thought to examine, as Gore and Giroux do when they retheorize pedagogy. As I hope my discussion of Gore's and Giroux's work suggests, such retheorizing can be quite useful, particularly when it enables readers to step back from commonsense understandings and reconsider both their assumptions and their practices. It has been one of the burdens of this study to argue, however, that the kinds of difficulties that I discuss in *Situating Composition* cannot be resolved solely or even primarily at the level of scholarly theorizing. We cannot retheorize away the material difficulties that many teachers of composition face in their daily work. We cannot retheorize away the conflicting positionings and double binds I describe in my analysis of the scenarios I present in chapter 1. We cannot retheorize away the differences between the ideologies of

THINKING THROUGH PRACTICE

the real, good, and possible that those engaged in the practice of theory and practice of teaching embrace, for these ideologies are embedded in and grow out of deeply held assumptions and practices.

We *can*, however, be more attentive to our own politics of location, and to the scholarly practices these politics encourage, particularly as they pertain to others who are less privileged in academic and cultural hierarchies of knowledge. Doing so encourages us to attempt to step back from our own assumptions and practices—something we can never, of course, entirely accomplish—and subject them to critique. It reminds us, as well, that there is no practice whose political effectivity can be guaranteed. Any practice—whether that of parenting, engaging in community activism, teaching a class, or writing an article or book—can work for progressive ends. It can also serve to maintain the status quo or to oppress. This is as true for the practice of theory as it is for the practice of teaching.

The political effectivity of theory is an issue that bell hooks discusses in "Theory as Liberatory Practice." In this essay, hooks provides a moving account of her own turn to theory, which happened in childhood. "I came to theory," hooks says, "because I was hurting" (59).[1] She emphasizes the positive role that the theory has played in her life and in her writing. This practice enabled hooks not only to survive a repressive childhood but also to "imagine possible futures, a place where life could be lived differently" (61). She adds that "This 'lived' experience of critical thinking, of reflection and analysis" became "a place where I worked at explaining the hurt and making it go away. Fundamentally, I learned from this experience that theory could be a healing place" (61). But not always. Theory, hook argues, "is not inherently healing, liberatory, or revolutionary. It fulfills this function only when we ask that it do so and direct our theorizing toward this end" (61).

In the remainder of her essay, hooks makes a nuanced argument about theory, particularly as it has been practiced within feminism, one that acknowledges the potential limitations and dangers of theory yet also avoids rejecting it. That hooks believes that theory holds potential dangers and limitations is clear. After discussing the development of women's studies programs and of feminist theory within the academy, hooks argues that often this work

> seems to have been formed and nurtured around common efforts to
> formulate and impose standards of critical evaluation that would be

used to define what is theoretical and what is not. These standards often led to appropriation and/or devaluation of work that did not "fit," that was suddenly deemed not theoretical—or not theoretical enough. (63)

The result, hooks observes, was the creation of an "intellectual class hierarchy where the only work deemed truly theoretical is work that is highly abstract, jargonistic, difficult to read, and containing obscure references" (64). To the extent that this has happened, hooks argues, feminist theory serves "to legitimize Women's Studies and feminist scholarship in the eyes of the ruling patriarchy, but it undermines and subverts feminist movements" (65).

These are harsh criticisms of the practice of feminist theory within the academy, yet hooks nevertheless argues that despite its potential dangers and limitations, theory is essential to feminism, for "despite its uses as an instrument of domination, it may also contain important ideas, thoughts, visions, that could, if used differently, serve a healing, liberatory function" (65). She asks feminists who are aware of the ways theory has circulated hegemonically within feminism to resist the temptation simply to reverse the theory-practice binary by "trashing theory" (65), for this practice widens the gap between theory and practice in feminism and "promote[s] the formation within feminist circles of a potentially oppressive hierarchy where all concrete action is viewed as more important than any theory written or spoken" (65–66). She argues forcefully that feminists "must do more than critique the conservative and at times reactionary uses some academic women make of feminist theory. We must actively work to call attention to the importance of creating a theory that can advance renewed feminist movements" (69–70).

I have discussed hooks's "Theory as Liberatory Practice" at such length because I see my effort in part 3 of *Situating Practice* as analogous to that of hooks. Like hooks, I have often found theory to be of great value, both personally and in my scholarly work. And yet I am aware that theory circulates in multiple ways in the academy, and that in composition, as in many other disciplines, theory sometimes dominates the practice of teaching. One way to resist the tendency for theory to dominate practice is to remember that theory itself if a practice—and that as Britzman argues, "practice makes practice" (240).

In the next chapter, I will provide some suggestions that scholars might consider as we attempt to enact Britzman's dictum in our scholarly work.

In this chapter, I want to continue my inquiry into the practice of theory in composition. I will begin this inquiry by considering some of the ideologies that most powerfully inform academic disciplines, including composition. Although many who came to the scholarly work of composition in the 1970s and 1980s saw themselves as in one way or another critical of and resistant to these ideologies, they nevertheless have exerted a powerful influence on the field. As a result, contradictions at times exist between the arguments that scholars in composition make and our scholarly assumptions and practices. Many theorists in composition, for instance, have strongly critiqued the liberal humanist subject assumed by Enlightenment notions of reason. They have not necessarily recognized—much less challenged—the extent to which the criteria for promotion and tenure take the autonomy of the individual for granted or the many other ways the autonomous individual is valorized in the academy.

In this and other ways, I hope to remind readers that no one, however politically, culturally, and ideologically aware, can escape the disciplining influence of ideology. Indeed, as I will point out shortly via an analysis of a Matt Groening cartoon from *School Is Hell*, "Lesson 19: Grad School—Some People Never Learn," those who willingly submit to the disciplining inherent in graduate study have been powerfully shaped by the hegemony of education—and continue to be so as teachers and scholars working within the academy. Recognizing our own immersion in ideologies we otherwise might wish to resist can remind scholars of the need to take care in commenting on the extent to which others are disciplined.

In the remainder of this chapter, I look again at the writing process movement, and I do so via a Burkean-inflected analysis that emphasizes the role that terministic screens play in any act of communication, including scholarly writing. This analysis illuminates at least some of the reasons why scholars in composition found it so natural first to valorize and then to reject this movement. I conclude by attempting to consider some of the limitations of my own textual practices in *Situating Composition*.

Disciplines, Disciplinarity, and Ideologies of the New

I want to begin this discussion with an extended excerpt from the introduction to *Knowledges: Historical and Critical Studies in Disciplinarity*, a collection of essays edited by Ellen Messer-Davidow, David Shumway, and David Sylvan. Here the editors attempt to convey some of the power of the ideologies that circulate within disciplines:

Socially and conceptually, we are disciplined by our disciplines. First, they help produce our world. They specify the objects we can study (genes, deviant persons, classic texts) and the relations that obtain among them (mutation, criminality, canonicity). They provide criteria for our knowledge (truth, significance, impact) and methods (quantification, interpretation, analysis) that regulate our access to it.

Second, disciplines produce practitioners, orthodox and heterodox, specialist and generalist, theoretical and experimental. They beget the tweedy dons and trendy young turks, plodders and paradigm-smashers, crackpots and classicists, who populate the academic bestiary.

Third, disciplines produce economies of value. They manufacture discourse in abundance: ephemeral conference papers, refereed articles, solid monographs, award-winning books, and ubiquitous discussion. They provide jobs: lavishly endowed chairs, minimally paid lectureships, exploitive graduate assistantships. They secure funding: research awards, contracts, laboratory budgets, scholarships, and salaries. They generate prestige: institutional rankings, department ratings, scientific and scholarly stars.

Finally, disciplines produce the idea of progress. They proliferate objects to study and improve explanations. They devise notions that command ever-growing assent: the conservation of mass, the class struggle, the irony of Jane Austen. They tell stories of progress, showing how knowledge advances within existing disciplines and by the establishment of new ones. (vii–viii)

As this description suggests, Enlightenment and modernist ideologies are hardly absent from academic disciplinarity. Despite the many changes scholars in English studies have seen in the last thirty years, for instance, most—though by no means all—scholars in the field continue to privilege texts that manifest the traits of consistency, coherence, parsimony, elegance, and originality. Though scholars argue about substantially different subjects than they did thirty years ago, and read substantially different texts, the deep structure, as it were, of English studies may not have changed as much as scholars would like to believe. Moreover, as I have argued throughout this study, assumptions about theory and practice in English studies—and in composition—are grounded in Enlightenment values that privilege disembodied theory over embodied practice.

There are other ways that ideologies of disciplinarity privilege Enlightenment and modernist values. As I noted earlier, despite the fact that both the individual subject and the author have been thoroughly critiqued, the ideologies of the academy (and, especially, of the humanities) take the autonomy of the individual—and of the author—for granted. And they do so in ways that encourage scholars not to notice potential contradictions between, say, poststructural and postmodern critiques of originality and the academy's traditional injunction that a PhD dissertation must represent an original contribution to a discipline. Whether one is an assistant professor working to meet explicit (and implicit) criteria for tenure and promotion or a senior faculty member striving to gain national recognition for his or her scholarly work, everyday practices in the humanities continue to ignore, or even to punish, collaboration, while authorizing work attributed to (autonomous) scholars.

In this and other ways, disciplines produce economies of value. Central to these economies is the notion of progress—of ever deepening, ever expanding knowledge. And key to the notion of progress is, of course, competition. Scholars who submit articles to journals compete with other scholars for publication, just as scholarly projects compete for disciplinary ascendancy. In this regard, composition has for the last thirty years been engaged in a gigantic contest with other areas within English studies for recognition—and for the professional and disciplinary rewards that come with that recognition.

The ideologies that circulate within disciplines run deep and inform both assumptions and practices in multiple ways. In *Work Time: English Departments and the Circulation of Cultural Value*, Evan Watkins provides a witty—and telling—example of disciplinary ideology in action. Watkins begins his analysis with a brief meditation on the term "work"— a term that, as he rightly points out—is "used a lot in English" (11). After all, scholars in English teach *works* of literature and participate in committee *work*. We read student *work*—and the time we spend doing so is figured into the number of hours of *work* per week that our university's accounting procedures assume when they calculate our paychecks. We also, of course, engage in the scholarly *work* of writing conference talks, articles, book chapters, and books.

Those in English studies not only understand the various meanings the term "work" can take but also intuitively understand the economies of value associated with these meanings. Such is not always the case with those outside the academy, Watkins points out, who might not understand "that when someone asks you what you are working on now, s/he usually expects a brief summary of your latest article or book manuscript, not a report on your intro to Am Lit class or a blow-by-blow account of how you typed up the minutes for the last faculty meeting" (11). It is faculty members' immersion in ideologies of disciplinarity—and outsiders' separation from these ideologies—that makes this usage so commonsensical as to be obvious to one group and puzzling to the other. Those who are immersed in ideologies of disciplinarity know without thinking that the work that really counts in the academy is work that can be identified on a vita as a publication, successful grant proposal, invited lecture, and so on.

In *Work Time,* Watkins attempts to expose, and then challenge, some of the ideologies that circulate in English studies. He does so because he wants to determine what might constitute (as the title of his concluding chapter puts it) "Cultural Work as Political Resistance" (248) for those in the field. Watkins believes that much work in English that hopes to achieve oppositional effects is mystified by what he terms "the dream of transubstantiation, of a cultural avant-garde suddenly and miraculously emerging as also a political vanguard" (28–29). Watkins connects the dream of substantiation with "ideologies of 'the new'" in English studies (15). Such ideologies, he argues, encourage those in English to take it for granted as obvious and commonsensical that "there's something 'new,' 'contemporary,' about *any* highly valued form of literary study in English" (15). It is hardly surprising, Watkins observes, that ideologies of the new should exert such a powerful force within English:

> In one sense, the pervasiveness of "the new" is no more than an indication of the specificity of formation of English departments as they now exist. For the study of "modernist" literature wasn't just grafted onto an older disciplinary structure, to bring it up to the present. Modernism was from the beginning the center of gravity of literary study in the English department. The organization of the work of literary study *in English* is always and everywhere modernist, whether the subject is Chaucer or Joyce, because as a location and an organization of work, literary study of all kinds in English was always tied in some way to the claims for modernism. (15)

Watkins emphasizes the power of "ideologies of the new" for those whose work is located in English and argues that these ideologies represent a significant problem for those who hope to effect political change through their work, for these ideologies "deny the specificity of location, "the way in which actual practices of resistance depend on specific working conditions" (28).

Watkins wants scholars to recognize more fully than many do that however politically motivated our teaching and research are, however much we hope that this work will serve progressive ends, given our location in the academy, our work circulates primarily within, not outside of, its institutional structures. He reminds scholars, as well, that "it's been altogether too convenient for theory to valorize as most important those changes in work practices that obligingly occur within territories where some direct, individual faculty control can be exercised" (4).

In these and other ways, Watkins argues—though he does not refer to Britzman or use her terminology—that practice makes practice. I believe that Watkins is correct, and that what he says of English studies is true of composition as well. But while Watkins's main focus is on political change in the culture at large and the relationship between those inside and outside the academy, I have been concerned with pedagogical change and the relationship between those engaged in the practice of theory and those engaged in the practice of teaching.

Watkins's analysis is a potent reminder that the ideologies that most powerfully influence us are those that circulate as common sense, in this case disciplinary common sense. While scholars can become more aware of the role that "ideologies of the new" play in authorizing some practices and not others, I do not believe it is possible for any scholar, myself included, to resist these ideologies entirely. Indeed, I am not sure that it is desirable to attempt to do so, for surely we need to retain some notion of progress, however critiqued and reconstructed, in our scholarly work. This sense of progress is, I would argue, something that scholars experience in multiple ways. We experience it when we have an individual or collaborative intellectual breakthrough or insight. And we experience it collectively when we read research in our field that seems to us to pose new questions or provide new insights into previous scholarly projects.

However much scholars critique the notion of progress as modernist and trace its lineage to Enlightenment values we no longer accept, we depend at times on rhetorical strategies that both reflect and grow out of ideologies of the new in our scholarly practice. The introduction to Andrea Lunsford's and my study of collaborative writing, *Singular Texts/ Plural Authors: Perspectives on Collaborative Writing,* is a good example of a dependence on such strategies:

In his essay "Common Sense as a Cultural System," Clifford Geertz argues that one of the most effective ways an anthropologist can begin to understand another culture is to study what that culture takes to be commonsense wisdom—the knowledge in our advanced Western society, for instance, that "rain wets and that one ought to come ⓘ in out of it, or that fire burns and one ought not play with it" (75). Such analysis can, Geertz notes, reveal how a "culture is jointed and put together" much better than traditional functionalist accounts (93). Not that such analysis is easy. "There is something," Geertz comments, "of the purloined-letter effect in common sense; it lies so artlessly before our eyes it is almost impossible to see" (92).

The research that led to this book began when we caught a glimpse of a purloined letter in our own field: the pervasive commonsense assumption that writing is inherently and necessarily a solitary, individual act. What caused us, six years ago, to look not through this assumption but at it, to see the purloined letter? (In Edgar Allan Poe's mystery of that name, detective C. Auguste Dupin locates a very important missing letter that has been "hidden" in plain view "upon a trumpery fillagree card-rack of pasteboard" and thus prevents a major political crisis [49].) The answer to our mystery is simple and even perhaps predictable: our own experience as coauthors. Most succinctly, our interest in collaborative writing grew out of the dissonance generated by the difference between our personal experience as coauthors and the responses of many of our friends and colleagues. (5)

As readers are undoubtedly aware, the rhetoric of this introduction presents Lunsford and myself as individuals who have been able to see through a commonsense assumption in composition that others have failed to recognize: the assumption that writing is inherently a solitary act. In so doing, this introduction draws heavily on values privileged by "ideologies of the new," for it takes rhetorical advantage of the potential value that such a "new" understanding holds for scholars in composition. And yet as Anne Ruggles Gere demonstrates in *Writing Groups: History, Theory, and Implications*—a study published before *Singular Texts/Plural Authors*—in an important sense our insight was hardly new at all. Gere's study includes an extensive bibliography of "a chronological listing of books and articles about writing groups" that "documents their history, as well as recommendations for and benefits assigned to these groups" (125). Granted, few if any of these studies argue for the value of

ⓘ Visiting Jerome, rain began - people walked outside to experience it first hand, get evidence for its reality

collaborative writing per se, but many explicitly or implicitly challenge the assumption that writing is inherently a solitary act.

Lunsford and I acknowledge Gere's study in *Singular Texts/Plural Authors*—but we nevertheless structure our introduction around the metaphor of the purloined letter, a metaphor that draws heavily on "ideologies of the new" for its persuasiveness. Though I am now aware of the extent to which Lunsford and I draw on ideologies of the new to authorize our study of collaborative writing, I am not sure that I would rewrite this introduction, had I the chance. It still seems to me accurately to represent our experience at that time. When Lunsford and I began coauthoring, the response to our efforts ranged from astonishment to concern about the negative consequences of our coauthoring for our careers. The strong resistance our collaboration engendered from colleagues encouraged us to see our interest in collaborative writing as something "new."

I will leave it to readers to determine if these comments are self-serving. At the very least, they are a reminder of the difficulties involved in any effort to revise scholarly practice. It is not unreasonable for scholars to want to call attention to the importance of their projects and to feel that these projects offer a new insight or opportunity for action. Often, as Lunsford's and my introduction attests, the rhetorical strategies that are most effective in meeting this need are empowered by "ideologies of the new." Thus though I believe scholars would benefit by attending to our immersion in ideologies of the new, I am not calling for a whole scale effort to reject these ideologies. I believe instead that we have no choice but to work within the ideologies of disciplinarity and professionalism that circulate in the academy. We can and should attempt to first see, critique, and (when appropriate) resist these ideologies, but we cannot entirely avoid them.

We can also attempt to recognize the most salient limitations and dangers that these ideologies present for scholarly work. When I think about these limitations and dangers, I am reminded of the definition of man [*sic*] that Kenneth Burke presents in his essay "Definition of Man." Here is Burke's definition—one with which many readers are doubtless already familiar:

> Man is
> the symbol-using (symbol-making, symbol-misusing) animal
> inventor of the negative (or moralized by the negative)
> separated by his natural conditions by instruments of his own mak-

ing
goaded by the spirit of hierarchy (or moved by the sense of order)
and rotten with perfection. (16)

In this essay, Burke explains that originally his definition did not include
the final "and rotten with perfection." Burke added this line, he explains,
because

The principle of perfection is central to the nature of language as
motive. The mere desire to name something by its "proper" name, or
to speak a language in its distinctive ways is intrinsically "perfectionist." What is more "perfectionist" in essence than the impulse, when
one is in dire need of something, to so state this need that one in effect "defines" the situation? (16)

The urge to define a situation is, of course, key to theoretical critique.
It informs this study, which attempts to redefine the role that the writing process movement played in composition's professionalization and
to raise questions about the practice of theory. Scholars cannot avoid
defining the situations about which we write. Sometimes, however, the
urge to define—driven as it can be by "the spirit of hierarchy" or a "sense
of order"—can cause scholars to overstate our case or decontextualize
or separate it from embodied complexities that resist its urge toward generalization and abstraction. Moreover, in our urge to define a situation,
scholars can ignore or undervalue the extent to which we are part of—
not separate from—the situation we are defining. Such happens, I believe, when scholars comment on the extent to which others are disciplined but ignore our own immersion in various ideologies—including
ideologies of disciplinarity and professionalism.

Who's Disciplining Whom?

As I worked on this chapter, I found myself returning again and again to
a cartoon that appears in Matt Groening's *School Is Hell*, for I have found
this cartoon to be a potent, if unusual, commentary on the ideologies of
disciplinarity and professionalism in the academy. The cartoon is titled
"Lesson 19: Grad School—Some People Never Learn." The cartoon has
nine boxed sections. I will share the text—but, alas, not the drawings—
from two of these sections. The first is the introduction to the cartoon
(assuming that one would read the cartoon from left to right). This section appears in the far middle upper column.

Should You Go to Grad School?

A Wee Test

T   F

☐ ☐   I am a compulsive neurotic.

☐ ☐   I like my imagination crushed into dust.

☐ ☐   I enjoy being a professor's slave.

☐ ☐   My idea of a good time is citing authorities.

☐ ☐   I feel a deep need to continue the process of avoiding life.

The second section of the cartoon appears at the center of the page immediately under the cartoon's title.

The 5 Secrets of Grad School Success

1. Do not annoy the professor.
2. Be consistently mediocre.
3. Avoid anything smacking of originality.
4. Do exactly what you are told.
5. Stop reading this cartoon right now and get back to work.

I have yet to share this cartoon with an academic who does not laugh out loud when he or she first reads it, for Groening wryly captures some of the angst associated with graduate school—especially with the course of study required to earn a PhD.

At least part of the humor of these texts, I would argue, derives from the fact that they emphasize *only* those aspects of graduate school that hold the potential to intellectually, emotionally, and physically discipline graduate students but make no reference to the satisfactions of not only graduate study but of life as a graduate student. (I'm thinking here, for instance, of the intense and long-lasting friendships that many students form in graduate school and the intellectual satisfaction of completing such major projects as theses and dissertations.) Why include these fragments from Groening's cartoon here? I do so as a reminder that those who complete graduate work and go on to careers in the academy are disciplined in *multiple* ways. In his analysis, Watkins emphasizes the role that "ideologies of the new" play in English studies. (Groening's cartoon with its emphasis on enforced mediocrity and of imaginations ground into dust may seem to challenge this emphasis. I believe, however, that it reminds readers of differences in ideologies of the real, the good, and the desirable within and without the academy. What strikes an English professor as a new and exciting theory of, say, gender relations in Henry James's *The Golden Bowl* may be viewed by those outside the academy as just another dry as dust interpretation of an obscure literary text.) Groening's cartoon calls attention to different ideologies at play, such as the power differential between professors and graduate students that many in the academy accept as commonsensical. It reminds readers, as well, of the physical disciplining of the body ("Stop reading this cartoon right now and get back to work") that graduate study can entail.

My point is simple: given the multiple ways that scholars in composition, like scholars in general, are disciplined both by our graduate educations and, later, by the ideologies that we must accept (however grudgingly) if we are to succeed in the academy, I believe that we should take care in assessing the extent to which others are disciplined. I don't mean to suggest that this should be a "hands off" subject. It is crucial that both scholars and teachers recognize the hegemonic forces at play in education, and in the culture, and that we inquire into these forces' effects. But particularly when we speak for those who are generally not authorized to speak back to us we need to do so with care.

When we do speak of the ways that others are disciplined, and when we are tempted to make highly generalized statements about the lived experiences of others, we might do well to think back to our own experiences as graduate students—and for that matter as tenure-line professors (assuming we were lucky enough to find such positions). While some graduate students might argue, as Sharon Crowley does of required first-year writing courses, that graduate school "considered as an institutional practice, has no content aside from its disciplining function," others might point out that this statement—while accurate from the perspective of institutional practice—does little to convey the specificity of their experience (*Composition* 11). Graduate students might observe, for instance, that although they recognized the ways their training required them to accept, and even embrace, professional and disciplinary norms, they were conscious agents who negotiated the demands of graduate education in order to gain the knowledge and credentials they desired. Some students might add that they actively found ways to resist the hegemony of professional and disciplinary norms. Some of these forms of resistance are relatively fleeting and trivial—I'm thinking here of humorous exchanges at parties and venting sessions in offices. Others are more consequential. Such is the case when a group of graduate students successfully petitions to change a departmental policy or academic regulation, or when a PhD student resists pressure from her major professor to write a dissertation on a particular topic and insists on writing about a different subject, one that matters deeply to her.

When we think about the power of ideologies to influence our thoughts and actions and the multiple ways that they can discipline even the most critical, vigilant person, it may be helpful to recognize that, in Burkean terms, we are all "rotten with perfection" ("Definition of Man" 16). We are all disciplined by ideologies of which we can at best be only partly conscious. And we all at one time or another intentionally and unintentionally contribute to the disciplining of others. (Two particularly relevant discussions of such disciplining are Marguerite Helmers's *Writing Students: Composition Testimonials and Representations of Students* and Marcy Taylor and Jennifer Holberg's "'Tales of Neglect and Sadism': Disciplinarity and the Figuring of the Graduate Student in Composition".)

A faculty member teaching a composition theory class that experienced public school teachers are required to take to upgrade their teaching certificates may not intend to discipline these teachers—to tell them that their knowledge of the pedagogy of their classrooms is inferior to that of the faculty member. The faculty member may work hard to find ways for students' embodied knowledge to play an important role in class discussions and assignments. She may also argue in department or college meetings that returning teachers should be empowered to enroll in whatever class they believe will most improve their teaching, or that they should be able to identify projects—within or without the academy—that they find relevant to their concerns as teachers that could be substituted for credit-bearing classes for credentialing purposes. (Teachers in an inner-city high school might argue, for instance, that they would benefit by participating in community service programs that would give them insights into the experience of not only their students but also of their students' families.) Nevertheless, as I observed earlier, the mere fact that teachers in the public schools are at times required to take classes from faculty members who are under no similar requirement to gain specific, concrete knowledge of their situations privileges scholarly knowledge and challenges or disciplines that of teachers.

If we are all disciplined by ideologies, we all have opportunities to resist these ideologies as well. Experienced teachers taking a required composition theory class may joke with colleagues about the professor's lack of understanding of the challenges facing public school teachers, and thus in a small but nevertheless significant way resist their positioning. As John Trimbur points out in "Resistance as a Tragic Trope," "ordinary people are wonderfully canny at playing the system, making do, and getting over in ways that carve out a measure of autonomy under the boss's or teacher's nose by using tools, texts, commodities, and places for their own ends" (13).

These same teachers may also develop innovative practices that subvert or in other ways resist the curricular and institutional forces that work to discipline their teaching. Such happens, for instance, when teachers who are compelled to follow standardized curricula that emphasize rote learning and assessment nevertheless find ways to engage students in significant learning experiences. Because teaching circulates primarily in the classroom and generally cannot be shared in the way that scholarly texts can, this teacher's professor will know about these activities only if the teacher chooses to write about them. That does not mean, however, that these activities are not happening.

Language as Symbolic Action: The Writing Process Movement (Again)

Can scholars find ways to remind ourselves of the limited and partial nature of our vision—of how our need to define a situation may cause us to oversimplify and decontextualize? Can we understand—truly understand—that teachers and students do not need to be immersed in the discourses of critical pedagogy, or of any other constellation of theories, to undertake teaching and learning that offer the potential for resistance to hegemonic forces and for positive educational, social, political, and cultural change? When I think about questions such as these, I find myself drawn to Kenneth Burke's concept of "terministic screens," for this concept has been a helpful reminder to me that any scholarly approach, including my own, necessarily has limitations. As many readers will recall, Burke develops this concept in a book chapter of the same name. Burke begins this chapter, which like "Definition of Man" appears in *Language as Symbolic Action,* by distinguishing between scientistic and dramatistic approaches to the nature of language. Scientistic approaches, Burke argues, "begin with questions of *naming,* or *definition*" (44). Burke's dramatistic approach, on the other hand, views language primarily "as an aspect of 'action,' that is, as 'symbolic action'" (44).

In his essay, Burke articulates some of the implications of a dramatistic view of language, one that emphasizes "the necessarily *suasive* nature of even the most unemotional scientific nomenclatures" (45). One such implication, Burke argues in an often-quoted passage, is that "if any given terminology is a *reflection* of reality, by its very nature as a terminology it must be a *selection* of reality; and to this extent it must function also as a *deflection* of reality" (45). Burke's formulation strikes me as a helpful mantra for those engaged in the work of theory, for it reminds us that no matter how important and productive the perspective or methodology we bring to our research, that which allows us to see and understand one thing simultaneously distorts, marginalizes, or disappears another.

The writing process movement is an excellent case in point. If we look at the events of the 1970s and early 1980s from one perspective, there is much to suggest that a movement is indeed occurring. As Lester Faigley points out in his 1986 "Competing Theories of Process: A Critique and a Proposal," "Slogans such as 'revising is good for you' are repeated in nearly every college writing textbook as well as in many secondary and elementary classrooms" (527). (This is as true now, I would argue—despite the field's purported shift to social and post-process theories of writing—as it was at the time Faigley's essay was published.) As I hope to have demonstrated in chapter 3, however, if we shift the perspective and take a materially grounded look at the broad range of research efforts underway during that period—and also at the diversity of theoretical and pedagogical projects that were generally viewed as part of the writing process movement—then what from one perspective looks like a unified movement takes on a different cast.

This shift in perspective is hardly arbitrary. In "Terministic Screens," Burke points out that "All terminologies must implicitly or explicitly embody choices between the principle of continuity [identification] or the principle of discontinuity [division]" (50). Burke points out as well that "Not only does the nature of our terms affect the nature of our observations, in the sense that the terms direct the attention to one field rather than to another. Also, *many of the 'observations' are but implications of the particular terminology in terms of which the observations are made*" (46). Since in Burke's view, language is fundamentally persuasive, these observations are inevitably *motivated*. Those who want to identify with others will "observe" shared features or understandings that encourage this identification; those who want to separate or distinguish themselves from others will "observe" differences.

As I hope my earlier discussion of the writing process movement suggests, the history of the writing process movement in composition demonstrates this principle in action. As I noted in chapter 3, scholars in composition have long expressed anxieties about the field's professional and disciplinary status. Such anxiety appears near the end of Faigley's essay, which heralds the turn from process to social process models of writing: "If the teaching of writing is to reach *disciplinary status*, it will be achieved through recognition that writing processes are, as Stanley Fish says of linguistic knowledge, 'contextual rather than abstract, local rather than general, dynamic rather than invariant'" ("Competing" 539, my emphasis). It appears as well in Patricia Bizzell, Bruce Herzberg, and Nedra Reynolds's preface to the fifth (2000) edition of *The Bedford Bibliography for Teachers of Writing:*

> The opening sentence of the preface to the first edition of *The Bedford Bibliography* in 1984 stated that "The study of composition is well established as a specialization in English, a serious discipline worthy of advanced graduate work." The former claim was based on the growing quantity and sophistication of scholarship in the field, on the rising numbers of composition specialists being hired and tenured, and on the appearance of more and more courses on composition theory and pedagogy in graduate school offerings. Still, the claim that the field was "well established" may have been just a little tendentious—a statement of confidence and hope rather than a clear fact. Today, though, despite continuing problems of acceptance by literary traditionalists in some English departments, the study of composition seems unequivocally well established. (iv)

As I read this statement, I see anxiety about composition's status expressed not only in the editors' recognition of the tendentious nature of the claim made in the first edition of the bibliography but also in the tendentiousness of their assertion that "the study of composition seems *unequivocally* well established" (my emphasis).

As I argued in chapter 3, these anxieties played a key role in the desire that motivated many scholars in the 1970s and 1980s, myself included, to identify with research on the writing process and to see this research as unifying the field. Given this desire, scholars at that time naturally "observed" and privileged whatever unifying aspects of the writing process movement we could identify. In this regard, it is anything but surprising that Faigley ends the first paragraph of "Competing Theories of Process" by arguing that for composition, "any disciplinary claims must be based on some shared definition of process" (527). As Faigley's article demonstrates, however, the logic of professionalization cannot accept such identification for long. For professionalization requires continual, ongoing progress—and progress requires change. In this sense, as I pointed out in chapter 3, "divisions *within* a professional group make that group stronger not weaker" (McCrea 204).

To maintain their status as disciplines, disciplines require new problems to work on and "solve." So in the mid- to late 1980s, scholars in composition identified a new series of problems. (Faigley begins the second paragraph of "Competing Theories of Process," for instance, by noting that "The problem, of course, is that conceptions of writing as a process vary from theorist to theorist" [527].) As they did so, scholars "observed" differences within the writing process movement that had not seemed apparent before. And they argued, as well, that these differences were highly significant. Hence the turn to social and post-process theories of writing.

In charting this Burkean-inflected history of the writing process movement, and of subsequent developments, I do not mean to devalue the scholarly work of composition during the last thirty years or to suggest that the developments I chart were fueled only by desires to professionalize composition. This research has been deeply significant to me, as it has to many in the field. Rather, I want to point out that as is inevitably the case, scholars have been motivated by desires that we have not always wished to claim. It will always be easier to recognize these motivations in hindsight. But if we keep in mind Burke's dictum that "if any given terminology is a *reflection* of reality, by its very nature as a terminology it must be a *selection* of reality; and to this extent it must function also as a *deflection* of reality," we might be more successful in recognizing at least some of these motivations as we enact them ("Terministic Screens" 45). After all, the epigraph included on the title page of Burke's *Grammar of Motives* is *ad bellum purificandum* ("toward the purification of war"). Scholars in composition have had theory wars aplenty in recent years. And we have also seen a widening in the gap between theorists and practitioners in composition.

I want to be clear about the limitations of any such effort, however. As I have repeated throughout *Situating Composition,* from the perspective of "practice makes practice," the consequences of theory for practice are limited. Scholars may write studies that are more aware of the problem of speaking for others, for instance—and clearly I would argue that this is a good thing—but as long as the working conditions of the majority of teachers of writing limit the time available for reading, reflection, and writing, scholarly texts will circulate primarily among those engaged in the practice of theory. The effort to rethink scholarly practice in composition could encourage scholars to be more modest in the claims we make for our scholarly work and more self-critical about our practices, but this would in no sense result in revolutionary changes in the practices of the majority of teachers of writing.

There are other potential limitations to any effort to reconsider scholarly practices in composition. Since as human beings we are "symbol-using (symbol-making, symbol-misusing) animals" who are also "rotten with perfection," efforts to enact alternatives to conventional disciplinary assumptions and practices could not operate in some pure space but would necessarily carry the motives of the scholars engaged therein (Burke, "Definition" 17). As a result, the consequences of such efforts for the scholarly work of composition are no more guaranteed than they are for composition's pedagogical work. It would be ironic if texts and arguments intended to resist ideologies of the new in composition would themselves circulate as the "new"—but such could happen. Indeed, as I pointed out earlier in this study, it is difficult if not impossible for a work to be published unless journal editors and book publishers believe that work makes a "new" argument or contributes in some way to "new" understandings.

On the Pedagogy of My Practice in *Situating Composition*

At various points in *Situating Composition,* I have argued that scholars would benefit by attending not only to the pedagogy argued for but also to the pedagogy of our arguments. What I ask of others, I should undertake myself. I hope that readers already recognize at least some of the ways that I have tried throughout *Situating Composition* to attend to the pedagogy of my argument. Wherever possible, for instance, I have tried to claim my participation in and commitment to the scholarly projects and practices I now wish to reconsider. I have attempted to situate my analysis at multiple levels of generalization, so that I could minimize (not avoid, for such strikes me as impossible) employing "a rhetoric of solutions and announcements" (Gore xv): thus the questions that appear in the introduction to part 1, the scenarios that begin chapter 1, the mixture of reflections on my own experience as a newly minted writing program administrator in the 1970s with analysis of materially grounded data from that time period in chapter 3, and the analysis of twenty-plus years of course descriptions in chapter 4. When I have made strong arguments and generalizations, I have attempted to qualify or in other ways limits and/or contextualize claims for their consequences.

These are, as I have mentioned, small, local revisions of scholarly practice. In many ways, *Situating Composition,* with its reliance on theoretical critique and historical analysis, is typical of much scholarly work in composition. I would now like to undertake a kind of analysis that is less common in scholarly work: I want to attempt to read against the grain of my own arguments and practices. I have already made some effort to do so. In previous chapters, I identified some of the limitations inherent to my approach. In chapter 2, for instance, I pointed out that some of the criticisms that have been made of Rich's "Politics of Location" may be relevant to my own work. I have written *Situating Composition* in an effort to hold myself and other scholars in composition accountable for our practices and to point out some of the ways the practice of theory is privileged over the practice of teaching. Even as I do so, however, I in some ways reinscribe the centrality of scholarly work of composition—if only because my primary focus is on this work. I have also reminded readers on several occasions that even if other scholars find my arguments persuasive, their consequences for scholarly practice are hardly clear. What does it mean, after all, to attempt to intervene in scholarly assumptions and practices at the level of style and method?

Given these potential limitations, why undertake this effort? Why not write, say, a study of the situated practice of teaching that makes that practice more visible? Why not write about one of the marginalized areas within composition, such as writing centers? These are questions that have troubled me as I worked on *Situating Composition.* Chapter 4 represents at least a gesture toward addressing the former question, but I have not found a way of addressing the second question in this study.

As someone who has directed a writing center for more than twenty years, and who is deeply committed to writing center work, I regret this. At times, this or that potential table of contents for this study included a chapter on writing centers and such other marginalized projects in composition as writing program administration. But as work on my manuscript progressed, its logic seemed to require a different focus. I want to encourage other scholars to recognize that there are many areas within composition that have been as marginalized vis-à-vis the scholarly work of composition as composition has been to English studies. Other areas in addition to writing centers and writing program administration include: English as a second language, writing assessment, basic writing, and writing-across-the-curriculum.[2] What might we learn from studying the ways various scholarly and pedagogical projects have been situated within composition? What would the history of composition look like if these projects were placed at the center, rather than on the margins, of our narratives?

As part of my effort to read against the grain of my own scholarly practices in *Situating Composition,* I would like to acknowledge several terminological problems. I mentioned one such problem in chapter 2: my inconsistent use of the pronouns "we" and "they." This inconsistency strikes me as particularly important given my discussion of the problem of speaking for others in chapter 5. (It reminds me, as well, of the sagacity of Rich's observation in "Notes Toward a Politics of Location" that "even ordinary pronouns" can "become a political problem" [224]). When I use "they," I am excluding myself and implicitly exempting myself from critique; when I use "we" I am including myself in the collective pronoun. What I came to think of as the pronoun problem was an issue that I struggled with from start to finish while working on this project— and it was an issue that I could resolve only through local decisions. Periodically I would move through this or that chapter changing all "we's" and "they's" to either "we" or "they"—but this never felt right and seemed to create new problems. The pronoun problem is one that scholars may increasingly experience as they (we?) attempt to develop more materially grounded analyses of theories and practices in composition, and to write as participants in (rather than detached observers of) the events and issues we explore. I encourage others who find more productive ways to address this problem to discuss their practice in future work.

A second terminological problem to which I wish to call attention is my reliance on several binary-driven descriptor terms. An example would be my decision in chapter 5 to describe what is often referred to as "theory" and "practice" as "the practice of theory" and "the practice of teaching." My primary reason for choosing these terms should be obvious: by referring to both of these activities as practices, I am better able to develop a materially and ideologically grounded analysis and to support my assertion that practice makes practice. This is an advantage, I would argue, over the more conventional dyad of theory and practice. My terms do not, however, avoid some of the problematic connotations associated with the traditional terms. My use of the terms "practice of theory" and "practice of teaching" might seem to suggest that I believe that teachers seldom engage in formal inquiry and that I want to marginalize the teacher-research that is an important part of many teachers' work. I want to emphasize that while I believe there are advantages to this terminology in the context of my study, this terminology also disappears the extent to which teachers engage in informal and formal research—and scholars teach classes of all sorts.

A related terminological problem involves my use of another set of binary-driven descriptors: the terms "scholar" and "teacher." I make this distinction to emphasize relevant material and ideological differences between the practice of theory and the practice of teaching in composition. But there is a fairly high price to pay for this advantage. I want to acknowledge that price here, and to do so in terms of my own experience. As I move through my day and life, I generally experience my work as a teacher, scholar, and writing program administrator not as a series of disconnected identity changes but rather as the enactment of multiple parts of my identity and positioning. While I suspect that there are some persons who might wish to claim only or primarily the identity of scholar or teacher, I believe that what is true of me is true of at least some others. And yet I could not find a way in this study to maintain a focus on differences in the material and ideological situations of those positioned in diverse ways in composition without relying on the scholar/teacher binary. If I could have devised an alternative to this binary, I would have. I invite readers, then, to think further about this issue. How can scholars enact a more materially focused analysis without letting certain features of a person's or group's material situation overdetermine what must be vastly more complex and situated identities and experiences?

There is an additional issue that I want to raise. I want to acknowledge that although I have called attention to the difficulties inherent in the material conditions of many teachers of writing, I have chosen to write a book that raises this issue—and does so in a peripheral rather than central way—rather than spending the time that I have worked on this book in activist projects focused on changing these conditions. In this sense, I am vulnerable to the criticisms that James Sledd raises in his 1991 "Why the Wyoming Resolution Had to Be Emasculated: A History and a Quixotism." I want to create a space in my text for Sledd's perspective, for though I believe that Sledd's position has limitations, it also has merits.

In this article—and in other writings—Sledd raises questions that ought to trouble scholars in composition. He points out, for instance, the ways that scholars, especially scholars of my generation, are "full of praise for themselves and their freshly bedoctored students but contemptuous of mere 'practitioners,' the teachers who do the work that the compositionists theorize about" (274–75). Sledd provides a number of examples of the devaluation of practitioners on the part of scholars, and he challenges how scholars have represented our work. Here is a typical Sledd volley at scholars in composition in general and at a statement by James Berlin in particular:

> They proudly maintain that they have opened a new field which "has clearly arrived at disciplinary status, complete with graduate programs, undergraduate majors, major conferences, and journals" (Berlin 217); but the content itself of that boast reveals that they have confused the externals of academic entrepreneurship with the intellectual elaborations of theory and method. (275; Berlin, "Writing Instruction 217)

Touché. I do not agree with all of Sledd's assessments, such as his claim that much research in composition is either "piddling" or "wildly overambitious" (275), nor do I believe that many scholars in composition are contemptuous of those who teach first-year and other required writing courses. But I appreciate his provocatively posed arguments, which have stimulated much thought on my part. Sledd is asking scholars in composition to be more accountable for our work and for our careers, and I would like to see more attention to the questions and issues that he raises.

There are a few additional issues that I would like to address in this effort to read against the grain of the pedagogy of my argument. One involves my repeated call for scholars to attend more carefully to the pedagogy of our arguments, to be more tolerant of multiple approaches to research on writing, to be more self-reflexive, self-critical, and modest in what we claim for ourselves and our scholarly work, and more generous toward the work of those whose location differs from our own—particularly when we find ourselves speaking for them. While I believe that these are laudable goals, they nevertheless raise a number of difficulties. As I mentioned earlier, there is no guarantee that efforts to revise scholarly practices in composition will not be taken up as "the new" by scholars—and thus circulate in ways that reinforce, rather than challenge, conventional disciplinary assumptions.

On a more practical level, any effort to revise scholarly practices holds its own challenges and difficulties. When I reflect on my individual and collaborative attempts to think and write differently than I have in the past, I am reminded that it often takes more time to compose a resistant text (however minor its resistances are) than it does to compose a more traditional academic argument. I am reminded as well that when I do attempt to enact alternative scholarly practices, I find it easy to make what in hindsight—and only in hindsight—I recognize to be significant rhetorical misjudgments. The introduction to part 1 of *Situating Composition,* for instance, originally comprised twenty-five, not ten, sets of questions. I hoped that these questions would serve as an invitation to readers and that the large number of questions would indicate my openness to multiple questions and perspectives. When an early anonymous reviewer indicated feeling "assaulted and battered" by the long list of questions, I realized that I had misjudged their effect. Though I subsequently reduced the number of questions, some readers may still prefer a more conventional introduction.

As this example suggests, scholars who are under the pressure of "publish or perish" may have good reasons for preferring more conventional academic genres—at least if they want to be promoted and granted tenure. Scholarly work that in one way or another resists disciplinary assumptions and practices may be more likely than traditional academic argument to generate an uncomprehending, mixed, or even hostile reception. Scholars who deviate from scholarly norms may also find it difficult to find suitable publishers for their work. This is a problem that bell hooks discusses in such early books as *Talking Back: Thinking Feminist, Thinking Black.*

Andrea Lunsford's and my experience writing "Representing Audience: 'Successful' Discourse and Disciplinary Critique" is another example of the kinds of difficulties that even experienced scholars can encounter when they deviate from conventional scholarly practices. In this article, Lunsford and I attempted to reconsider our earlier "Audience Addressed/

Audience Invoked: The Role of Audience in Composition Theory and Pedagogy" (AA/AI)—but to do so in an unusual way. As we note in our later article, in revisiting our earlier essay "we wish[ed] neither to reject nor defend AA/AI but rather to embrace multiple understandings of it, and to acknowledge the extent to which any discursive moment contains diverse, heterodox, and even contradictory realities" (169).

"Representing Audience" was one of the most difficult and time-consuming articles we have ever undertaken, going through many drafts before we first submitted it to a journal. We also had a difficult time placing this article. Though "Representing Audience" was eventually published in *College Composition and Communication (CCC)*, which had also published AA/AI, the editor's first response to our essay was to summarily reject it. Lunsford and I revised multiple times before "Representing Audience" was accepted. Ironically, in one of the few published references to "Representing Audience" of which we are aware, Geoffrey Sirc in "Never Mind the Tagmemics, Where's the Sex Pistols?" characterizes our article as an effort to "auto-mutilate 80s Composition classic-rock as *mea culpa*" (27). Even though we affirmed as many aspects of AA/AI as we critiqued, readers such as Sirc felt compelled to iron out the complexities of the story that we attempted to tell of our earlier effort.

When Lunsford and I embarked on "Representing Audience," we were already tenured professors with strong publication records. Indeed, those reputations may well have played a role in the then-editor of *CCC*'s ultimate decision to accept and print our article. In a study that calls attention to the politics of location in composition, it seems crucial for me to acknowledge that efforts like *Situating Composition* and "Representing Audience" may not represent viable models for those differently situated in the scholarly work of composition. As Min-Zhan Lu observes at the conclusion of "Redefining the Literate Self: The Politics of Critical Affirmation," a reflection on her own writing practices, those who call for change in scholarly practices need to remember "the specific, privileged, material conditions sustaining the type of reading and writing" we are "posing" (193). Lu goes on to argue that her essay

> needs to be scrutinized on not only the extent to which I am practicing the kind of critical affirmation I pose but also the usefulness of such a forum of self-education for teachers and scholars at different institutional locations and at different points of their professional and personal lives. (193)

I wish to make the same point about *Situating Composition*. In this study, I have attempted not to argue that other scholars *ought* to follow this or that practice—and certainly not that they ought to, in effect, do as I do here. Rather, I have tried (as Lu says of her own effort) to "put my self on the line so that I might stay on line with voices that matter" (193). The issues that I discuss in *Situating Composition* matter in deeply personal, as well as professional, ways to me. As someone whose career has "tracked" composition's professionalization, I have puzzled many times over how scholars can best understand the nature and consequences of this transformation. I have puzzled, as well, about what it means to enact progress in a field committed to pedagogical, and well as scholarly, action. *Situating Composition* represents my effort to write myself into a better understanding of these, and other, puzzlements.

7 Situated Knowledges
Toward a Politics of Location in Composition

Habits of mind can be difficult to change, and yet it is at the level of habits of mind—of stylistic, methodological, and argumentative preferences, values, and commitments—that ideologies of disciplinary and professionalism operate most powerfully. In our daily lives, we can easily undervalue the hold that various physical habits have in our lives. Just because I have a cup of coffee every afternoon at 3 p.m., I may tell myself, doesn't mean that I *need* to have that coffee or am in the grips of caffeine addiction. And yet I regularly appear at the coffeehouse across from my office most work days at 3 p.m. We can similarly undervalue the role that our intellectual habits of mind play in our scholarly work. After all, when scholars write texts, we are most conscious of the argument that we are developing. It is much harder to recognize the extent to which ideologies of disciplinarity and professionalism may encourage us to *need*, say, to develop our critique in ways that "perfect" our argument in terms of disciplinary norms but cause us to ignore such issues as the problem of speaking for others.

Before developing this idea further, I should note a few caveats. The first is that in discussing the relationship between ideology, experience, and discourse, I assume that this relationship is always in flux. There is no singular engine that drives these relationships, which I see as contingent and discontinuous. Although in an important sense, ideology, experience, and discourse are mutually constitutive, their relationship is as likely to manifest contradiction and tension as congruence and influence. In this regard, though I believe that my comparison between physical habits and intellectual habits is a helpful reminder of the way that desires of all sorts can work through us, I do not mean to represent ideologies of disciplinarity and professionalism as driving scholarly habits of mind in any unilateral, univocal, or totalizing way. The relationship

THINKING THROUGH PRACTICE

between these ideologies and any discursive act cannot be adequately represented by the body's desire for a 3 p.m. cup of coffee or a post-dinner cigarette—though, again, the fact that we can so easily turn away from the significance of these desires for our physical habits is telling.

I do want to argue that these ideologies can at times influence scholars to fail to recognize contradictions between consciously held theories and the practices that we enact when we engage in theoretical critique. (Other forms of contradiction are, of course, possible. Such occur when scholars who critique Enlightenment and modernist notions of the subject and of the author refuse to allow students to write collaboratively.) Consider, for instance, potential contradictions between the social constructionist epistemology that many scholars in composition avow and our actual textual practices. At the level of theory, many scholars in composition—like many scholars in the humanities—argue that the self or subject is socially constructed and is "always already" immersed in multiple and competing ideologies. No one, postmodern and social constructionist theories argue, can exist free of ideology; all perspectives are partial.

In practice, however, as I hoped to have demonstrated at various points in this study, scholars at times write as if we are somehow exempt from the disciplining force of ideologies we critique in others. We also at times make statements that suggest that our knowledge is anything but situated and partial. We do so not because we are lack theoretical sophistication but because materially and ideologically embedded disciplinary assumptions and practices encourage—or at least allow—us to exempt ourselves from our critique. In this sense, ideologies that inform scholarly practice at the level of habits of mind can at times prove more powerful than consciously held beliefs—as Bordieu's concept of habitus suggests.[1]

Because we are all influenced by assumptions, practices, and forces of which we can only partly be aware, scholars in composition cannot address issues surrounding the politics of our location in the academy solely or primarily at the level of theory but must rather inquire into our own practices, and into the ideologies that ground them. Theory can certainly inform and aid this effort. In this regard, for instance, I have found Donna Haraway's emphasis on situated knowledges helpful. As Haraway argues in *Simians, Cyborgs, and Women: The Reinvention of Nature*, a view of knowledge as situated represents an alternative both to totalizing claims to epistemic authority and to relativism. Different as the latter are, Haraway notes, both views of knowledge "deny the stakes in location, embodiment,

and partial perspective" (191). An understanding of knowledge as situated views knowledge as plural—as knowledges. Such knowledges are,
as Haraway observes, "partial, locatable, critical knowledges sustaining
the possibility of webs of connections called solidarity in politics and
shared conversations in epistemology" (191). As this comment suggests,
Haraway's formulation is motivated at least in part by a utopian desire
for change. Indeed, Haraway observes that she "does not seek partiality
for its own sake, but for the sake of the connections and unexpected
openings situated knowledge makes possible" (196).

I find Haraway's discussion of situated knowledges persuasive—but
even more powerful, I believe, are comments in *Simians, Cyborgs, and
Women* that are directed less toward theory and more toward practice.
Like many feminists, for instance, Haraway has been concerned about the
virulence of debates within feminist theory. In reflecting on these debates,
Haraway focuses as much on practice as on theory, pointing out the extent to which "Taxonomies of feminism produce epistemologies to police deviation from official women's experience" (156). Feminists,
Haraway argues, require "a knowledge tuned to resonance, not to dichotomy" (194–95). They also need to consider what a feminist understanding of the critical might look like and be like—at least if they wish
to resist the agonism that is inherent in the academy.

Haraway discusses this and many other issues in *How Like a Leaf: An
Interview with Thyrza Nichols Goodeve*, a book-length dialogue between
Haraway and Goodeve. At one point in their conversation, Goodeve com-
ments that Haraway's

> notion of criticality is strikingly different from the traditional notion
> of critical meaning breaking down arguments and seeing where power
> lies. . . . Looking only for the flaws or the absences seems like such a
> weird way to learn. In fact it seems like the opposite of learning. (111)

Goodeve then asks Haraway why so many academics "think that is the
only way of being critical" (11). Haraway responds as follows:

> Part of it is competition and the fear of looking dumb if you haven't
> made the criticism first. I actually think some of the really bad race
> politics works out of the same principle where people are intent on
> calling other people racist first lest they be judged. It's as though they
> think racism is something you can expel easily by a few statements.
> You can't do away with racisms by various kinds of mantras or by

pointing out how this article didn't deal with race in such a way and then sit back and think look how I'm free because I noticed. In other words, *because I saw I am not there.* (111, my emphasis)

Haraway's cautionary words about how easy it is for scholars to think "because I saw I am not there" resonate deeply for me. They remind me of the extent to which the disciplinary habits of mind that most powerfully influence the practice of theory in the academy—even such theories as postmodernism, poststructuralism, cultural studies, critical pedagogy, and feminism—encourage scholars to distance ourselves from that which we are critiquing, to assume that because we understand this or that phenomenon we are somehow exempt from its workings.

I want to say more about problems and lost opportunities that can result when scholars assume that "because I saw I was not there." Before doing so, however, I would like to identify several other habits of mind that I believe are rooted in ideologies of disciplinarity and professionalism. One such habit I might term "theory hope." In using this term, I do not intend to evoke arguments over the nature and status of theory, such as Stanley Fish undertakes in *Doing What Comes Naturally: Change, Rhetoric, and the Practice of Theory in Literary and Legal Studies.* Rather, I refer to the general hope that I believe many scholars in composition, myself included, hold that if only we can work through an idea or issue at the level of theory, it will inevitably have significance for practice. This is a hope that from one perspective scholars must have if we are to undertake projects that matter to us. But such a hope can become so powerful that it encourages scholars to forget how complex and situated the messy and impure world of teaching is. Such happens when scholars articulate zero-sum arguments about the consequences of this or that theory for practice or establish unreasonable litmus tests that theories must pass at the level of practice if they are to be considered valid.

Evan Watkins refers to a variant of theory hope in *Work Time: English Departments and the Circulation of Cultural Value*: this is what Watkins terms "dreams of transubstantiation"—the belief that work done in one location can somehow have direct and immediate consequences for another location. Scholars in composition subscribe to these dreams when we argue that theories and practices in composition will necessarily lead not only to productive educational change but also to broad political, economic, social, and cultural changes. As was the case with theory hope, scholars cannot, I would argue, entirely forego dreams of transubstantiation. After all, from the classical tradition to the present day, at their strongest and most vital moments, rhetoric and writing have been concerned with the larger political, cultural, and social good. Scholars can, however, learn to develop some healthy suspicions about these dreams, which, as Watkins points out, tend to "deny the specificity of location, the way in which actual practices of resistance depend on specific working conditions" (28).

When I think of the third intellectual habit that I want to identify, I find myself drawn back in memory to advertisements for General Electric that appeared on television in the 1960s and 1970s. "Progress," the announcers in these ads intoned, "is our most important product." In the academy, ideologies of disciplinarity and professionalism whisper these words in scholars' ears constantly, if almost imperceptibly, for in a very important sense, progress is indeed academic disciplines' most important product. We cannot entirely do away with the desire for progress, just as we cannot do away with the desire for our work to have significance for others. But when the desire for progress requires the metaphorical killing of our disciplinary mothers and fathers, whose work must (by its logic) be overturned in order for our own to have value, we would do well to question its role in our assumptions and practices: such "murders" ignore the extent to which our forefathers' and foremothers' research has literally made our own work possible.

Too often, I would argue, scholars in composition enact progress by establishing "killer" dichotomies that reduce complicated and situated scholarly projects to opposing "camps" that we then either oppose or advocate. The creation of these camps does violence to scholarly work in a number of ways. It takes projects that are loosely aligned, such as various projects that in one way or another were concerned with the writing process in the 1970s and 1980s, and fuses them in ways that do not reflect their material, situated complexity. The creation of opposing camps also tends to obscure or ignore many other important scholarly efforts that are underway at the same time, creating master narratives that obscure, rather than clarify, the multifaceted work of composition.

In these and other ways, habits of mind that are grounded in ideologies of disciplinarity and professionalism encourage scholars—even scholars who agree with Donna Haraway that knowledge is best viewed as both plural (as knowledges) and as situated—to ignore the situatedness and partiality of our own theories and practices. Though many scholars

187

in composition are highly critical of Enlightenment notions of progress as they have circulated in the culture in general and in such institutions as the public schools, we have proven less able to recognize the way that these same notions circulate within academic ideologies of disciplinarity and professionalism. Similarly, though scholars have recognized the need to refigure the relationship of theory and practice in the practice of theory, we have proven less able to refigure this relationship in the practice of teaching, or in other professional relationships. We have been quick to comment on the extent to which others are disciplined by various ideologies—but much less willing and able to recognize our own immersion in ideologies of disciplinarity and professionalism.

"A Knowledge Tuned to Resonance"

What would it take for scholars in composition not only to *understand* that knowledge is socially constructed—and hence always partial and situated—but also to *enact* this knowledge in our theoretical critique? To do so, scholars would need, at the very least, "a knowledge tuned to resonance, not to dichotomy" (Haraway, *Simians* 194–95). What might this knowledge look like at the level of scholarly practice? In asking these questions, I do not mean to suggest that contradictions between understanding and action are endemic to theoretical critique in composition but rather that at times they exist as gaps and fissures—as eruptions of the disciplinary unconscious, as it were—in our texts. I am not arguing, in other words, that there is a crisis in scholarly work that requires the overturning of earlier theories—and theorists. Indeed, the problems that I have discussed in this study are relevant only to some work in composition. Rather, I am asking scholars to work together to inquire into our practices, to see if what are finally relatively minor revisionary changes might make a difference in the accuracy, power, and relevance of our critique.

One step in this direction would be for scholars in composition to remind ourselves of the partial and limited nature of any effort to understand both writing and the teaching of writing. Surely both are so complex and multivalent—so full of tensions, contradictions, and other desires and practices—that no single theory or approach can ever fully explain or account for them. Such an understanding would encourage scholars to view different theories and approaches to both writing and the teaching of writing as terministic screens that provide insights into some—but not all—aspects of their subject. Rather than engaging in theory wars, scholars approaching similar topics from diverse perspectives could attempt to learn from and with each other.

Such an effort might result in some surprising "connections and unexpected openings" (Haraway, *Simians* 196). An example could help clarify my point. In chapter 3, I cited a passage from Gary Olson's foreword to Andrea Greenbaum's *Insurrections*. In his foreword, Olson notes that "This book is particularly timely, emerging as it does at a time of increasing hegemonic struggle over how the field of composition studies should be defined" ("Resistance" xi–xii). Olson's depiction of this struggle pits those who, in Olson's terms, "define composition studies as a field committed to critical (not just functional) literacy" against advocates of "teaching writing creatively" and declares that the special issue of *College Composition and Communication* on this topic (51.1, 1999) represents "an opening salvo in what will undoubtedly will come to be known as 'the new theory wars'"(xi). Olson argues as well that the scholars in this special issue, as well as other "boss compositionists," are "struggling desperately to set back our disciplinary clock" (xii).

This is a particularly striking example of rhetorical strategies that work to establish the very struggle that Olson decries. Consider, for instance, the dichotomy that undergirds Olson's argument: one must be either for or against critical literacy. When Olson characterizes those on the privileged side of his dichotomy as committed to critical literacy, readers rely upon their own understanding of what critical literacy is and does to elaborate the meaning of this statement. ("Critical literacy" is a particularly malleable term in this regard. Who, after all, would claim that they do not want to foster critical literacy?) Unless readers are familiar with James Sledd's use of the term "boss compositionist" in "Return to Service," it too is strikingly elastic.[2]

In setting up this dichotomy, Olson rules out the possibility that scholars might be engaged both in the work of critical literacy and of creative writing—might see these two projects, in fact, as linked or mutually reinforcing, as indeed many of the scholars whose work appeared in the special issues of *College Composition and Communication* on creative writing do. He establishes an agonistic opposition when he could work toward common ground. Such common ground does, I believe, potentially exist, at least in one arena—though Olson's assertion that those who published articles in this special issue are "struggling desperately to set back our disciplinary clock" makes such a rapprochement unlikely.

Olson has been a strong advocate of post-process theories of writing. In "Toward a Post-Process Composition: Abandoning the Rhetoric of Assertion," for instance, Olson argues that

> The problem with process theory, then, is not so much that scholars are attempting to theorize various aspects of composing as it is that they are endeavoring (consciously or not) to construct a model of the composing process, thereby constructing a Theory of Writing, a series of generalizations about writing that supposedly hold true all or most of the time. (8)

My own reading of process theory differs from that of Olson. In their 1981 "A Cognitive Process Theory of Writing," for instance, Linda Flower and John Hayes characterize their effort to build a model of the writing process in much less grandiose terms, noting that "a model is a metaphor for a process: a way to describe something, such as the composing process, which refuses to sit still for a portrait" (368). This statement as I read it differentiates their effort to construct a working model of the writing process from a larger effort to construct a totalizing Theory of Writing.

Although I am resistant to Olson's argument, in my experience, the creative writing faculty and MFA students with whom I have worked are much less so. When I teach studies such as Flower and Hayes's article in composition theory classes, MFA students express strong and sustained resistance to any effort to study the writing process which, they argue, is unknowable. I have heard many visiting creative writers assert that writing cannot be taught—at least not in the way that most other subjects can. As these comments suggest, if Olson had been able to work toward "a knowledge tuned toward resonance," he might have identified those involved with creative writing as allies in his effort to critique process theories of writing (Haraway, *Simians* 194–95). Instead, he positions them as opponents. The resistance that creative writing faculty and students have to efforts to study the writing process has different sources and takes different forms than does Olson's, but it represents an enthymematic common ground that those working from both perspectives could explore.

For this to occur, however, Olson—and other scholars, for this example from Olson's foreword is hardly unique—would need to redefine some of the goals he (and we) bring to our work and develop ways to resist some of our intellectual habits of mind, such as our tendency to create "perfect" arguments by creating opposing camps and pitting them against each other. We would need to first *want to*, and then *find ways to*, practice not just theoretical critique but what Min-Zhan Lu, echoing Cornell West, refers to as critical affirmation. As Min-Zhan Lu observes in "Redefining the Literate Self: The Politics of Critical Affirmation":

> Within the academic nervous system, scholarly activity remains the primary source of our cultural capital. Critical analysis of oversights in the work of others remains more lucrative than critical reflections on similar oversights in one's own work, on problems facing one another's work, and on how to help one another address these problems. (193)

We would need to learn to be more sensitive to the ways that ideologies of disciplinarity and professionalism, which none of us can entirely escape, encourage scholars to take advantage of various strategies of *reductio ad simplifacationem* (Cintron 376) and to privilege "the new" over previous or ongoing theories and practices. We would also have to be more willing to grant that rather than representing a problem to be deplored, the existence of multiple approaches to and understandings of both writing and the teaching of writing represents a strength to be taken advantage of.

Toward a Politics—and Rhetoric—of Critical Affirmation

In part 3 of *Situating Composition*, I have argued that scholars would benefit by acknowledging more than we currently do that, as Britzman argues, "practice makes practice" (240). I have done so because I believe, with Britzman, that this perspective—while anything but a universal guarantor of scholarly efficacy—nevertheless helpfully reminds us of the importance of attending to "the complex dialogue between practice and theory, biography and social structure, knowledge and experience, and differences and commonalities" (240). In recent years, I have attempted to find ways of enacting this understanding in my scholarly work, both individual and collaborative. I would like to share some of the strategies that I have explored. More importantly, I would like to invite other scholars to share their own efforts to (paradoxically) both resist certain aspects of—yet also contribute to—the scholarly work of composition.

I present these strategies because I want to be as specific and concrete as possible in articulating suggestions other scholars might consider. I have read too many books that spend the majority of their effort and space on critique and leave only the last three to five pages to articulate

PROCESS

a constructive vision of productive change; I want to create a larger space in my text for such a vision. I worry, however, that the rhetoric of these suggestions may strike some readers as problematic, for in addressing readers directly, I may seem to be suggesting that readers *should* and *must* follow a specific suggestion, when I mean only to encourage readers to consider the advantages and disadvantage of particular practices for their own scholarly inquiry. I experimented with alternative ways of expressing my suggestions—ways that did not involve directly addressing readers—but the suggestions as rewritten seemed less focused and specific. I could not find a way to resolve this dilemma, so I settled for the clearest and most concrete articulation of suggested strategies. I hope that readers can experience these suggestions as part of a conversation between colleagues who share similar interests and concerns and not as a series of admonitions.

Strategy 1: Apply Jameson's well-known admonition "Always historicize" to your own work as well as to the work of others. If you are writing a critique of the writing process movement, for instance, and you once identified with and advocated for that movement, acknowledge that previous experience in your critique—if only briefly—and attempt to use it to think through your analysis. You might even consider returning to work you have written in the context of earlier identifications and convictions to see what you can learn from it.

According to Richard Fulkerson, for instance, "The first college composition text to have the word 'process' in its title was Susan Miller's *Writing: Process and Product* published in 1976" (96). What if Miller had acknowledged her earlier affiliation with the writing process in *Textual Carnivals* and clarified subsequent changes in her thinking? At the very least, such a discussion might have repositioned her less as a scholar who has "always already" understood the limitations of the writing process and more as a scholar whose thinking and practice have evolved, as teachers' thinking and practices similarly evolve.

Strategy 2: Remember that efforts to generalize about the scholarly work of this or that time period foreground some theories and practices while backgrounding others. Such partiality of vision and representation is inevitable, but the more we are aware of it, the more we can attempt to recover at least some of the material complexity and situatedness of a particularly scholarly and/or pedagogical moment.[3] Doing so reminds us, as Marita Sturken points out in *Tangled Memories: The Vietnam War, the AIDS Epidemic, and the Politics of Remembering,* that "all memories are 'created' in tandem with forgetting" (7). Chapter 3 demonstrates, I hope, the "forgetting" that played a critical role in the "remembering" of the writing process movement in the 1980s and later.

Strategy 3: Be cautious about speaking for others, whether those others are students, classroom teachers, or other scholars. As I argued in chapter 5, scholars in composition cannot avoid speaking for others. Indeed, at times we must do so. But given the variety of needs, desires, and situations that both students and teachers bring to our classrooms, we might think carefully before we make totalizing statements about teachers, students, or teaching practices. We make such statements when we argue, for instance, that this or that practice will necessarily be liberating or infantilizing no matter what the situation.

It will always be difficult to step outside of our own ideologically and materially grounded experiences. At the least, as you develop scholarly arguments, try to read your work from the perspective of those whose experiences you are describing. After all, most scholars are also teachers. If you find yourself articulating a totalizing argument about someone else's teaching, take a moment to imagine how you would respond to such an analysis about your own teaching. As Alcoff suggests, it might also be helpful to undertake "a concrete analysis of the particular power relations and discursive effects involved" in your analysis (24). Doing so may remind you that language is indeed symbolic action and help you to see ways that the "perfection" of your argument distorts or mystifies the experiences of others.

Strategy 4: Attempt, in other words, to read against the grain of your own work and to find spaces for paradox and multiplicity as well as for more conventional forms of critique. Such an effort is, to put it mildly, difficult, for in the heat of the moment, it is hard to resist, rather than to embrace, the logic of passionately held convictions. In *Whose Science? Whose Knowledge? Thinking from Women's Lives,* Sandra Harding discusses the role that developing what she terms "'traitorous' identities and social locations" can play in such an effort (288). Harding's particular focus is on the role that identity politics has at times played in feminist theory.

These politics have caused some to feel that only lesbians can write about the lesbian experience, only African Americans about African American experience, and so on. Harding argues that such prohibitions are unhelpfully restricting and that (for example) "whites *as whites* can provide 'traitorous' readings of the racial assumptions in texts—literature, history, science—written by whites" (289). Such an effort enables white feminists to

> activate their full identities and social situations as whites and to let us see how they are taking responsibility for their identity as whites, how they are discovering the causal connections between their own social situation as whites as the situations of blacks in the past and today. (289–90)

What might we better understand about the work of composition if scholars *as scholars* attempted at times to enact "'traitorous' identities and social locations"?

There are additional ways that scholars might helpfully read against the grain of our own work. We can remind ourselves, for instance, that *any* scholarly practice entails both potential benefits and potential limitations. This is as true of efforts to resist conventional disciplinary assumptions and practices in composition as it is of efforts that depend upon and enact them. And we can attempt to develop conventions that might enable and encourage scholars to read against the grain of our arguments. What might such a reading look like in practice? Is it realistic to imagine that such a reading could become as common as, say, the review of literature that so often appears in scholarly work? What disadvantages, as well as advantages, might the establishment of such a practice entail?

Strategy 5: Try to identify—and draw upon—research in other scholarly areas that can help you gain distance from and perspective on the body of research with which you most strongly identify. As readers of *Situating Composition* are aware, this is a strategy that I have employed often in this study. My reading of the work of such feminists as Donna Haraway, Sandra Harding, Jane Flax, Sandra Gubar, and Adrienne Rich—and of such differently situated scholars as Deborah Britzman, Kenneth Burke, Jennifer Gore, Henry Giroux, and Evan Watkins—has played a key role in my thinking and writing. As I watched Gubar attempt to come to terms with the theory wars that have played so prominent a role in feminist theory, for instance, I gained a helpful perspective on the theory wars in composition. Donna Haraway's recognition that "rhetorical strategies, the contest to set the terms of speech, are at the centre of feminist struggles in natural science" reinforced my sense that such was also the case in composition (*Simians* 72). When I read Sandra Harding's observation that scientists have often "found it convenient to overlook the deep ties between science and war making," I found a metaphorical heuristic—the question of what various disciplines have found "convenient to overlook"—that I have found helpful in considering the scholarly work of composition (33).

I need to acknowledge, however, that the material conditions of many scholars in composition, many of whom have high teaching loads while they also direct writing programs and negotiate demanding family and community responsibilities, does not allow for such wide reading—especially since it can be particularly difficult to tell whether reading this or that study outside your immediate field will bear intellectual fruit. This is one of many reasons why, as I noted earlier in this chapter, I do not present my own practices as a model that others should follow. Because the process of thinking analogically has been so helpful to me, however, I include it in the list of possible—not required or necessarily helpful—strategies.

Strategy 6: At the same time, recognize the importance of claiming what Jacqueline Jones Royster refers to as scholars' "passionate attachments" (280). As Royster observes, such acknowledgment "reminds us that knowledge has sites and sources and that we are better informed about the nature of a given knowledge base when we take into account its sites, material contexts, and points of origin" (280). Royster argues eloquently for the importance of claiming one's "passionate attachments":

> My point here is that knowledge is produced by someone and that its producers are not formless and invisible. They are embodied and in effect have passionate attachments by means of their embodiments. They are vested with vision, values, and habits; with ways of being and ways of doing. These ways of being and doing shape the question of what counts as knowledge, what knowing and doing mean, and what the consequences of knowledge and action entail. It is important, therefore, to specify attachments, to recognize who has produced the knowledge, what the bases of it are, what the material circumstances

of its production entail, what consequences of implications are suggested by its existence, and for whom the consequences and implications hold true. (280)

In arguing that scholars should acknowledge our "passionate attachments," Royster is in effect arguing for a small but critical change in scholarly work. If scholars were to follow her advice, the result would hardly constitute a revolutionary change in scholarly practice—but it might help contextualize and ground our efforts and remind us of the situatedness of our own scholarly interests.

Strategy 7: Treat theories and practices that you find in one or another way suspicious as opportunities for learning as well as opportunities for critique. Royster's argument about the importance of acknowledging passionate attachments is a reminder that the reverse can also be true. As scholars, we can find ourselves instinctively suspicious of certain scholarly and pedagogical practices. Rather than simply "believing" these suspicions, we can benefit from "doubting" them as well. Readers familiar with Peter Elbow's work will recognize that in referring to "believing and doubting," I am evoking a common "turn" in his thinking, one that informs not only his "The Doubting Game and the Believing Game" but much of his writing.

I mention Elbow because the strategy I am discussing here—that of doubting one's suspicions (or believing that which one doubts)—has played a key role in my response to Elbow's work. Like a number of scholars in composition, in the 1980s and early 1990s, I found myself largely persuaded by critiques of Elbow. Talking with teachers whom I knew to be gifted, successful teachers of writing about Elbow's work convinced me that I needed to reread his work with greater attentiveness to its articulated aims and audience. I now read Elbow's work, I believe, with greater understanding, recognizing that more than many scholars in composition, Elbow is open to multiple perspectives and to both/and reasoning. I recognize, as well, the importance of the fact that throughout his career, Elbow has often attempted to speak to and with—rather than for—both teachers and students.

Strategy 8: Try to resist the agonism and zero-sum thinking that have played a key role in some of the most prominent scholarly work in composition in recent years. How can scholars in composition benefit from the many strengths of theoretical critique without relying upon a rhetoric of agonism? This is a question that feminists have faced as well—for as many readers are aware, in recent years, academic feminism, like composition, has been rocked by vehement and polarizing debates. In this regard, I find Susan Brown Carlton's observation about debates over essentialism within feminism compelling. Carlton argues for the value of reconstructing what strikes many as a philosophical impasse that pits essentialists against postmodernists "as a map of rhetorical options available for voicing the feminist stance" (240). Doing so encourages feminists to recognize, Carlton argues, that "no single mode of voicing can ever accommodate the myriad discourse situations confronting feminists." It also encourages feminists to "move among rhetorics of advocacy, possibility, and intervention . . . and imagine rhetorics that remain as yet unformulated" (240). It also recognizes, as Elizabeth Flynn observes in *Feminism Beyond Modernism,* that theories and movements represent orientations "that often overlap and intersect and that are plural rather than singular" (4). If scholars in composition were to adopt such an understanding, we might be less likely to charge that this or that scholarly project threatens to derail composition's disciplinary progress and recognize instead that "no single mode of voicing can ever accommodate the myriad discourse situations confronting" compositionists (Carlton 240).

Strategy 9: Remember that no matter how critical scholars are, we are nevertheless subject to the "bandwagon effect." Scholars sometimes like to think of ourselves as exempt from the limitations of "ordinary" people, who can be swayed by the "bandwagon effect" to vote for this or that person or party or to purchase a much-touted consumer good. But scholars are, as Burke reminds us, human—and thus as "rotten with perfection"as any man or woman we pass on the street ("Definition" 16). We may be highly resistant to commercial or political advertising, but we can nevertheless have our scholarly opinions swayed by the "bandwagon effect." For this reason, when an idea or scholarly development appears particularly obvious or "friendly," we might do well to be on our guard. In *The Social Construction of What?* Ian Hacking comments on the way theories and practices of social construction have circulated in the academy:

> Social construction has in many contexts been a truly liberating idea, but that which on first hearing has liberated some has made all too many others smug, comfortable, and trendy in ways that have become

merely orthodox. The phrase has become code. If you use it favorably, you deem yourself rather radical. If you trash the phrase, you declare that you are rational, reasonable, and respectable. (vii)

Scholars can never be free from the temptation of the "bandwagon effect." My own commitment to feminist theory in some ways demonstrates its influence, in the sense that I am predisposed to favor feminist research. We can, however, work to recognize the ways the "bandwagon effect" can influence our thinking and writing. (This is, of course, easier to do in hindsight than at the present moment.) Doing so might enable scholars to avoid the kind of pendulum swings that first valorize, and then devalue, scholarly and pedagogical projects such as the writing process movement. It might also encourage us to be more critical of the way that scholarly work in the humanities in general circulates.

As scholars, we cannot avoid valorizing some terms and projects over others. One potential criticism of *Situating Composition*, for instance, is that I have valorized teaching over research since I have directed my critique primarily toward the latter. We can, however, attempt to recognize the ways that terms and projects "hail" us and influence our thinking and writing. How can scholars benefit from various theoretical and pedagogical projects and yet remain aware of the ways these projects can "hail" us and influence our thinking and writing in ways of which we are unaware?

Strategy 10: Be realistic about what any scholarly project can accomplish given the diverse locations in which the work of composition takes place. Is it realistic to expect that the writing process movement, or any other scholarly or pedagogical project, could dramatically transform the teaching of writing in all its various sites and locations—or that it could, as Crowley argues, have "change[d] the institutional situation of composition" via a reduction in the workload of teachers and abolition of the required first-year writing requirement (*Composition* 213)? Given the many factors that influence the practice of teaching—from budgetary and other institutional and curricular constraints to the diverse nature of various student populations and the training and teaching loads of instructors—the answer to this question, I would argue, is no. If we remember that theory circulates primarily among scholars, we may develop more realistic criteria for evaluating scholarly projects than such litmus tests present. Doing so might also remind us that change or "progress" in the practice of theory often proceeds in different ways and takes different forms than it does in the practice of teaching.

Strategy 11: Explore ways of reaching a wider range of addressed and invoked audiences. Acknowledging the forums in which scholarly work does—and does not—circulate might also encourage scholars to invest more time and energy in efforts to reach a wider range of audiences. The premise here is simple. If scholars want our work to circulate more broadly than it currently does, we have to take seriously the needs and situations of diversely situated readers. It has been all too convenient for scholars in composition to blame others—teachers in the schools, or scholarly movements with which we disagree—when our work has not had the material consequences at the level of practice that we believe it should have had.

I want to be clear about my point here: in raising this issue, I am not asking scholars to water down our thinking and writing or turn away from theoretical critique. I am asking scholars to bring issues of audience and rhetorical situation more strongly into focus in our writing. Doing so might encourage us to be more attentive to the rhetoric, politics, and ethics of our *own* practices. It might also encourage scholars in composition to think creatively about genres and strategies that might reach audiences who have been resistant (or have had limited access) to scholarly work. As an example of such an effort, I would point to the *Teacher's Introduction to . . .* series published by the National Council of Teachers of English. (Sharon Crowley's *A Teacher's Introduction to Deconstruction* was published as part of this series and is a helpful and thought-provoking analysis of a complex theoretical project.) Another example of a text that attempts to meet the needs of readers who are not usually addressed in scholarly work in composition is Paul Heilker and Peter Vandenberg's *Keywords in Composition Studies.* This collection of brief discussions of keywords in the field makes scholarly work more available to those new to this work, such as teaching assistants taking required composition theory classes, and it does so without diminishing various keywords' theoretical and pedagogical complexity. Other examples of texts that productively explore alternatives to traditional scholarly argument include such literacy narratives as Mike Rose's *Lives on the Boundary,* Keith Gilyard's *Voices of the Self: A Study of Language Competence,* and Victor Villanueva's *Bootstraps: From an American Academic of Color.*

Strategy 12: Experiment with ways of expanding scholarly genres and of resisting the conventional ways that knowledge circulates in composition— but recognize the potential difficulty and complexity of such efforts. What if more scholars attempted to move back and forth from traditional scholarly work to texts intended to reach a broader audience? Would efforts such as this "count" for untenured assistant professors, or would they necessarily be limited to those who have already proven their scholarly mettle? What other revisions of scholarly practice might we productively identify? Might scholars work together to experiment with and authorize new scholarly genres—genres that interrupt the usual circulation of knowledge in composition and/or reach diverse audiences?

What might such a genre look like? As an example, I would point to the "Course Designs" articles that appear in the journal *Composition Studies*. As the description of this feature that appears on the journal's web site indicates, each course design includes the following:

- A syllabus, preferably the same document distributed to students.
- A critical statement, written specifically for journal readers, in which the author explains the course's theoretical frame and its relationship to the pedagogy announced in the syllabus.
- A statement of locale, in which the author elaborates a relationship between the course and/or its specific design and the needs, desires, or focus of the program, department, institution, community, or region in which the course is offered.
- A critical, post-course reflection on the design, in which the author assesses strengths, acknowledges weaknesses, and proposes adjustments or modifications based on outcomes. (<http://condor.depaul.edu/~compstud/cd.htm>)

As this description suggests, "Course Designs" articles disrupt the usual circulation of knowledge in composition by bringing knowledge that often circulates locally into the scholarly work of the field. They also model a way of theorizing teaching that encourages scholars to embrace theory not only in the practice of theory but also in the practice of teaching. As Roskelly and Ronald observe in *Reason to Believe: Romanticism, Pragmatism, and the Teaching of Writing,* often "teachers embrace theory wholeheartedly *in theory,* but do not use theory to reflect on or change their own classrooms or implications for re-reading literature" (17).

In an earlier draft of this chapter, I called on readers to work together to contribute to and develop such innovative scholarly practices, and mentioned others that have occurred to me over the years. (Wouldn't it be wonderful, I mused, if scholars regularly published discussions of our teaching failures?) Only later did I recognize an obvious irony: I have not contributed an article to *Composition Studies'* "Course Designs" feature— and though I once drafted the start of an article on a particularly signifi- cant teaching failure, I did not complete it.

This reflection on my own scholarly work reminds me that there is an *economics* as well as a politics, ethics, and rhetoric of scholarship in the academy. In referring to the economics of scholarly work, I hope to evoke multiple realities. One reality is of course economic in the most literal sense. There are English departments and writing programs where pub- lishers, scholarly journals, and other indicators of professional success are ranked and where the consequences of these rankings for one's sal- ary are immediately evident. In this regard, a major theoretical article in *College Composition and Communication* is "worth" more than a relatively brief contribution to *Composition Studies* "Course Designs" series when salary and merit increases are determined. But there is a more general economics at work in the academy as well. This economics says that an article, book chapter, or book that in some significant way revisions or revises previous scholarly work—contributes to a "new" understanding of this or that topic—is more important than one that explores a more local and situated practice, such as a particular course that is situated in a particular university in a particular program, department, institution, community, and region.

Scholars who wish to resist these and other conventions of the academy need to be realistic about the power that these conventions hold. Thus while I would encourage such resistance, I do not hold it out as a model that others should follow. As I know from my own experience as a coauthor, there can be a price to pay for resisting the conventions of the academy. These conventions are deeply entrenched, and the success that a limited number of scholars may have in resisting these conventions can do little to dislodge them. Thanks to the efforts of the many scholars in composi- tion who have both advocated for and modeled collaborative writing prac- tices in composition, it is now somewhat easier for those in composition who wish to write collaboratively to do so. It is important to recognize, however, that these relatively local and marginalized changes have done little to affect the most deeply and strongly held conventions of authorship in the academy. It is still generally not possible for PhD students in composition to write collaborative dissertations—though a number have argued strongly that they should be allowed to do so—and the single-authored monograph remains the "gold standard" in scholarly work.

It will take considerable effort on the part of many scholars to make even modest changes in the conventions that govern academic writing—and even then it is not clear what the consequences of such efforts might be. Nevertheless, some scholars have begun this undertaking. On numerous occasions, bell hooks has written about her determination to write scholarly books that "ordinary" people can read. As a consequence of her refusal to follow such scholarly conventions as footnoting, hooks's work has at times been challenged. In "Theory as Liberatory Practice," hooks observes that "Students at various academic institutions often complain that they cannot include my work on required reading lists for degree-oriented qualifying exams because their professors do not see it as scholarly enough" (71).

In citing hooks's practice and the price she has paid for it, I do not mean to suggest that I believe that the resistance that her (or anyone else's) writing manifests to the conventions that govern academic writing is automatically or necessarily progressive and liberating. Such a judgment is situated. While it seems praiseworthy that hooks has attempted to reach a diverse audience, readers of her work may at times wonder, as I have, whether a format and purpose that in her early years of publication seemed innovative and risk-taking have in recent years become somewhat formulaic and repetitive. Though I am sympathetic to the efforts of bell hooks, Jane Tompkins, Nancy K. Miller, and other scholars who are attempting to address broader and more diverse audiences, I recognize the limitations that at times accompany these efforts. When I read Jane Tompkins's *A Life in School: What the Teacher Learned*, for instance, I often found intimate details about Tompkins's personal relationships to be an intrusion into, rather than a helpful part of, her inquiry into her experiences as a student and teacher.

I repeat: the question of what constitutes a progressive and helpful act of resistance in the practice of theory is situated and thus cannot be determined on an *a priori* basis. Moreover, a practice that from one perspective seems progressive can reasonably be read in other ways; indeed, given our complexity as humans, it seems likely that many acts of resistance work for multiple ends.

Another example may help to clarify the situated and arguable nature of any intervention in the practice of theory. This example grows out of well-known literary scholar Sander Gilman's efforts to establish a new Humanities Laboratory at the University of Illinois at Chicago—one that would emphasize collaboration and would attempt to broaden the forms of and audiences for scholarly work. As an article by Danny Postel in the *Chronicle of Higher Education* explains, Gilman's efforts received a mixed reception from junior faculty at his university: "Junior faculty members . . . have told" Gilman "that 'this is a great idea, but we're dead if we do it.'" In the promotion and tenure process, they point out, almost every university requires a scholarly monograph, published by a peer-reviewed academic press." Such monographs must, of course, be single-authored.

As Postel explains, Gilman's response to this situation has been to "help young scholars publish their first" single-authored "books by underwriting some of the publication costs. In collaboration with the Humanities Laboratory, the University of Illinois Press plans a series of first books by faculty members on the Chicago campus." Does this underwriting effort represent a much-needed intervention into the realities of academic publishing, one that serves as a necessary "transitional step to" Gilman's "larger vision of revolutionizing the humanities"? Or does it reinforce and enable assumptions about authorship that ought to be resisted? These are questions about which scholars can reasonably disagree. Before we can do so, however, we need to raise these and related questions more often than we currently do.

Strategy 13: Draw upon your own experiences to interrogate your scholarly assumptions and practices. Such an effort might alert scholars to moments when the "perfection" of our arguments tempts us to generalize in unhelpful ways about the experiences of others. Doing so might also provide opportunities to refine or complicate our thinking in productive ways. (When Andrea Lunsford and I were working on "Representing Audience," a pivotal moment occurred when we looked at that article through the terminological screen of our personal experience and realized that we had written "Audience Addressed/Audience Invoked" out of our experiences as what we termed "academic good girls" (171), students and writers who instinctively sought approval. This insight powerfully informed our rereading of our article and caused us to see ways that our identification limited our understanding of audience.) Before we argue, in other words, that this or that teaching practice necessarily infantilizes or liberates either students or teachers, we might consider this generalization in light of our own experience. Doing so might encourage us to resist totalizing generalizations and to acknowledge the complexity of lived experience. When I think about my own experiences as a student, teacher, and writing program administrator, for instance, I am quickly reminded that there is no pedagogy that cannot be perverted—and that this "perversion" can be grounded in many sources, from a teacher's inexperience to his or her pedagogical or personal rigidity to the working conditions that constrain or enable his or her practice. I am reminded, as well, that a gifted teacher can overcome many difficulties—from personal limitations to curricular and institutional constraints to such material limitations as inadequate resources and texts—and that there is an art to effective teaching that can be informed by, but not limited to, one's consciously held pedagogical views.

In calling attention to the variable consequences of any pedagogical theory, I do not mean to suggest that scholarly theorizing on pedagogical issues is irrelevant to the practice of teaching. Rather, I want to remind readers that when theory is taken up by teachers, it is enacted in highly specific locations where a multitude of assumptions, practices, and constraints—from the personal to the institutional—are at play. What is true of the practice of teaching is also of course true for the practice of theory. Just as teachers need to develop ways in interrogating their practices, so too do scholars. While personal experience can be deployed to resist critique and to shore up one's commonsense understandings, the opposite can also be true.

Strategy 14: Particularly if you are writing about teaching, try to find ways to enact scholarly arguments at multiple levels of generalization—from the relatively specific and concrete to the more general and abstract. In *Changing the Subject in English Class,* Marshall Alcorn provides a striking example of how this strategy can help scholars clarify and enrich their arguments, and he does so via an analysis of a response that James Berlin once made to Alcorn's critique of his work. Before discussing this example, however, I would like to clarify the nature of Alcorn's general project. In *Changing the Subject,* Alcorn argues that those who take a cultural studies approach to composition, such as Berlin, have often adopted "an insufficiently complex understanding of subjectivity" and that "This oversimplification hinders our ability to make progress in cultural change" (2). Alcorn argues that he doesn't want so much to challenge the work of Berlin and others as to "take up the discussion that Berlin began" so Alcorn can "connect the political aspirations of composition more thoroughly to psychological goals" that Alcorn believes "are important for both writing and political justice" (3).

As part of this effort, Alcorn reconsiders Berlin's "Poststructuralism, Cultural Studies, and the Composition Classroom: Postmodern Theory in Practice." Alcorn observes that his analysis in *Changing the Subject* in many respects follows that of an article he submitted to *Rhetoric Review* in 1995. He points out as well the role that Berlin, serving as an anonymous reviewer for that journal, played in helping him to formulate his thesis. Here is his description of that experience as described in the conclusion of his 1995 article. (This conclusion is reprinted in *Changing the Subject.*)

> This article has had a somewhat unusual history in going to press. My present essay begins with the claim: "If Berlin had allowed his description of classroom behavior to become more fully integrated with his theoretical claims, he might have been prompted to formulate a more Lacanian description of the subject that would lead, I believe, to more useful ideas both for negotiating the ideological conflicts generated in the classroom and for achieving the cognitive power which Berlin seeks." When I originally wrote this sentence it was a hypothetical claim, responding to an anonymous reader's suggestion for sharpening the focus of my argument. I accepted this suggestion as essentially correct without worry about much more than the ability of the sentence to reflect my understanding of Berlin's essay and my desire to summarize the argument I wanted to developed.
>
> What I did not know at the time was that the reviewer who suggested this wording was in fact James Berlin himself. (*Changing the Subject* 23–24)

Alcorn goes on to say that Berlin argued strongly that Alcorn's essay should be published and offered to write a response that could appear with Alcorn's essay. Unfortunately, Berlin died before he could write this response.

In *Changing the Subject,* Alcorn argues that Berlin is correct in diagnosing a significant problem in the argument of his essay. If Berlin had explored his ideas on multiple levels of generalization—from reflections on classroom experiences to theoretical critique—he might have recognized, Alcorn argues, that his argument "describe[s] a constructed subject in theory but a free subject in classroom practice" (12). Berlin is, I would argue, hardly the only scholar in composition who would benefit from staging his argument at multiple levels of generalization and from interrogating his ideas vis-à-vis his own experiences as a teacher.

There is another reason why it might be helpful for scholars who are writing about teaching—at least those scholars who hope to reach an audience not only of other scholars but also of classroom teachers—to develop our ideas via multiple levels of generalization and abstraction: doing so might make our work more relevant to the teachers we wish to reach. As I have argued earlier, I am not suggesting that we turn away from difficult and complex ideas and arguments. Rather, I am suggesting that we take the interests and needs of these teachers seriously and attempt more often than we currently do to write in ways that speak *to* rather than *for* or *about* teachers. Since, as I suggested in chapter 5, teachers may well hold different understandings of the real, the good, and the possible than scholars do, we might—if we want genuinely to communicate with teachers—at least gesture toward these understandings in our writing.

Given the diversity of research in composition, not all scholars are engaged in writing projects of potential relevance to classroom teachers. If it is not already clear that I value this research and do not believe my advice is relevant to it, I want to make that point now. I also want to acknowledge that there are multiple ways that scholars can demonstrate their respect for and interest in teaching (and in such related subjects as writing program administration) to readers. Some recent studies that strike me as successful in doing so include Elizabeth Boquet's *Noise from the Writing Center,* Russell Durst's *Collision Course: Conflict, Negotiation, and Learning in College Composition,* Katharine Haake's *What Our Speech Disrupts: Feminism and Creative Writing Studies,* Kay Halasek's *A Pedagogy of Possibility: Bakhtinian Perspectives on Composition Studies,* Anne Herrington and Marcia Curtis's *Persons in Process: Four Stories of Writing and Personal Development in College,* Paul Kameen's *Writing/Teaching: Essays Toward a Rhetoric of Pedagogy,* Barbara Kamler's *Relocating the Personal: A Critical Writing Pedagogy,* Karen Surman Paley's *I Writing: The Politics and Practice of Teaching First-Person Writing,* Marilyn Sternglass's *Time to Know Them: A Longitudinal Study of Writing and Learning at the College Level;* David Wallace and Helen Rothschild Ewald's *Mutuality in the Rhetoric and Composition Classroom,* and Nancy Welch's *Getting Restless: Rethinking Revision in Writing Instruction.*

This is a diverse group of scholarly studies that employ a variety of methods to connect theoretical analysis with the life of the classroom—and also at times with the authors' embodied experiences. The positions that these authors take vary considerably, but all are clearly looking for ways to connect the practice of theory with the practice of teaching and (in the case of studies devoted to writing center work) of tutoring. I find it heartening that so much work along these lines has been undertaken in recent years. I include this work here both to call attention to it—some of these studies have received a strong scholarly reception and circulated broadly in the field; others have not—and to make the point that there is much work already underway in composition that explicitly or implicitly addresses the concerns that I raise here.

Strategy 15: Whatever your project, try to keep in mind the power that scholars hold to map, name, and establish agendas. This is an issue that Adrienne Rich addresses in "Notes Toward a Politics of Location," and it is one that bell hooks also takes up in "Theory as Liberatory Practice," where hooks observes that

> the privileged act of naming often affords those in power access to modes of communication and enables them to project an interpretation, a definition, a description of their work and actions, that may not be accurate, that may obscure what is really taking place. (62)

This is not a problem that scholars can retheorize away. As scholars, we cannot undertake our work without mapping, naming, and establishing agendas. We can, however, be more cognizant of the multiple, and potentially contradictory, tensions and contradictions that power holds.

On Practicing Theory and Theorizing Practice

The preceding reflections—and much of this book—have focused primarily on the practice of theory in composition. Because my effort to think through practice has influenced not only my thinking about the practice of theory but also my understanding and enactment of the practice of teaching, I want to discuss this subject, however briefly, here.

Thinking through practice about my teaching has, for instance, helped me to find ways to resist an unproductive tendency to mistake form for content in my teaching. As a scholar heavily invested in theories and practices of collaborative learning and collaborative writing, for instance, I have too often mistaken external aspects of my classroom situation— Are we sitting in a circle? Am I discussing this or that issue or reading with students and not lecturing?—with more key features. Rather than worrying about whether we are sitting in a circle, for instance, I might more helpfully ask myself who speaks in my classroom, how often, and for what purpose? And who writes, and for what purpose?

Thinking through practice about my teaching has been simultaneously a profoundly rewarding—but also at times disorienting—experience. The more I think through practice about collaborative learning and writing, for instance, the harder I find it is to first recognize and then evaluate these practices. Doing so was easy when I focused on external, observable aspects of my teaching—when I conducted as many classes as I possibly could in seminar formats, with students and myself awkwardly arranging our chairs in a large and unwieldy circle. I do not want to suggest that observable characteristics of a classroom such as these are irrelevant—but I still remember what I learned when, as part of a peer review, I visited the classroom of a colleague whose teaching students praised highly. In this class, my colleague stood in the front of the class: in this sense the class looked traditional. But when I paid attention to the conversational turns that my colleague and her students took, I realized that what counted was not how my colleague and her students were configured but who felt empowered to speak. When my colleague left her class early so I could talk with students about their experience, this observation was confirmed. "This is a class where I feel that I can say whatever I think," one student said. "This is a class where my professor respects me as a person," another added. I had to acknowledge that in my colleague's class, I observed students who felt freer to disagree with their teacher, or to raise questions that interested them (but had not even occurred to her) than in my own classes.

This was a powerful understanding. Another powerful understanding came to me when I began attempting to look at my classes not from my perspective but rather from that of my students. Though I couldn't have quite articulated it this way then, this was an early effort to consider my teaching not from the perspective of theory but rather from the perspective of practice. I wanted to learn more, in other words, about what the practice of my teaching was telling students about my goals as a teacher, rather than what my explicit theorizing was expressing.

This effort to focus on my practice as a teacher, as well as on the theories that undergird my practice, quickly reminded me that in an important sense, what I *do* as a teacher is at least as important to students as what I *say* at the level of explicit theory. I may talk eloquently about the power and benefits of collaborative learning and writing, but if I fail to enact this understanding moment-by-moment, assignment-by-assignment in my teaching, my students will quickly recognize the contradiction—and they will believe what I do, not what I say. In this regard, when I teach, as when I write scholarly articles and books, practice makes practice.

This recognition has encouraged me to give greater attention to the performative and situated nature of teaching. It has encouraged me, in other words, to attempt to devise ways to demonstrate my theoretically grounded pedagogical intentions to my students. Here is an example of such a demonstration. As a teacher interested in collaborative learning and writing, I want my students to experience the benefits of working together. I want to disrupt the circulation of knowledge as it operates in most classes, where the teacher's knowledge and/or skills go from her to the students, and the students' knowledge and skills return solely to the teacher. Since just about every aspect of the educational system—but especially grading—works to keep the conventional circulation of knowledge in place, I realize that if I want to disrupt this cycle I must do so quickly and decisively.

Hence the brief writing assignment that now begins many of my classes. The specific nature of this assignment varies. In advanced composition, students write a literacy narrative. In the composition theory classes that I teach, they write a personally grounded exploration of the topic they hope to focus on in their seminar paper. In all cases, however, students know that on the day that the essay is due, they will bring enough copies of their essay (which is limited to a single page of single-spaced, double-sided text) for the rest of the class, that we will assemble their essays as our first class "book," and that this book will comprise one of the early readings for the course. They know as well that on the day that we will discuss our "book"—and we spend one entire course period doing so—they must bring a brief response (two to three sentences is fine) to each of their peers' essays to class. When students distribute these

209

responses to their peers, the energy in the room is palpable—as is the controlled chaos as students mill about the room passing them out. After all the responses are distributed and students begin reading what their peers have written about their essay, there is always an intense, focused period of silence as students digest these comments.

I don't want to make any great claims for this assignment, which is hardly original and which represents only a momentary act of resistance to the conventional way knowledge circulates in my classroom. I am, after all, still the teacher—and, perhaps more importantly in students' eyes— still the grader in our classroom. I do believe, however, that this assignment at least partly succeeds in demonstrating to students that I want the circulation of knowledge in our classroom to differ from that of more traditional classes. Though the effect of this assignment varies from class to class—seeming more powerful in some classes, less so in others—students typically voice their pleasure in having the opportunity to read what others have written. Most students comment that they have never before had the opportunity to read all other students' responses to an assignment. Often, they refer to essays that appear in our class "book" throughout the term, so that they become a continuing motif in the class.[4]

I have just used the word pleasure in relation to my students' experience of our first assignment—and this reminds me that a second major shift as I have attempted to think through practice about my teaching is a greater concern for affect in both learning and teaching. This concern is expressed in several ways. Perhaps the most important has to do with my increased recognition that students' resistance to various readings and assignments—and, sometimes, to the general project of theory itself— is an opportunity for *my* learning, and that I can use this resistance in productive ways in my teaching if my students and I can develop a classroom culture where students feel that they can safely articulate it.

At times, my effort to think through and understand students' resistance has caused me to make significant changes in my teaching. This is certainly the case with my approach to collaborative writing assignments. As a scholar who regularly writes collaboratively, and as an advocate of collaborative writing, I very much want my students to experience the benefits of collaboration. In the past, I have regularly required students to coauthor at least one essay for a class—a practice that most students strenuously resisted. Once I credited this resistance as arguable and worked hard to understand it, I recognized that by insisting that students experience explicit coauthorship, I was failing to acknowledge a number of legitimate difficulties that students faced in doing so.[5] Moreover, I was failing to take advantage of opportunities to help students experience the implicit benefits of collaboration.

I am now less likely to require that students coauthor a project. Instead, I attempt to find ways to help students experience the benefits of collaboration with less risk. The brief writing assignment that serves as an early text for many of the classes that I teach is an example of such an effort. Another assignment engages groups of students in the collaborative process of choosing a reading to which all students write individual response essays. Students meet first to choose a reading, and then again to discuss it. Students then meet a third time to discuss the approach that each student plans to take in his or her response to the reading; they work together to troubleshoot potential strengths and limitations of each student's approach. Students then draft their essays, which they bring to a group meeting for peer response. Before submitting their individual essays to me, group members write a collaborative letter describing and evaluating their group effort.[6]

I still at times find myself thinking that if I were a better, more creative teacher, I would somehow find a way to develop required collaborative writing assignments that would work. (And, yes, I recognize the vagueness inherent in the term "work.") Assignments such as the one I have just described represent my current compromise. In the case of this assignment, my hope is that the process of working together on their essays demonstrates the powerful role that collaboration can play in writing, while giving students a sense of safety and of control. I do know that as I have backed off from requiring major (and thus from students' perspective, high risk) collaborative writing assignments and attempted to find other ways to help students experience the benefits of collaboration, more students have taken advantage of the statement on my syllabus that informs them that they always have the option of writing any essay collaboratively. The number of students who do so is small in comparison with the larger number of students in the course—but the fact that they have chosen to collaborate seems significant.

By thinking through practice about my teaching, then, I have learned that collaboration can take more forms than I had previously realized, and that I need to think in complex ways about how best to enact my own desire that students experience its benefits. Thinking through practice about my teaching has also helped me learn to be more explicit in articulating my intentions for various courses and to recognize that any course in effect represents a negotiation between the interests and desires that both the students and the teacher bring to a class. Here, for instance, is the description of the major assignments for Current Composition Theory, a 400/500 (senior/MA level) class that I sometimes teach. The texts for this class, which I most recently taught during spring term of 2002, were Russell Durst's *Collision Course: Conflict, Negotiation, and Learning in College Composition,* Joseph Harris's *A Teaching Subject: Composition since 1966,* Victor Villanueva's *Cross-Talk in Comp Theory,* and Paul Heilker and Peter Vandenberg's *Keywords in Composition Studies.* Following the description of the assignments—and also appearing on the syllabus—is an explanation of the logic of the course design.

Major assignments:

Journal of informal writing and learning activities: 20% of final course grade

The majority of your journal entries will take the form of responses to prompts I give you at the start of each class. These entries should be written after you've done the reading for the next day's class, and you should bring your entry to class. Upon occasion, there will be additional entries. You'll write a prospectus for your seminar paper, for instance, which will be part of your journal. At the midterm and end of term I'll ask you to review and introduce your journal. Using a rubric that I have developed, you will also grade your journal.

I-search essay on the topic of your seminar paper: 20% of final course grade

I'm using the term "I-search" loosely here, as I'll explain in class. Basically, this essay will provide an opportunity for you to engage the topic of your seminar paper via your personal experience. My hope is that this kind of personally grounded engagement will give added richness and passion to your seminar paper, as well as providing questions for you to consider as you research and write about your topic. This essay should be one single-spaced, double-sided page long and will be photocopied and shared with the rest of the class. We will discuss our class "book" early in the term.

Entering-the-conversation paper: 20% of final course grade

This assignment is designed to help you engage more fully with the topic of your seminar paper, while also encouraging you to make timely progress on it. As the title of this assignment indicates, your concern in this paper is with entering the scholarly conversation on your topic. Later I will give you a more detailed assignment sheet, but for now you may find it helpful to know that you will organize your paper around these headings: 1) Description of your topic and discussion of its significance; 2) Relationship of your topic to your intellectual, gendered, academic, literate, cultural, professional, and perhaps even your emotional development; 3) Conception of your topic and of the methodology you will use to explore it; 4) Results of your inquiry thus far; 5) Plan of work; 6) Annotated bibliography. Suggested page length: 8–10 pages not counting the annotated bibliography.[7]

Seminar paper: 40% of final course grade

This is the final project for the course and builds on the previous two assignments. There needs to be a research-based component to your seminar paper, but the nature of that research and the form your paper might take can vary considerably. Research could include not only library research but such field methods as interviews and observations. Although some students' seminar papers may take the form of relatively traditional academic essays, others might be more personal—and even experimental—in nature. You can also direct your project to a specific audience. A teaching assistant writing about how to respond effectively to student essays might develop a "best practices" guide for other graduate students, for instance.

Some thoughts about these assignments

We will discuss these assignments more fully in class, but for now you might think of them as representing my effort to negotiate the demands of the class with you. My strongest goal for our class is that you engage the readings and class discussions as fully and deeply as you can. In order to facilitate this engagement, I have limited our readings to four texts, one of which (*Keywords*) serves primarily as a resource. These texts cannot convey the many conversations that make up current composition theory, but they can give you a sense of what it means to theorize about the teaching of writing. Such theorizing encourages you to step back from your commonsense understanding of teaching and writing and pose questions that can help you make effective choices as you teach. And this ability is what I hope you will take away from this class. One way I have attempted to negotiate the demands of our class with you, then, is to limit the readings, so you can have time to engage them. In order to emphasize the importance of this engagement, I am asking you to complete informal write-to-learn assignments, which as your journal will constitute 20% of your final course grade. As our syllabus explains, I will provide prompts for this informal writing. In most cases, you'll be able to choose from among a series of prompts.

You don't have a choice in the readings, and you have limited choices in the topics of your journal entries. I have tried to balance these restrictions by giving you as much choice as possible with the remaining assignments. As the syllabus indicates, these assignments are linked. The topic of these assignments is, moreover, open not only to multiple subjects but also to multiple approaches. So here, in a nutshell, is my vision of how I hope we can negotiate the demands of this class. In return for your serious engagement with the course readings and class discussions, I am offering you considerable latitude in the assignments that make up 80% of the course grade.

As with the assignment that I shared earlier, I make no special claim for this assignment sequence. Those teaching courses like Current Composition Theory often ask students to complete seminar papers, and I can hardly be the first teacher to have experimented with linking this paper to earlier assignments. I have included this assignment sequence because I want to try to articulate the role that thinking through practice has played in my teaching.

Though I do believe that my effort to think through practice about my teaching has improved my teaching, I do not claim to be an exemplary teacher. Indeed, I am so aware that my assignments and other teaching practices are anything but inventive or extraordinary that I almost did not discuss them here. I did so because I want to encourage myself and others to find ways of making our teaching more visible in our scholarly work. I also hope that this discussion of my teaching demonstrates that thinking through practice can be helpful to teachers as well as to scholars. In my case, doing so helped me, I believe, to tap back into certain commonsense understandings of teaching that I had come dangerously close to forgetting, such as the powerful role that affect plays in learning and the need to provide an environment where risks and challenges to students are in some way balanced with opportunities for safety and individual control. It also encouraged me to be more attentive to the politics of my location in my classroom.

As a teacher, I continue to have many questions and concerns. When I teach composition theory classes, for instance, I worry that I am not rigorous enough in my expectations, particularly in terms of the amount of reading that I require. I have at times exchanged syllabi with colleagues teaching similar courses at other universities, and even when I factor in the reduced number of weeks available on the ten-week term that my university follows, I am typically asking students to read fewer texts than these colleagues are asking. Particularly in the case of MA students who want to continue on for their PhD, am I hindering these students' development?

I also worry that the assignment sequence that I have just described gives students too much choice. The freedom to work on a topic of individual interest has obvious benefits, but it has disadvantages as well. Graduate students who are in their first term or first year of teaching writing will generally choose topics that are of most immediate concern to them, such as the question of how best to respond to student writing, the role that personal narratives should play in first-year writing classes, how best to teach revision, and the nature of voice in writing. If only because they are first learning about them in my course, few choose to inquire into political and ideological issues that many scholars in the field find central to current debates.

As a teacher, I must constantly inquire into my practices, asking myself questions and making decisions. How do I decide when I should learn from students' resistance, revising my teaching practices accordingly? How do I decide when to in effect resist students' resistance, as I often do? These are questions I wrestle with continually.

Some Concluding Reflections and Questions

As a teacher, I have learned to live with questions and with doubts, knowing that the moment I think I know for certain how to teach this or that course is the moment when I am most dangerously close to shutting down as a teacher. As a teacher and as a scholar, I must constantly inquire into my practices—paradoxically somehow both believing in and doubting them—if I am to continue to grow. Even if I wanted to, I could not undertake this ongoing inquiry alone, for as Hannah Arendt has observed, "For excellence . . . the presence of others is always required" (49). This is true for me as a teacher—and it is true for me as a scholar as well.

As I begin this concluding section of *Situating Composition,* I want to encourage others to share insights they have gained as a result of inquiring into their own practices. Some of these insights will undoubtedly conflict with or challenge my own. I invite such alternate perspectives, for I know that they will enrich my understanding. In the remaining pages of this chapter (and book), I want to explore some additional issues that grow out of my inquiry into the politics of location in composition. This effort has led me to call for greater self-reflexivity and modesty on the part of scholars in composition, and to urge scholars to explore alternatives to the agonistic rhetoric that at times has played such a powerful role in our arguments. It has led me, as well, to suggest that if scholars would attempt more often to think *through* practice—recognizing that practice makes practice—we might be less likely to enact some of the problems and limitations in the practice of theory that I have described throughout this study. We might be less likely, for instance, to develop "killer" dichotomies that encourage wholesale rejections of past practices and uncritical acceptance of current efforts. We might be more aware of the situated and partial nature of our own understandings—

which might encourage scholars both to take greater care when we speak for others and to work harder to identify unexpected openings and alliances with those who are diversely situated in the work of composition.

While I believe that the changes I have just described would be helpful, I do not mean to suggest that scholarly work would somehow be transformed as a result. In this regard, I will say one final time that I am not calling for revolutionary changes in the practice of theory in composition. Rather, I am calling for greater attention to the diverse ways any scholarly practice can be deployed, and the potentially diverse consequences of any such practice. If we remind ourselves that practice makes practice, we are more likely to recognize the socially constructed nature of all practices, including our own. Doing so might remind scholars of the potential value of reading both against and with the grain of these practices and of attending to the politics of our location in the academy.

What I propose is no easy task. (Indeed, from a Burkean perspective, it is literally an impossible task, for if we work to "perfect" some aspects of our scholarly work, we inevitably obscure other aspects.) It is difficult indeed both to advance an argument and to reflect on and critique that argument at the same time. I can easily imagine instances where undertaking the latter might imperil—or be irrelevant to—the former. The same holds true for my attempt to question conventional disciplinary assumptions about and enactments of progress in composition. As I argued in chapter 5, scholars in composition—as other scholars in the academy—must hold to some notion of progress, even as we critique its immersion in Enlightenment and modernist values. Moreover, scholars need ways to identify our allegiance to certain assumptions and practices and to challenge others.

How can we acknowledge these identifications and inquire into the validity and helpfulness of various assumptions and practices without dramatically oversimplifying or in other ways significantly distorting them? As Lynn Worsham observes in "On the Rhetoric of Theory in the Discipline of Writing: A Comment and a Proposal," "the struggle for power in a discipline is always a struggle to define its limits and boundaries, a struggle to possess the legitimate terms of recognition and representation" (394). Given our human nature and its "rotten with perfection" state, the basic terms of this struggle are unlikely to change. Can scholars nevertheless undertake this struggle with greater care, both for the articulation of our arguments and also for their consequences for those who are diversely situated in the work of composition?

As I have argued at various points in this study, composition cannot return to a predisciplinary, preprofessional past. Nor, I believe, can it enact a thoroughly postdisciplinary, postprofessional future. How can scholars in composition work together to inquire into the ethics, politics, rhetoric, and economics of our situation? In raising this question, I do not mean to suggest that others should be excluded from this inquiry; scholars have a good deal to learn from voices that are not often heard— and we might do well to attempt to create more space for these voices. Rather, I do so to emphasize that given the privilege of our academic location, scholars might do more to, in Rich's terms, hold ourselves accountable for our practices.

How can scholars whose primary identification and location is with the practice of theory forge productive connections with and learn from those who identify primarily with the practice of teaching? How can we contribute to—and learn from—teachers' ongoing efforts to increase their own knowledge and skills, and those of their students? What form might these efforts most productively take?

In the May 1988 issue of *CCC*, Lucille Schultz, Chester Laine, and Mary Savage discussed questions such as these in an article titled "Interaction among School and College Writing Teachers: Toward Recognizing and Remaking Old Patterns." The authors begin their article by commenting on current efforts on the part of college writing teachers to explore "options for collaborating with secondary school teachers about the teaching of writing" (139). As examples of these efforts, they point to the numerous sites of the National Writing Project, as well as to a number of other collaborations. And yet, the authors note, "much of this work has been marked by acrimony, and the projects have often been less than successful" (141). After considering some historical examples of these efforts, the authors argue that for more productive change to occur, teachers of writing need "to move toward an understanding of school-college interaction as a complex cultural phenomenon in which writing teachers in both groups are more than likely acting in response to the options allowed them by their respective cultures" (144).

One way to do so, the authors argue, is to acknowledge the differential access that teachers in the public schools and teachers in colleges and universities have to "time, material goods," and "rewards" (145). These differences are surely one of the primary reasons that efforts to collaborate between college and secondary writing teachers founder, the authors observe. After all, "daily routines, career patterns, and rewards are so organized that they can militate against joint action, and both cultures may espouse barely hidden beliefs which are fundamentally incompatible with an authentic collaborative effort" (149). Schultz, Laine, and Savage argue that those who want to undertake productive collaborations will need to find ways to first represent and then reflect upon factors such as these, and they offer the following recommended critical practices. (The references included in several of these practices are to studies cited in the article's bibliography.)

1. The encouragement of autobiographical and biographical writing accounts by participants in such projects to reflect on their formation in their cultural scenes and project alternatives (Traver 443–52);
2. The use of stories and rituals to highlight incongruities ordinarily obscured by asymmetrical relations within a collaborative project (Pitman 31–32);
3. The conscious exploration of limnality, the recognition that persons on the margins of a society are pregnant with possibilities for transforming that society (Pitman 24, 30–31; Miller 3–12); college writing teachers, for example, who lead a kind of marginal existence in many English departments, may be crucial agents for transforming the isolated and hierarchical character of academic knowledge;
4. The conscious search for the kinds of coalitions between token and marginalized persons which precipitate change (Pitman 30); the fact that writing instruction is devalued in the academy and that both writing teachers and high school teachers tend to be women may be a source of strength in this regard;
5. The encouragement of "neighborliness," a teacher from one culture working for the sake of teachers in another culture as an agent for transforming consciousness about writing as a transformative social act (Savage 8–17). (151)

I have quoted here this list of "initiatives for critical practice" (150) because they strike me as powerful and thought-provoking; those differently situated in the work of composition might use these suggestions to begin to explore the ways practice makes practices—and as a result

create openings for dialogue and, possibly, change. The authors' suggestion that autobiographical and biographical narratives might enable
those engaged in collaborative efforts "to reflect on their formation in
their cultural scenes and project alternatives," for instance, suggests a
potentially radical use for personal narration, which is criticized by some
scholars as expressivist or in other ways insufficiently sociopolitical. The
same is true of their advocacy of the "use of stories and rituals to highlight incongruities ordinarily obscured by asymmetrical relations within
a collaborative project" (151).

I include these suggested critical practices as well because they raise a
number of difficult questions in my mind. These suggested critical practices encourage both scholars and teachers to attend more carefully than
we have in the past to the politics of our locations. And yet as I read the
scholarly work of composition, it seems to me that scholars have generally not followed up on these authors' suggestions. Admittedly, these
suggestions are directed toward those engaged in school-college collaborations, but they strike me as having potentially broader implications and
applications. Rather than writing arguments that speak *for* teachers of
writing, for instance, why haven't more scholars attempted to establish
dialogue *with* teachers by reflecting on our formation in cultural or disciplinary scenes? Such might be a helpful and even necessary first step
in embarking on more productive textual and material interactions with
teachers. Why have we not done more to recognize the potential intellectual and disciplinary contributions of teachers and instead have at
times represented these teachers as working at "site[s] for the discipline
of punishment" (Lewiecki-Wilson and Sommers 439)?

Why has it seemed commonsensical and obvious to many that rather
than considering such issues as our relationship with teachers, we should
instead take a broader and more general political turn, one that encourages scholars to work to effect significant political change in our society
at large? Why has this broader political effort, which is demonstrably even
more demanding than the kind of collaborations that Schultz, Laine, and
Savage hope to enable, seemed so much more important to scholars?
What might the turn toward politics *in theory* but the continuation of
business-as-usual in the politics of location *in practice* reveal to scholars
about our own impulses and desires?

This is a difficult question for me to pose, for I have largely shared the
utopian vision—and I will claim it as utopian—that Patricia Bizzell,

James Berlin, John Trimbur, Min-Zhan Lu, Bruce Horner, and others have so eloquently advocated for composition. This is a vision that puts composition at the center of efforts to, as Bizzell observes in the afterword to *Academic Discourse and Critical Consciousness,* "find more ways to promote social justice—that is, at least, to work against economic inequality and rampant hatred of difference" (283). I believe in the value of this effort, one that can be forwarded only if significant numbers of teachers of writing join with scholars in pursuing this goal. But I am troubled by my awareness that a project focused on raising *teachers'* critical consciousness about the need for general political change has generally not been accompanied by an awareness of the need to attend to such issues as the ways that *scholars* represent and speak for teachers of composition.

Another difficult question involves the attention that scholars have—and have not—given to the actual teaching of writing in recent years. In "How I Teach Writing: How to Teach Writing? To Teach Writing?," for instance, Susan Miller observes that "composition's successes, in my experience, have generated less and less discussion of teaching writing among those who have gotten 'up'" and that "few discussions of writing pedagogy take it for granted that one of our goals is to teach how to write" (480). Why has so little scholarly attention been paid to the actual teaching of writing in recent years? Such work certainly exists, but in many cases, this work does not circulate as powerfully in the field as does more theoretical work. And what role should attention to the products of writing play in the teaching of writing? Should we be concerned that, as Joseph Harris observes in "Beyond Community: From the Social to the Material," "an increasing interest in the workings of power" in scholarly work in composition "seems often to have been accompanied by a decreasing attention to the workings of texts" (7)?

These are for me real questions, not rhetorical questions. I want to close this study with some additional questions, for if *Situating Composition* contributes to the scholarly work of composition, it does so at least in part by raising questions that others find meaningful. The following, then, are questions that I have found heuristic as I have attempted to read both with and against the grain of the scholarly work of composition during the last thirty years:

What narratives about its mission and development have scholars in composition tended to construct? What gaps or contradictions might a different reading of these narratives reveal? Why, for instance, have scholars found it convenient to emphasize the role that the writing process movement played in composition's professionalization, while commenting little on the role that the project that we have come to call basic writing played in helping establish the field during this same time period? Concerns about basic writing led to the development of many important programs and initiatives, a number of which played both direct and indirect roles in composition's professionalization. Yet in comparison with the writing process movement, this role has been much less recognized. Moreover, currently research on basic writing is marginalized within composition—as are a number of other scholarly and pedagogical projects—and debate over the fate of basic writing programs, many of which are under attack, has circulated only in limited ways in the practice of theory. What might this marginalization tell scholars about our own predilections and desires? How can we distinguish between a kind of forgetting that is powered by ideologies of the new and an appropriate moving on from one scholarly and pedagogical project to another?

What have scholars in composition at times found it convenient to ignore? In *Radical Departures: Composition and Progressive Pedagogy,* Chris Gallagher notes one potential candidate, writing program administration. As Gallagher observes, "institutional resources are typically allocated to compositionists as a result of an unspoken but mutually understood bargain"—the agreement that most if not all scholars in composition will direct first-year and other writing programs (110). As I have argued elsewhere in this study, based on my personal experience, I have benefited in important ways from my experiences as a writing program administrator. Not all in such positions feel this way, however. Why is this mutually understood bargain so little discussed in the practice of theory? What else might scholars in composition have found it convenient to ignore?

What have scholars typically viewed as oxymorons, contradictions in terms?[8] Thanks to the efforts of Susan Miller and others, scholars are aware of the extent to which the term "student writer" has functioned as an oxymoron. But what other oxymorons might we identify? Teacher researcher? Writing program administrator scholar? Something else?

What obsessions might scholars in composition be said to have?[9] To what extent have scholars engaged in theoretical critique been caught up in what Judith Butler, John Guillory, and Kendall Thomas refer to in the introduction to *What's Left of Theory? New Work on the Politics of Literary*

Theory as "projects of purity" (x)? Might scholars' desire to control the consequences of the teaching of writing for students represent another obsession? What is a scholar like Geoffrey Sirc assuming when he argues that teachers of writing "can allow students the seduction of texts in a carnival classroom, or we can train them to create writing that can be used in the production and marketing of bombs"? (*English Composition* 225). Sirc's dichotomous claim is admittedly extreme—but he is hardly the only scholar in composition to leave students' own goals out of the equation when talking about the teaching of writing or to assume that students will learn, and experience our writing classes, on our terms, rather than on their own. To what extent have scholars been obsessed with directing and controlling students' learning in writing classes? How can we differentiate between the reasonable desire to set goals for our teaching and the desire to control aspects of students' learning that might best be left to students to determine?

In what ways have scholars paradoxically desired both to claim—and to escape—composition's location in the academy? We have been highly motivated to achieve disciplinary and professional success, and in many respects we have done so. But to what extent have scholars attempted to "escape" composition's pedagogical location in the academy? How can scholars in composition best understand our field's traditional commitment to the teaching of first-year and other writing courses? How can scholars hold on to our utopian goals for composition—goals that are directed toward broad social, political, and cultural change—without allowing these goals to distance us in unhelpful ways from the scene of writing and teaching? What unexpected alliances and opportunities might we see if scholars could unsettle conventional hierarchies of theory and practice in composition?

What does it mean, after all, to enact progress in a field that is committed to pedagogical, as well as scholarly, progress?

NOTES
WORKS CITED
INDEX

NOTES

Preface

1. Oregon State University is a Research I university; the majority of such universities offer PhDs in most academic departments. Oregon State University is an exception. When I arrived in 1980, there were no MA or PhD programs in the humanities. In the years since, a number of departments, including the English department, have developed MA programs—and two or three now offer PhDs. The majority of PhD programs at Oregon State are in the sciences, business, and applied sciences.

1. What Are We Talking about When We Talk about Composition?

1. Some of the scenarios I present portray repeated and ongoing experiences. Though the first scenario evokes (as all the scenarios do) a particular experience, in my current teaching, most graduate students continue to be intimidated by "theory." Other scenarios, such as the third and fifth scenarios, represent experiences that time has altered. The Center for Writing and Learning survived the budget crisis that I describe in the third scenario, for instance; currently, we have an adequate recurring budget. (My dean's comment about the protection that my scholarly work provides the center does, I believe, still obtain.) The situation in regard to the fifth scenario has changed as well. This past spring, when faculty in my department worked together to expand our web pages for various areas, the senior scholar in literature and culture included my name on a list of faculty members with expertise in this area.

2. All tenure-line faculty in my department teach one or more "service" or general education courses as part of our teaching assignment. Our required first-year writing course is, of course, also a service course, but because the introduction to fiction class enrolls sixty to seventy students, while our first-year writing courses are limited to twenty-seven students, tenure-line faculty teach the introductory literature classes and graduate teaching assistants teach first-year writing.

3. In this regard, it is no accident that the first two faculty members to direct the Center for Excellence in Teaching, Learning, and Research in the College of Liberal Arts at Oregon State University were faculty in composition studies.

4. For a related discussion of the ways composition's professionalization has required a disciplinary division of labor, one that tends to "disappear" the work of those in such areas as ESL, see Matsuda.

5. Even Sirc's study is organized around a central motif of composition's professionalization—only in Sirc's case, he laments rather than praises this development. Other studies that question composition's commitment to traditional academic disciplinarity include Gallagher's *Radical Departures: Composition and Progressive Pedagogy* and Horner's *Terms of Work for Composition: A Materialist Critique*.

6. For a discussion of this and related issues, see Richard E. Miller's *As If Learning Mattered: Reforming Higher Education.*

2. Situating Myself—And My Argument

1. As I will explain later in this study, I am not opposed to local inquiries into the benefits and disadvantages of required first-year writing courses at specific sites but question the helpfulness of efforts to determine this issue at a national level.

2. In making this point, I do not mean to devalue much important work done previous to this time—work that made the consolidation and legitimation that both composition and feminism experienced in the academy in the 1970s and 1980s possible.

3. For another assessment of the strengths and limitations of Rich's formulation, see Kirsch and Ritchie.

4. This perspective on location is shared by scholars in critical geography. For an introduction to research in critical geography and its potential application to composition see Johnathon Mauk's "Location, Location, Location: The 'Real' (E)states of Being, Writing, and Thinking in Composition" and Nedra Reynolds's "Composition's Imagined Geographies: The Politics of Space in the Frontier, City, and Cyberspace."

3. Paradigms Lost: The Writing Process Movement and the Professionalization of Composition

1. The first paragraph of this article gives a good sense of its inflammatory rhetoric:

> If your children are attending college, the chances are that when they graduate they will be unable to write ordinary, expository English with any real degree of structure and lucidity. If they are in high school and planning to attend college, the chances are even less than even that they will be able to write English at the minimal college level when they get there. If they are not planning to attend college, their skills in writing English may not even qualify them for secretarial or clerical work. And if they are attending elementary school, they are almost certainly not being given the kind of required reading material, much less writing instruction that might make it pos-

sible for them eventually to write comprehensible English. Willy-nilly, the U.S. educational system is spawning a generation of semiliterates. (58)

The article cites declining test scores as evidence for assertions such as these. It also attacks such diverse projects as an emphasis on teaching creativity in writing in the 1960s, the influence of structural linguistics, and the CCCC's 1974 "Students' Rights to Their Own Language" resolution. The article does not mention the fact that during this time period many students who previously would not have attended college were doing so under "open admissions" policies at various universities. It did not recognize, in other words, that test scores might reflect not a decline in the literacy skills of all students but rather the presence of a new group of students on college campuses—those who represent the first generation of their family to embark on higher education.

2. At SUNY Brockport, as at many universities, until the 1970s, the responsibility for directing first-year or other writing programs was viewed as a service to the department rather than an academic area of expertise; as such, it was often considered an appropriate assignment for untenured assistant professors or tenured associate professors with weak records of scholarly publication. Given the pressures that the literacy crisis of the mid-1970s placed on university administrators—and the then-generous budgets for higher education—many English departments created new positions for specialists in composition to direct writing programs. Since there were few PhD-granting institutions in composition at that time, those who could argue that they had some expertise often filled these positions.

3. Though I believe the results of my inquiry into the disciplinary training of faculty who accepted tenure-line positions from 1969 to 1980 are telling, I am not claiming that they are systematic or complete. A word about my method: I drew upon a number of resources, including my memory, to develop a list of faculty who completed their PhDs in the period from 1969–1980 and who subsequently became engaged with the scholarly work of composition. After developing this list, I then determined the faculty member's dissertation topic by consulting *Dissertation Abstracts*. When a dissertation title clearly announced a standard literary topic and approach, I assumed that not only the scholar's dissertation but general PhD work involved literary training. In instances where I was unsure of the nature of the PhD dissertation and academic training, I consulted the scholar directly.

Of course not everyone who became engaged with the scholarly work of composition in the period from 1969 to 1980 had literary training. A number of scholars completed PhDs in recently developed PhD programs in composition, or in such related areas as English education, linguistics, and rhetoric. Examples include: Miriam Chaplin, Bob Connors, Charles Cooper, Barbara Couture, Frank D'Angelo, Vivian I. Davis, Richard Enos, Sarah Freedman, John Gage, Barry Kroll, Andrea Lunsford, Ronald Lunsford, Thomas Newkirk, Stephen North,

Lee Odell, Louise Wetherbee Phelps, Geneva Smitherman, Nancy Sommers, Marilyn Sternglass, Sandra Stotsky, C. Jan Swearingen, and Lynn Quitman Troyka.

4. Jasper Neel's 1978 *Options for the Teaching of English: Freshman Composition* and Carol Hartzog's 1986 *Composition and the Academy: A Study of Writing Program Administration* provide helpful information about writing program administration during this period.

5. In the preface to *Reinventing the Rhetorical Tradition,* Freedman and Pringle comment on "the sense of excitement evinced at the conference" and add that "In large measure this is due to the extent to which those who attended discovered the strength of their commonality" (ix–x).

6. In an e-mail response to my query about the Pennsylvania State University conference, Jack Selzer commented on its multiple effects. The conference played an important role for scholars in composition at Penn State, which developed one of the early PhD programs in composition. "Through the conference," Selzer observed, "I got to know so many people whose work I had been reading, and I developed relationships with a lot of them—personal and professional—over subsequent years." Many faculty members in the region attended the conference regularly, so that it constituted an ongoing opportunity for scholarly conversation. And the conference also impacted graduate students at Penn State. For many of its early years, consultant speakers taught six-week seminars in conjunction with the conference. When the graduate program in composition was in its early years of development, these seminars supplemented regular offerings.

7. From this volume, in "The Curious Case of Harry Caplan's Hat, or, How I Fell in Love With Rhetoric," Richard Enos describes how three early experiences—"my early years growing up in an Italian neighborhood, the Catholic Church, and the scholastic education I received through high school"—predisposed him to his passion for rhetoric (66). He describes, as well, the difficulty and reward of putting together a course of study in classical rhetoric as a graduate student in a traditional English department at Indiana University, a department that offered no rhetoric courses. Other chapters in *Living Rhetoric and Composition* tell different stories. In "Heart of Gold," Wendy Bishop narrates a tale of serendipity, of being "in the right place at the right time," and of how her work in composition enabled her to make sense of both her intellectual and personal life (33). In "On Being a Writer, Being a Teacher of Writing," Ed White tells another story of "great good luck" (178), of completing a PhD in literature at Harvard, getting a job as "a conventional lit-crit man" at Wellesley College, and almost on a whim moving to a newly built state university in San Bernadino, California—a move that as White says "forced me to rethink what I thought I knew about composition" and ultimately led to his engagement with the field (181).

8. Warnock provides additional details about this meeting in "The Discipline and the Profession: *It's a Doggy Dog World,*" including this description of the genesis of this meeting:

The meeting came about because Ross Winterowd, Dick Young, and I thought that something significant was happening in a number of places across the country and also that some people might want to get together to see if we could get a better sense of what this was and how we might nourish it. (72–73)

Present, in addition to its organizers, were Pat Sullivan, E. D. Hirsch, Janice Lauer, Frank D'Angelo, and George Yoos, all of whom paid their own way to participate in the institute (73). The phrase "a need in search of a discipline" also appears in the introduction to Young, Becker, and Pike's *Rhetoric: Discovery and Change* (8).

9. Indeed, as Jack Selzer points out in "Exploring Options in Composing," "the earliest researchers on the subject resisted the temptation to offer prescriptive formulas for composing" (277). As examples, Selzer cites the research of Gordon Rohman and Janet Emig.

10. As another example, consider Richard L. Graves's *Rhetoric and Composition: A Sourcebook for Writers*. The original edition, published in 1976, was divided into sections with the following titles: "Introduction," "Motivating Student Writing," "A Reluctant Medium: The Sentence," "The Paragraph and Beyond," "The Pedagogy of Composition," and "The Uses of Classical Rhetoric." The subsequent edition, published in 1984, maintains the same first four section titles. It combines the sections on pedagogy and classical rhetoric ("The Pedagogy of Composition: From Classical Rhetoric to Current Practice"). And it presents a new section: "New Perspectives, New Horizons." Several—though by no means all—of the essays in this section focus on the composing process.

11. According to Goggin, the *Rhetoric Society Newsletter* was compiled by the RSA's executive secretary, Nelson J. Smith III and "consisted of two mimeographed sheets stapled together and distributed free to names supplied by the RSA board of directors" (86). The newsletter appeared sporadically from 1968 to 1972, when George Yoos took over as editor. A number of other journals had similarly rocky initiations and survived only, as Goggin puts it, because of the "intense commitment" of a limited number of persons (86).

12. In 1992, the name of this journal was changed to *Composition Studies/ Freshman English News,* and in 1997 it was changed yet again to *Composition Studies.*

13. In "Centering in on Professional Choices," Muriel Harris describes the serendipitous founding of the *Writing Lab Newsletter:*

At the 1977 Conference on College Composition and Communication, after several of us finished a presentation of our perspectives on writing labs and listened to the wealth of valuable insights audience members were offering, the need to continue networking and sharing was evident. As people waiting to start the next session poured into the room, I grabbed a sheet of paper and asked for names of those who wanted to keep in touch via some sort of newsletter (email was still far in the future), and thus was born *The Writing Lab Newsletter.* . . . (433–34)

14. Founding dates for some of these associations are approximate, for what started as an informal identification of like-minded peers could take time to develop into a more formal association. In responding to my query about the founding date of the National Network of Writing Across the Curriculum Programs, for instance, Chris Thaiss replied that this association "started with a mailing list of about 15 names that Bob Weiss of West Chester State (PA) put together in 1979 and a meeting at C's that year that came out of the list. I took the list over from Bob in 1980 and put together a Consultants Board for a new SIG at C's in 1981."

15. In stating this I do not mean to suggest that there were no assumptions shared by most or all of those who saw themselves as part of writing process movement. Cognitivists, expressivists, and those doing rhetorically grounded work all shared a strong interest in invention, for instance—although preferred methods of invention could vary considerably.

16. In "Writing Theory: : Theory Writing," Susan Miller explicitly challenges paradigm hope:

> This [her preferred] way of entering theory—questioning our observations, our opinions, and our principles in light of the complete matrix of circumstance that localize contemporary writing—would encourage a slow and recursive interplay of assertions, applications, resistances, and further assertions that describe intellectual movement more accurately than 'paradigm shift' can. (78)

17. As Olson acknowledges, he draws the term "boss compositionist" from James Sledd, who uses this term in "Return to Service."

4. On Process, Social Process, and Post-Process

1. When I came to OSU in 1980, the English department's Advanced Composition class was numbered WR 316. In the mid-1980s, when the department began to work toward the establishment of an MA program, the course was renumbered as WR 416, so that it could eventually be offered as a combined upper-level/graduate course. I taught Advanced Composition at OSU, then, with three different course numbers: WR 316, WR 416, and WR 416/516.

2. I taught both first-year and advanced composition at SUNY Brockport, but I brought only scattered course materials with me when I moved to Oregon. Hence my decision to focus on my teaching since moving to Oregon State University.

3. Based on the class materials I have—and I do not have copies of syllabi for every class I taught during this period—the variations that exist seem to reflect changes in interest or a desire to experiment with a new topic rather than a more systematic or deep-seated alteration in a course's purpose or structure. In the fall of 1988, for instance, I required students in my advanced composition class to complete four major assignments: the first was a history of themselves as a writer; the second, a response to or critique of Richard Rodriguez's *Hunger of Memory;* the third, an argument; and the fourth, an open topic. The

following spring I similarly required students in my first year composition class to complete four major writing assignments. The first assignment was identical to that in advanced composition. The second assignment was a response/critique essay, but in this case, students responded to one or more essays in *Northwest Variety: Personal Essays by Fourteen Regional Authors,* a collection of essays about place edited by Lex Runciman and Steven Sher. The third essay was a critical review; the fourth, an argument.

4. These course descriptions were written solely for sections of first-year and advanced composition that I taught. For the first six years that I taught at Oregon State, I served as Director of Composition, but since my department did not at that time have teaching assistants, I did not develop course descriptions or syllabi for general use.

5. Kent might well not agree with my discussion here, for he does not mention the rhetorical tradition in his discussion of post-process theory. Because of his desire strongly to differentiate process and post-process theories, he would also disagree with my suggestion that advocates of the writing process see writing as public. I believe that his three criteria are open to multiple interpretations.

6. In this regard, it can be helpful to turn to concrete descriptions of previous teaching practices. In *1977: The Cultural Moment in Composition,* Brent Henze, Jack Selzer, and Wendy Sharer remind readers that

> at many colleges and universities during the 1970s the composition class comfortably doubled as an introduction to Great Ideas or to canonical literary texts that were part of an established literary canon that provided 'content' for students to write about. A number of composition-and-literature textbooks accommodated these courses, as they had for decades [Crowley, *Composition,* chapter 5]. If the courses did not always emphasize explicitly literary genres of poetry, drama, and fiction, then they often offered up an analogous 'canon' of 'artistic' nonfiction or an introduction to Great Ideas in the sciences, the arts, and the humanities that could generate material for student essays. The best-selling 1977 edition of *The Norton Reader,* for example, accommodated both approaches. (26–27)

7. In the most recent advanced composition class that I taught, for instance, I presented the students with four major writing assignments. The first two assignments were intended to address questions raised in the course description and overview; they were intended, in other words, to encourage students to look at writing from a social perspective. These assignments—which are anything but original—were to write a literacy narrative, and then to write a second essay that in some way responded to one or more of the literacy narratives we read at the start of the term. The final two assignments for the course were entirely open except for the inclusion of a length requirement.

8. I opened the class by having students read and discuss Winston Weathers's "Grammars of Style: New Options in Composition" and Carl Leggo's "Questions I Need to Ask Before I Advise My students to Write in Their Own Voices,"

an essay that enacts its thesis by presenting readers with a list of ninety-nine unanswered questions designed to "court contradiction and confusion and consternation in" Leggo's "commitment to shake up and explode the notion of voice in writing" (143). Students also read a variety of professional and student literacy narratives. Once students had written their own literacy narratives, these were compiled into a photocopied book, *Writing/Reading/Life,* that became a text for the class. By the middle of the term, however, the focus was entirely on the students' own work in progress. (See the previous note for a fuller explanation of the reading and writing assignments for this class.)

9. Here, for instance, is an excerpt of an assignment that I gave in my 1994 advanced composition class. This assignment had two parts: a collaborative oral presentation and an individually written essay. The following are part of the instructions I provided for the collaborative project.

Academic Discourse Community Assignment

For this first part of the assignment, you will join with a team of other interested students to study an academic discourse community in the university. To do so, you may choose to study an academic discipline as broadly defined—to focus on the discourse of historians, for instance, or psychologists or sociologists. Or you may focus on an area of specialization within a discipline, such as the discourse of social psychologists or historians of science. There are advantages and disadvantages to each choice—just as there are advantages and disadvantages to studying a discipline you already have considerable knowledge of versus one that is more or less new to you. We'll discuss issues such as these in class.

Most broadly, in studying your discourse community you will be asking three related questions:

What assumptions and practices do members of this discourse community share?

In "Does Coming to College Mean Becoming Someone New?" Kevin Davis argues that members of a discourse community: 1) are able to recognize and employ certain shared textual conventions; 2) have learned to think in the ways valued by community members; 3) have developed writing strategies that enable them to respond to the challenges of writing in that community; 4) have identified personally and intellectually with the community (238). Using these statements as starting points, investigate the commonalities shared by those in the discourse community you are studying.

What disagreements or differences in assumptions and practice exist in this discourse community?

This question invites you to shift your focus from commonalities to differences. Although all members of a particular discipline or sub-discipline may share certain assumptions and practices, and thus can be viewed as members of the same discourse community, other differences may exist. Some differences may reflect differences in subject matter and/or method and may be accepted as more or less "natural" within the larger community. Other differences may reflect substantial disagreements about the goals of research, writing, and/or teaching currently being debated in the field. How do members of the discourse community view you are studying view these differences? To what extent do these differences challenge the coherence and viability of the larger discourse community?

What kind of transitions must students make as they attempt to become accepted members of this community?

This question encourages you to investigate the experiences of students as they move from their lower-division to upper-division and (in the cases of some) graduate student courses in a discipline—as they attempt, in other words, to move from being outsiders to insiders in a discourse community. You'll also want to look at this issue from the perspective of those who, by virtue of their position as teachers, are explicitly or implicitly introducing students to writing in their field. To what extent do faculty and students share the same understanding of the characteristics of effective student writing in this community? Do teachers generally ask students to do the same kinds of writing they themselves do, or do they devise different kinds of assignments? Why? What understanding do students working on assignments have of the relationship between the writing they are doing and the writing done by faculty members and/or professionals in their discipline?

In working on your group investigation, you should collect and analyze examples of written discourse in this community, locate published discussions about its conventions of writing in the discourse community you are studying (as can be found in various professional association's style and documentation guides, for example), and interview a number of informants from this community.

Further instructions for this part of the assignment, and for the related individual project, follow.

10. A similar line of reasoning caused me sometime in the early 1990s to abandon my portfolio grading system—a system whereby I did not give individual student essays letter grades but rather graded the entire portfolio—for conventional grading practices.

11. In stating this, I don't mean to deny the possibility of large and significant pedagogical shifts. If the director of a first-year writing program with a mandated curriculum and texts decided to make a dramatic change in textbooks, for instance, or to abandon traditional writing classes for a service-learning program, these would indeed be significant changes. They are also, however, imposed changes—changes that teachers may embrace or in various ways resist.

Introduction to Part 3: Practice Makes Practice

1. One interview was conducted in person; the others were either telephone, written, or e-mail interviews. Those interviewed include Rhonda Grego, Sylvia A. Holladay, Melissa Sue Kort, Helen Raines, Stephen Ruffus, Ira Shor, and Mary Soliday. (461–62). Lewiecki-Wilson and Sommers do not claim that their interviews yielded generalizable information about teaching in open access institutions.

2. Stephen Ruffus is an exception. According to Lewiecki-Wilson and Sommers, he characterized his teaching as "post-process" (454).

3. Horner points out, for instance, that North "ends up writing lore out of the work of Composition in the very attempt to legitimize it, because the terms for the legitimation of work he applies are drawn from the discourse of academic professionalism" ("Traditions" 379).

4. In the introduction to *Under Construction: Working at the Intersections of Composition Theory, Research, and Practice,* editors Christine Farris and Chris M. Anson make a related observation: the "notion that theory, research, and teaching are all *practices* providing a location from which to view and critique the others is one that appeals to us in constructing this volume and one which offers a way out of battling binaries" (3).

5. On Theory, Theories, and Theorizing

1. For an analysis of the early years of the field's development, see my introduction to *On Writing Research: The Braddock Essays 1975–1998.*

2. For information on the Wyoming Resolution, see "CCCC Initiatives on the Wyoming Conference Resolution: A Draft Report" and "The Wyoming Conference Resolution Opposing Unfair Salaries and Working Conditions for Post-Secondary Teachers of Writing" by Linda R. Robertson, Sharon Crowley, and Frank Lentricchia.

3. The studies in composition that have most strongly engaged my thinking will be evident to readers of *Situating Composition,* so I will not cite them here. I do want to acknowledge studies outside of composition that have played an important role in provoking thought. Some of the most important of these include: Jane Flax's *Thinking Fragments: Psychoanalysis, Feminism, and Postmodernism in the Contemporary West;* Jennifer Gore's *The Struggle for Pedagogies: Critical and Feminist Discourses as Regimes of Truth;* Sandra Harding's *Whose Science? Whose Knowledge? Thinking from Women's Lives;* Donna Haraway's *Simians, Cyborgs, and Women: The Reinvention of Nature;* bell hooks's *Talking Back: Thinking Feminist, Thinking Black;* James Sosnoski's *Token Professionals and Master Critics: A Critique of Orthodoxy in Literary Studies* and *Modern Skeletons in Postmodern Closets: A Cultural Studies Alternative;* Trinh T. Minh-ha's *Woman, Native, Other;* and Evan Watkins's *Work Time: English Departments and the Circulation of Cultural Value.*

4. Understandings of theory can vary not only from person to person but also within individuals. As a scholar attempting to understand the relationship

of theory and practice in composition, I am drawn to characterizations of theory that emphasize its cultural, rhetorical, and material situatedness. But in different situations I hold—and act on—other understandings of "theory." At times, I use the term metonymically to stand in for the critical projects that have been at the forefront of much scholarly work in the humanities in recent years. If a friend who teaches elsewhere described a colleague as someone who "does theory," I know what she means—even if I don't know what specific kind or kinds of theory the person "does." At other times I participate in commonsense understandings of theory, understandings that sometimes cause both academics and non-academics to comment that "Theoretically that should be correct, but in practice it doesn't work that way."

5. I should note that neither Crowley nor Miller limits her analysis to theoretical critique. A number of the chapters in Crowley's *Composition in the University* are grounded in historical research. In *Textual Carnivals*, Susan Miller includes "The Status of Composition: A Survey of How Its Professionals See It." She also at times discusses the material conditions of teachers of writing and considers the history of first-year writing courses.

6. Many teachers of writing would not, it is important to point out, cite mastering correct English as the major goal of their composition classes.

7. I make this point because depending on your perspective, the power that scholars have could seem either substantial or— if not trivial—then much less significant. In graduate programs and in the various forums for research, scholarly views dominate. In recent years, for instance, graduate students in certain graduate programs knew that to admire the work of Peter Elbow or Linda Flower meant exposing themselves to substantial criticism. Outside these programs and forums, the situation can differ considerably. Many teachers are simply unaware of the battles between various camps of theorists in composition; others view them with varying degrees of interest. For many, textbooks may play a much more powerful role in influencing their teaching than any scholarly text.

8. Berlin does add that "the overall effect of these tend to support the hegemony of the dominant class" ("Rhetoric and Ideology" 479).

9. I should also add that I experienced what I think of as the pronoun problem with particular intensity in writing this section of chapter 5. I am fortunate to be able to move back and forth between the identity of teacher and that of scholar. Actually, I should add a third identity here—that of WPA. As I worked on this discussion, I moved back and forth between "we"s and "they"s. Part of me wanted to claim my affiliations with both identities and practices. But another part of me felt that scholarly detachment finally called for "they." I remain uneasy with this solution.

10. Wall is quoting from James Berlin's *Rhetoric and Reality: Writing Instruction in American Colleges, 1900–1985*, page 166. She does not cite the page number here because the complete statement from which she draws excerpts here is prominently featured earlier in her essay.

6. Who's Disciplining Whom?

1. The term "theory" is used by hooks in at least two ways in this essay. When speaking of her childhood turn to theory, for instance, hooks is clearly referring not to a specific scholarly project, such as deconstruction or feminist theory. Rather, she refers to the activity of theorizing, which enabled her "to look at the world differently . . . to challenge the status quo" (59–60). Elsewhere she uses the term to refer to the general project of theory in the humanities in its various forms, including feminist theory.

2. In this regard, see Paul Kei Matsuda's "Composition Studies and ESL Writing: A Disciplinary Division of Labor" and Jeanne Gunner's "Identity and Location: A Study of WPA Models, Memberships, and Agendas."

7. Situated Knowledges: Toward a Politics of Location in Composition

1. In "Re-Centering Authority: Social Reflexivity and Re-Positioning in Composition Research," Ellen Cushman and Teresa Guinsatao Monberg characterize Bordieu's notion of habitus as follows: "The habitus includes those actions and discourses that identify us as belonging to particular social and cultural groups. People feel more comfortable around those who act and speak in ways similar to theirs" (177). Habitus encourages individuals to remain within ideologies they inhabit rather than to step outside them. "We think," Cushman and Monberg argue, "this conception of a habitus rigid to alternative ways of constructing the world describes many academics (and upper-class whites) well" (178).

2. Olson's appropriation of Sledd's term strikes me as questionable. As I read Sledd's work—as exemplified in "Return to Service"—Sledd uses the term broadly to refer to "a new group of hierarchs" who have made careers for themselves in tenure-line positions in composition (11). Sledd charges that boss compositionists have subordinated a concern for teaching to a concern for theory and for individual career advancement, and he argues vigorously that scholars should, as his title suggests, "Return to Service" and devote themselves primarily to "the teaching of general literacy" (28). Sledd generally does not discuss current scholarly debates within composition—unless to dismiss them as irrelevant, pretentious, or harmful. In his work, then, the term "boss compositionist" applies broadly to anyone in a tenure-line position in composition who no longer teaches required writing courses and identifies him- or herself primarily with the practice of theory.

3. For examples of such an effort see: Robin Varnum's *Fencing with Words: A History of Writing Instruction at Amherst College During the Era of Theodore Baird, 1938–1966,* Lucille Schultz's *The Young Composers: Composition's Beginnings in Nineteenth-Century Schools,* and Susan Kates's *Activist Rhetorics and American Higher Education, 1885–1937.*

4. Other teachers sometimes ask me how students whose writing is clearly less successful than others feel about sharing their work with peers. This is a reasonable concern, and one that I had when I first began to assign this essay. I

have been surprised and pleased to discover that students express little concern about this issue—at least to me. Students whose writing is not as strong as others in the class have expressed gratitude at being able to see other students' writing, so they can recognize and learn from its strengths. The fact that I also require students to write *positive* responses to their peers may also help allay this concern. I do recognize that just because students have not expressed reservations about sharing their writing this does not mean that some may not in fact have reservations, perhaps strong ones. No assignment is perfect, but in my experience the benefits of having students share writing early in the term outweighs the potential disadvantage of students' discomfort in sharing their writing.

5. These range from such factors as the brevity of my university's ten-week term, which makes it difficult for students to have the time to get to know each other and to work through the difficulties inherent to collaboration, to the fact that ultimately students receive individual grades for their courses.

6. I used to count this collaborative letter as a small part of students' final grade. I experimented with not doing so one term, and I discovered that students still took the writing of the letter seriously. Ideally this would be because they had developed a strong sense of collaborative responsibility. But the fact that I require each student to hand sign the letter may also help.

7. I developed this assignment collaboratively with my former colleague and friend Cheryl Glenn, who now teaches at Pennsylvania State University.

8. The second and third questions are drawn from *Whose Science? Whose Knowledge? Thinking from Women's Lives,* by Sandra Harding. In her analysis Harding notes, for instance, that scientists have often found it "convenient to overlook the deep ties between science and warmaking" (33). She also comments on the extent to which until recently the phrase "woman scientist" appeared to be a contradiction in terms (20).

9. My use of the term "obsessions" is drawn from Michelle Fine's *Disruptive Voices: The Possibilities of Feminist Research,* where Fine explores the question of whether "psychology's obsessions" are "compatible with notions of feminist epistemology" (2).

WORKS CITED

Abbott, Andrew. *The System of Professions: An Essay on the Division of Expert Labor.* Chicago: U of Chicago P, 1988.

Alcoff, Linda. "The Problem of Speaking for Others." *Cultural Critique* 37 (1991): 5–32.

Alcorn, Marshall W., Jr. *Changing the Subject in English Class: Discourse and the Constructions of Desire.* Carbondale: Southern Illinois UP, 2002.

Arendt, Hannah. *The Human Condition.* Chicago: U of Chicago P, 1958.

Axelrod, Rise B., and Charles R. Cooper. *The St. Martin's Guide to Writing.* 5th ed. New York: St. Martin's, 1997.

Bartholomae, David. "Response." *CCC* 46 (1995): 84–87.

———. "What Is Composition and (If You Know What That Is) Why Do We Teach It?" *Composition in the Twenty-First Century: Crisis and Change.* Ed. Lynn Z. Bloom, Donald A. Daiker, and Edward M. White. Carbondale: Southern Illinois UP, 1996: 11–28.

———. "Writing with Teachers: A Conversation with Peter Elbow." *CCC* 46 (1995): 62–71.

Bartholomae, David, and Anthony Petrosky. *Ways of Reading: An Anthology for Writers.* 4th ed. Boston: Bedford, 1996.

Bazerman, Charles. "Looking at Writing; Writing What I See." *Living Rhetoric and Composition: Stories of the Discipline.* Ed. Duane H. Roen, Stuart C. Brown, and Theresa Enos. Mahwah: Erlbaum, 1999. 15–24.

———. "Theories That Help Us Read and Write Better." *A Rhetoric of Doing: Essays on Written Discourse in Honor of James L. Kinneavy.* Ed. Stephen P. Witte, Neil Nakadate, and Roger D. Cherry. Carbondale: Southern Illinois UP, 1992. 103–12.

Beach, Richard, and Lillian S. Bridwell, eds. *New Directions in Composition Research: Perspectives in Writing Research.* New York: Guilford, 1984.

Berlin, James A. "Poststructuralism, Cultural Studies, and the Composition Classroom: Postmodern Theory in Practice." *Rhetoric Review* 11 (1992): 16–33.

———. "Rhetoric and Ideology in the Writing Class." *College English* 50 (1988): 477–94.

———. *Rhetoric and Reality: Writing Instruction in American Colleges, 1900–1985*. Carbondale: Southern Illinois UP, 1987.

———. *Writing Instruction in Nineteenth-Century American Colleges*. Carbondale: Southern Illinois UP, 1984.

Berlin, James A., and Robert P. Inkster. "Current-Traditional Rhetoric: Paradigm and Practice." *Freshman English News* 8 (1980): 1–4, 13–14.

Berthoff, Ann E. "Killer Dichotomies: Reading In/Reading Out." *Farther Along: Transforming Dichotomies in Rhetoric and Composition*. Ed Kate Ronald and Hephzibah Roskelly. Portsmouth: Heinemann-Boynton, 1990. 12–24.

Bishop, Wendy. "Heart of Gold." *Living Rhetoric and Composition: Stories of the Discipline*. Ed. Duane H. Roen, Stuart C. Brown, and Theresa Enos. Mahwah: Erlbaum, 1999. 25–35.

Bizzaro, Patrick. "What I Learned in Grad School, or Literary Training and the Theorizing of Composition." *CCC* 50 (1999): 722–42.

Bizzell, Patricia. *Academic Discourse and Critical Consciousness*. Pittsburgh: U of Pittsburgh P, 1992.

———. "Cognition, Convention, and Certainty." *Pre/Text* 3 (1982): 213–43. Rpt. in *Academic Discourse and Critical Consciousness*. Ed. Patricia Bizzell. Pittsburgh: U of Pittsburgh P, 1992. 75–104.

Bizzell, Patricia, Bruce Herzberg, and Nedra Reynolds, eds. *The Bedford Bibliography for Teachers of Writing*. 5th ed. Boston: Bedford/St. Martin's, 2000.

Bloom, Lynn Z., Donald A. Daiker, and Edward M. White, eds. *Composition in the Twenty-First Century: Crisis and Change*. Carbondale: Southern Illinois UP, 1996.

Booth, Wayne C. *The Rhetoric of Fiction*. Chicago: U of Chicago P, 1961.

Boquet, Elizabeth H. *Noise from the Writing Center*. Logan: Utah State UP, 2002.

Brereton, John C., ed. *The Origins of Composition Studies in the American College, 1875–1925*. Pittsburgh: U of Pittsburgh P, 1995.

Britzman, Deborah P. *Practice Makes Practice: A Critical Study of Learning to Teach*. Albany: State U of New York P, 1991.

Brown, Stuart C., Paul R. Meyer, and Theresa Enos. Preface. *Rhetoric Review* 12 (1994): 240–51.

Brown, Wendy. "The Impossibility of Women's Studies." *Women's Studies on the Edge*. Spec. issue of *Differences* 9.3 (1997): 79–101.

Burke, Kenneth. "Definition of Man." *Language as Symbolic Action: Essays on Life, Literature, and Method*. Berkeley: U of California P, 1966. 3–24.

———. *A Grammar of Motives*. Berkeley: U of California P, 1969.

———. *The Philosophy of Literary Form*. Berkeley: U of California P, 1973.

———. "Terministic Screens." *Language as Symbolic Action: Essays on Life, Literature, and Method*. Berkeley: U of California P, 1966. 44–62.

Butler, Judith, John Guillory, and Kendall Thomas, eds. *What's Left of Theory? New Work on the Politics of Literary Theory.* New York: Routledge, 2000.

Carlton, Susan Brown. "Voice and the Naming of Woman." *Voices on Voice: Perspectives, Definitions, Inquiry.* Ed. Kathleen Blake Yancey. Urbana: NCTE, 1994: 226–41.

Carr, Jean Ferguson. "Rereading the Academy as Worldly Text." *CCC* 45 (1994): 93–97.

Carver, Raymond. "What We Talk about When We Talk about Love." *The Story and Its Writer: An Introduction to Short Fiction.* Compact 6th ed. Ed. Ann Charters. Boston: Bedford/St. Martin's, 2003. 98–107.

"CCCC Initiatives on the Wyoming Conference Resolution: A Draft Report." *CCC* 40 (1989): 61–72.

Chapman, David W., and Gary Tate. "A Survey of Doctoral Programs in Rhetoric and Composition." *Rhetoric Review* 5 (1987): 124–33.

Charney, Davida. "Empiricism Is Not a Four-Letter Word." *CCC* 47 (1996): 567–93.

Christensen, Francis. "A Generative Rhetoric of the Sentence." *CCC* 14 (1963): 155–61.

Cintron, Ralph. "Wearing a Pith Helmet at a Sly Angle: Or, Can Writing Researchers Do Ethnography in a Postmodern Era?" *Written Communication* 10 (1993): 371–412.

Clifford, John, and Elizabeth Ervin. "The Ethics of Process." *Post-Process Theory: Beyond the Writing-Process Paradigm.* Ed. Thomas Kent. Carbondale: Southern Illinois UP, 1999. 179–97.

Clifford, John, and John Schilb, eds. *Writing Theory and Critical Theory.* New York: MLA, 1994.

Code, Lorraine. *Rhetorical Spaces: Essays on Gendered Locations.* New York: Routledge, 1995.

Connors, Robert J. "The Abolition Debate in Composition: A Short History." *Composition in the Twenty-First Century: Crisis and Change.* Ed. Lynn Z. Bloom, Donald A. Daiker, and Edward M. White. Carbondale: Southern Illinois UP, 1996. 47–63.

———. "Composition History and Disciplinarity." *History, Reflection, and Narrative: The Professionalization of Composition, 1963–1983.* Ed. Mary Rosner, Beth Boehm, and Debra Journet. Stamford: Ablex, 1999. 3–21.

———. *Composition-Rhetoric: Backgrounds, Theory, and Pedagogy.* Pittsburgh: U of Pittsburgh P, 1997.

———. "Composition Studies and Science." *College English* 45 (1983): 1–20.

Connors, Robert J., Lisa S. Ede, and Andrea A. Lunsford, eds. *Essays on Classical Rhetoric and Modern Discourse.* Carbondale: Southern Illinois UP, 1984.

Cooper, Charles R., and Lee Odell, eds. *Research on Composing: Points of Departure.* Urbana: NCTE, 1978.

Cooper, Marilyn M. "The Ecology of Writing." *College English* 48 (1986): 364–75.

Corbett, Edward P. J. *The Little Rhetoric and Handbook.* 2d ed. Dallas: Scott, 1982.

"Course Designs." *Composition Studies.* Oct. 5, 2002. <http://condor.depaul.edu/'compstud/cd.htm>.

Crowley, Sharon. *Composition in the University: Historical and Polemical Essays.* U of Pittsburgh P, 1998.

———. *A Teacher's Introduction to Deconstruction.* Urbana: NCTE, 1989.

Cushman, Ellen, and Terese Guinsatao Monberg. "Re-Centering Authority: Social Reflexivity and Re-Positioning in Composition Research." *Under Construction: Working at the Intersections of Composition Theory, Research, and Practice.* Ed. Christine Farris and Chris M. Anson. Logan: Utah State UP, 1998. 166–80.

D'Angelo, Frank. "Professing Rhetoric and Composition: A Personal Odyssey." *History, Reflection, and Narrative: The Professionalization of Composition, 1963–1983.* Ed. Mary Rosner, Beth Boehm, and Debra Journet. Stamford: Ablex, 1999. 269–82.

Daniell, Beth. "Theory, Theory Talk, and Composition." *Writing Theory and Critical Theory.* Ed. John Clifford and John Schilb. New York: MLA, 1994. 127–40.

Davis, Kevin. "Does Coming to College Mean Becoming Someone New?" *The Subject Is Writing: Essays by Teachers and Students.* Ed. Wendy Bishop. Portsmouth: Heinemann-Boynton, 1993. 235–41.

Dobrin, Sidney I. *Constructing Knowledges: The Politics of Theory-Building and Pedagogy in Composition.* Albany: State U of New York P, 1997.

Durst, Russell K. *Collision Course: Conflict, Negotiation, and Learning in College Composition.* Urbana: NCTE, 1999.

Ede, Lisa, ed. *On Writing Research: The Braddock Essays, 1975–1998.* New York: Bedford/St. Martin's, 1999.

———. *Work in Progress: A Guide to Academic Writing and Revising.* 6th ed. New York: Bedford/St. Martin's, 2003.

———. "Writing Centers and the Politics of Location: A Response to Terrance Riley and Stephen M. North." *Writing Center Journal* 16 (1996): 111–30.

Ede, Lisa, and Andrea A. Lunsford: "Audience Addressed/Audience Invoked: The Role of Audience in Composition Theory and Pedagogy." *CCC* 35 (1984): 155–71.

———. *Singular Texts/Plural Authors: Perspectives on Collaborative Writing.* Carbondale: Southern Illinois UP, 1990.

Elbow, Peter. "Being a Writer vs. Being an Academic: A Conflict in Goals." *CCC* 46 (1995): 72–83.

———. "The Doubting Game and the Believing Game—An Analysis of the

Intellectual Enterprise." *Writing Without Teachers.* New York: Oxford UP, 1973. 147–91.

———. "Response." *CCC* 46 (1995): 87–92.

———. *Writing Without Teachers.* New York: Oxford UP, 1973.

Emig, Janet. *The Composing Processes of Twelfth Graders.* Urbana: NCTE, 1971.

———. *The Web of Meaning: Essays on Writing, Teaching, Learning, and Thinking.* Ed. Dixie Goswami and Maureen Butler. Upper Montclair: Boynton, 1983.

Enos, Richard Leo. "The Curious Case of Harry Caplan's Hat, or, How I Fell in Love with Rhetoric." *Living Rhetoric and Composition: Stories of the Discipline.* Ed. Duane H. Roen, Stuart C. Brown, and Theresa Enos. Mahwah: Erlbaum, 1999. 65–74.

Faigley, Lester. "Competing Theories of Process: A Critique and a Proposal." *College English* 48 (1986): 527–42.

———. *Fragments of Rationality: Postmodernity and the Subject of Composition.* Pittsburgh: U of Pittsburgh P, 1992.

Farris, Christine, and Chris M. Anson, eds. *Under Construction: Working at the Intersections of Composition Theory, Research, and Practice.* Logan: Utah State UP, 1998.

Fine, Michelle. *Disruptive Voices: The Possibilities of Feminist Research.* Ann Arbor: U of Michigan P, 1992.

Fish, Stanley. *Doing What Comes Naturally: Change, Rhetoric, and the Practice of Theory in Literary and Legal Studies.* Chapel Hill: Duke UP, 1990.

Flax, Jane. *Disputed Subjects: Essays on Psychoanalysis, Politics, and Philosophy.* New York: Routledge, 1993.

———. *Thinking Fragments: Psychoanalysis, Feminism, and Postmodernism in the Contemporary West.* Berkeley: U of California P, 1990.

Flower, Linda. *The Construction of Negotiated Meaning: A Social Cognitive Theory of Writing.* Carbondale: Southern Illinois UP, 1994.

———. *Problem-Solving Strategies for Writing.* 4th ed. Fort Worth: Harcourt, 1993.

Flower, Linda, and John R. Hayes. "The Cognition of Discovery." *CCC* 31 (1980): 21–32.

———. "A Cognitive Process Theory of Writing." *CCC* 32 (1981): 365–87.

Flynn, Elizabeth A. *Feminism Beyond Modernism.* Carbondale: Southern Illinois UP, 2002.

Foster, David. "What Are We Talking about When We Talk about Composition?" *JAC* 8 (1988): 30–40.

Freedman, Aviva, and Ian Pringle, eds. *Reinventing the Rhetorical Tradition.* Conway: L and S; Canadian Council of Teachers of English, 1980.

Fulkerson, Richard. "Of Pre- and Post-Process: Reviews and Ruminations." *Composition Studies* 29 (2001): 93–119.

Fulwiler, Toby, and Art Young, eds. *Language Connections: Writing and Reading Across the Curriculum*. Urbana: NCTE, 1982.

Fuss, Diana. *Essentially Speaking: Feminism, Nature, and Difference*. New York: Routledge, 1989.

Gale, Frederick G. "An Interview with Janice Lauer." *Composition Forum* 11 (2000): 1–12.

Gallagher, Chris W. *Radical Departures: Composition and Progressive Pedagogy*. Urbana: NCTE, 2002.

Gerber, John C. "The Conference on College Composition and Communication." *CCC* 1 (1950): 12.

Gere, Anne Ruggles. *Into the Field: Sites of Composition Studies*. New York: MLA, 1993.

———. "Kitchen Tables and Rented Rooms: The Extracurriculum of Composition." *CCC* 45 (1994): 75–92.

———. "The Long Revolution in Composition." *Composition in the Twenty-First Century: Crisis and Change*. Ed. Lynn Z. Bloom, Donald A. Daiker, and Edward M. White. Carbondale: Southern Illinois UP, 1996. 119–32.

———. "Practicing Theory/Theorizing Practice." *Balancing Acts: Essays on the Teaching of Writing*. Ed. Virginia A. Chappell, Mary Louise Buley-Meissner, and Chris Anderson. Carbondale: Southern Illinois UP, 1991. 111–21.

———. *Writing Groups: History, Theory, and Implications*. Carbondale: Southern Illinois UP, 1987.

Gibson, Walker. "Writing Programs and the Department of English." *ADE Bulletin* 61 (1979): 19–22.

Gilyard, Keith. "Basic Writing, Cost Effectiveness, and Ideology." *Journal of Basic Writing* 19 (2000): 36–42.

———. *Voices of the Self: A Study of Language Competence*. Detroit: Wayne State UP, 1991.

Giroux, Henry A. "Who Writes in a Cultural Studies Class? Or, Where Is the Pedagogy?" *Left Margins: Cultural Studies and Composition Pedagogy*. Ed. Karen Fitts and Alan W. France. Albany: State U of New York P, 1995. 3–16.

Goggin, Maureen Daly. *Authoring a Discipline: Scholarly Journals and the Post–World War II Emergence of Rhetoric and Composition*. Mahwah: Erlbaum, 2000.

Gore, Jennifer M. *The Struggle for Pedagogies: Critical and Feminist Discourses as Regimes of Truth*. New York: Routledge, 1993.

Graves, Donald H. "An Examination of the Writing Processes of Seven-Year-Old Children." *Research in the Teaching of English* 9 (1975): 227–41. Rpt. in *Landmark Essays on Writing Process*. Ed. Sondra Perl. Davis: Hermagoras. 23–38.

Graves, Richard L., ed. *Rhetoric and Composition: A Sourcebook for Teachers*. Rochelle Park: Hayden, 1976.

———, ed. *Rhetoric and Composition: A Sourcebook for Teachers and Writers.* New edition. Upper Montclair: Boynton, 1984.

Gray, Donald. "New Ideas about English and Departments of English." *English Education* 18 (1986): 147–52.

Greenbaum, Andrea, ed. *Insurrections: Approaches to Resistance in Composition Studies.* Albany: State U of New York P, 2001.

Groening, Matt. "Lesson 19: Grad School—Some People Never Learn." *School Is Hell.* New York: Pantheon, 1982. N. pag.

Gubar, Susan. *Critical Condition: Feminism at the Turn of the Century.* New York: Columbia UP, 2000.

Gunner, Jeanne. "Identity and Location: A Study of WPA Models, Memberships, and Agendas." *WPA* 22 (1999): 31–54.

Haake, Katharine. *What Our Speech Disrupts: Feminism and Creative Writing Studies.* Urbana: NCTE, 2000.

Hacking, Ian. *The Social Construction of What?* Cambridge: Harvard UP, 1999.

Hairston, Maxine. "The Winds of Change: Thomas Kuhn and the Revolution in the Teaching of Writing." *CCC* 33 (1982): 76–88.

Halasek, Kay. *A Pedagogy of Possibility: Bakhtinian Perspectives on Composition Studies.* Carbondale: Southern Illinois UP, 1999.

Haraway, Donna J. *How Like a Leaf: An Interview with Thyrza Nichols Goodeve.* New York: Routledge, 2000.

———. *Simians, Cyborgs, and Women: The Reinvention of Nature.* New York: Routledge, 1991.

Harding, Sandra. *Whose Science? Whose Knowledge? Thinking from Women's Lives.* Ithaca: Cornell UP, 1991.

Harkin, Patricia. "The Postdisciplinary Politics of Lore." *Contending with Words: Composition and Rhetoric in a Postmodern Age.* Ed. Patricia Harkin and John Schilb. New York: MLA, 1991. 124–38.

Harris, Joseph. "Beyond Community: From the Social to the Material." *Journal of Basic Writing* 20 (2001): 3–15.

———. "Meet the New Boss, Same as the Old Boss: Class Consciousness in Composition." *CCC* 52 (2000): 43–68.

———. "The Rhetoric of Theory." *Writing Theory and Critical Theory.* Ed. John Clifford and John Schilb. New York: MLA, 1994. 141–47.

———. *A Teaching Subject: Composition since 1966.* Upper Saddle River: Prentice, 1997.

Harris, Muriel. "Centering in on Professional Choices." *CCC* 52 (2001): 429–40.

———. *Tutoring Writing: A Sourcebook for Writing Labs.* Glenview: Scott, 1982.

Hartzog, Carol P. *Composition and the Academy: A Study of Writing Program Administration.* New York: MLA, 1986.

Hays, Janice N., Phillis A. Roth, Jon R. Ramsey, and Robert D. Foulke, eds. *The Writer's Mind: Writing as a Mode of Thinking.* Urbana: NCTE, 1983.

Heilker, Paul, and Peter Vandenberg, eds. *Keywords in Composition Studies.* Portsmouth: Heinemann-Boynton, 1996.

Helmers, Marguerite. *Writing Students: Composition Testimonials and Representations of Students.* Albany: State U of New York P, 1994.

Henze, Brent, Jack Selzer, and Wendy Sharer, with Brian Lehew, Shannon Pennefeather, and Martin Schleuze. *1977: The Cultural Moment in Composition.* Unpublished MS.

Herrington, Anne J., and Marcia Curtis. *Persons in Process: Four Stories of Writing and Personal Development in College.* Urbana: NCTE, 2000.

Hillocks, George, Jr. *Research on Written Composition: New Directions for Teaching.* Urbana: NCRE; ERIC, 1986.

Holberg, Jennifer L., and Marcy Taylor. "Editors' Introduction." *Pedagogy* 1 (2001): 1–5.

hooks, bell. *Talking Back: Thinking Feminist, Thinking Black.* Boston: South End, 1989.

———. "Theory as Liberatory Practice." *Teaching to Transgress: Education as the Practice of Freedom.* New York: Routledge, 1994. 59–76.

Horner, Bruce. "Resisting Academics." *Insurrections: Approaches to Resistance in Composition Studies.* Ed. Andrea Greenbaum. Albany: State U of New York P, 2001. 169–84.

———. *Terms of Work for Composition: A Materialist Critique.* Albany: State U of New York P, 2000.

———. "Traditions and Professionalization: Reconceiving Work in Composition." *CCC* 51 (2000): 366–98.

Jarratt, Susan C. "As We Were Saying . . ." Introduction. *Feminism and Composition Studies: In Other Words.* Ed. Susan C. Jarratt and Lynn Worsham. New York: MLA, 1998. 1–18.

Jarratt, Susan C., and Lynn Worsham, eds. *Feminism and Composition Studies: In Other Words.* New York: MLA, 1998.

Kameen, Paul. *Writing/Teaching: Essays Toward a Rhetoric of Pedagogy.* U of Pittsburgh P, 2000.

Kamler, Barbara. *Relocating the Personal: A Critical Writing Pedagogy.* Albany: State U of New York P, 2001.

Kaplan, Caren. "The Politics of Location as Transnational Feminist Critical Practice." *Scattered Hegemonies: Postmodernity and Transnational Feminist Practices.* Ed. Inderpal Grewal and Caren Kaplan. Minneapolis: U of Minnesota P, 1994. 137–52.

———. *Questions of Travel: Postmodern Discourses of Displacement.* Durham: Duke UP, 1996.

Kasden, Laurence N., and Daniel R. Hoeber, eds. *Basic Writing: Essays for Teachers, Researchers, Administrators.* Urbana: NCTE, 1980.

Kates, Susan. *Activist Rhetorics and American Higher Education, 1885–1937.* Carbondale: Southern Illinois UP, 2000.

Kent, Thomas. "The Consequences of Theory for the Practice of Writing." *Publishing in Rhetoric and Composition.* Ed. Gary A. Olson and Todd W. Taylor. Albany: State U of New York P, 1997. 147–61.

———, ed. *Post-Process Theory: Beyond the Writing-Process Paradigm.* Carbondale: Southern Illinois UP, 1999.

Kinneavy, James L. *A Theory of Discourse: The Aims of Discourse.* New York: Norton, 1971.

Kirsch, Gesa E., and Joy S. Ritchie. "Beyond the Personal: Theorizing a Politics of Location in Composition Research." *CCC* 46 (1995): 7–29.

Kroll, Barry, and Roberta J. Vann. *Exploring Speaking-Writing Relationships: Connections and Contrasts.* Urbana: NCTE, 1981.

Larson, Magali Sarfatti. *The Rise of Professionalism: A Sociological Analysis.* Berkeley: U of California P, 1977.

Lather, Patti. *Getting Smart: Feminist Research and Pedagogy with/in the Postmodern.* New York: Routledge, 1991.

Lauer, Janice M. "Composition Studies: Dappled Discipline." *Rhetoric Review* 3 (1984): 20–29.

———. "Disciplinary Formation: The Summer Rhetoric Seminar." *JAC* 18 (1998): 503–8.

Lee, Amy. *Composing Critical Pedagogies: Teaching Writing as Revision.* Urbana: NCTE, 2000.

Leggo, Carl. "Questions I Need to Ask Before I Advise My Students to Write in Their Own Voices." *Rhetoric Review* 10 (1991): 143–52.

Lewiecki-Wilson, Cynthia, and Jeff Sommers. "Professing at the Fault Lines: Composition at Open Admissions Institutions." *CCC* 50 (1999): 438–62.

Lloyd-Jones, Richard. "Who We Were, Who We Should Become." *CCC* 43 (1992): 486–96.

Lu, Min-Zhan. "Redefining the Literate Self: The Politics of Critical Affirmation." *CCC* 51 (1999): 172–94.

Lunsford, Andrea A, and Lisa Ede. "Representing Audience: 'Successful' Discourse and Disciplinary Critique." *CCC* 47 (1996): 167–79.

Macrorie, Ken. *Uptaught.* Rochelle: Hayden, 1970.

Mailloux, Steven. *Rhetorical Power.* Ithaca: Cornell UP, 1989.

Martin, Biddy. "Success and Its Failures." *Women's Studies on the Edge.* Spec. issue of *Differences* 9.3 (1997): 102–31.

Matsuda, Paul Kei. "Composition Studies and ESL Writing: A Disciplinary Division of Labor." *CCC* 50 (1999): 699–721.

Mauk, Johnathon. "Location, Location, Location: The 'Real' (E)states of Being, Writing, and Thinking in Composition." *College English* 65 (2003): 368–88.

McComiskey, Bruce. *Teaching Composition as a Social Process.* Logan: Utah State UP, 2000.

McCrea, Brian. *Addison and Steele Are Dead: The English Department, Its*

Canon, and the Professionalization of Literary Criticism. Newark: U of Delaware P, 1990.

McQuade, Donald, ed. *Linguistics, Stylistics, and the Teaching of Composition.* Akron: L and S; Department of English, U of Akron, 1979.

Messer-Davidow, Ellen. *Disciplining Feminism: From Social Activism to Academic Discourse.* Durham: Duke UP, 2002.

Messer-Davidow, Ellen, David R. Shumway, and David J. Sylvan. *Knowledges: Historical and Critical Studies in Disciplinarity.* Charlottesville: UP of Virginia, 1993.

Micciche, Laura. "The Role of Edited Collections in Composition Studies." *Composition Forum* 12 (2001): 101–24.

Miller, Marilyn M. "The Ecology of Writing." *College English* 48 (1986): 364–75.

Miller, Nancy K. *Getting Personal: Feminist Occasions and Other Autobiographical Acts.* New York: Routledge, 1991.

Miller, Richard E. *As If Learning Mattered: Reforming Higher Education.* Ithaca: Cornell UP, 1998.

Miller, Susan. "Composition as a Cultural Artifact: Rethinking History as Theory." *Writing Theory and Critical Theory.* Ed. John Clifford and John Schilb. New York: MLA, 1994. 19–32.

———. "The Death of the Teacher." *Composition Forum* 6 (1995): 42–52.

———. "How I Teach Writing: How to Teach Writing? To Teach Writing?" *Pedagogy* 1 (2001): 479–88.

———. *Textual Carnivals: The Politics of Composition.* Carbondale: Southern Illinois UP, 1991.

———. *Writing: Process and Product.* Cambridge: Winthrop, 1976.

———. "Writing Theory: : Theory Writing." *Methods and Methodology in Composition Research.* Ed. Gesa Kirsch and Patricia A. Sullivan. Carbondale: Southern Illinois UP, 1992. 62–83.

Mitchell, Donald. "Breakthrough Books on Geography." *Lingua Franca* May/June 1999: 16–17.

Moss, Beverly J. "Theory, Theories, Politics, and Journeys." *Writing Theory and Critical Theory.* Ed. John Clifford and John Schilb. New York: MLA, 1994. 341–47.

Murray, Donald. "Teach Writing as a Process Not Product." *Leaflet* Nov. 1972: 11–14. Rpt. in *Cross-Talk in Comp Theory: A Reader.* Ed. Victor Villanueva Jr. Urbana: NCTE, 1997. 3–6.

———. *Write to Learn.* New York: Holt, 1984.

Myers, Miles, and James Gray, eds. *Theory and Practice in the Teaching of Composition: Processing, Distancing, and Modeling.* Urbana: NCTE, 1983.

Neel, Jasper, ed. *Options for the Teaching of English: Freshman Composition.* New York: MLA, 1978.

Nelms, Gerald. "Reassessing Janet Emig's *The Composing Processes of Twelfth Graders:* An Historical Perspective." *Rhetoric Review* 13 (1994): 108–30.

North, Stephen M. "The Idea of a Writing Center." *College English* 46 (1984): 433–46.

———. *The Making of Knowledge in Composition: Portrait of an Emerging Field.* Upper Montclair: Boynton, 1987.

———. "Revisiting 'The Idea of a Writing Center.'" *Writing Center Journal* 15 (1994): 7–19.

Nystrand, Martin, Stuart Greene, and Jeffrey Wiemelt. "Where Did Composition Studies Come From? An Intellectual History." *Written Communication* 10 (1993): 267–333.

Olson, Gary A. "Resistance and the Work of Theory." Foreword. *Insurrections: Approaches to Resistance in Composition Studies.* Ed. Andrea Greenbaum. Albany: State U of New York P, 2001. xi–xii.

———. "Toward a Post-Process Composition: Abandoning the Rhetoric of Assertion." *Post-Process Theory: Beyond the Writing-Process Paradigm.* Ed. Thomas Kent. Carbondale: Southern Illinois UP, 1999. 7–15.

Paine, Charles. *The Resistant Writer: Rhetoric as Immunity, 1850 to the Present.* Albany: State U of New York P, 1999.

Paley, Karen Surman. *I Writing: The Politics and Practice of Teaching First-Person Writing.* Carbondale: Southern Illinois UP, 2001.

Park, Stephen. *Class Politics: The Movement for the Students' Right to Their Own Language.* Urbana: NCTE, 2000.

Perl, Sondra. "The Composing Processes of Unskilled College Writers." *Research in the Teaching of English* 13 (1979): 317–36.

Petraglia, Joseph. "Is There Life after Process? The Role of Social Scientism in a Changing Discipline." *Post-Process Theory: Beyond the Writing-Process Paradigm.* Ed. Thomas Kent. Carbondale: Southern Illinois UP, 1999. 49–64.

Phelps, Louise Wetherbee. *Composition as a Human Science: Contributions to the Self-Understanding of a Discipline.* New York: Oxford UP, 1988.

———. "Composition Studies." *Encyclopedia of Rhetoric and Composition: Communication from Ancient Times to the Information Age.* Ed. Theresa Enos. New York: Garland, 1996. 123–34.

Phillips, Donna Burns, Ruth Greenberg, and Sharon Gibson. "*College Composition and Communication:* Chronicling a Discipline's Genesis." *CCC* 44 (1993): 443–65.

Postel, Danny. "Hot Type." *Chronicle of Higher Education* Sept. 27, 2002: A17.

Probyn, Elspeth. *Sexing the Self: Gendered Positions in Cultural Studies.* New York: Routledge, 1993.

Ray, Ruth E. *The Practice of Theory: Teacher Research in Composition.* Urbana: NCTE, 1993.

Reither, James A. "Writing and Knowing: Toward Redefining the Writing Process." *College English* 47 (1985): 620–28.

Reynolds, Nedra. "Composition's Imagined Geographies: The Politics of Space in the Frontier, City, and Cyberspace." *CCC* 50 (1998): 12–35.

Rich, Adrienne. "Notes Toward a Politics of Location." *Blood, Bread, and Poetry: Selected Prose, 1979–1985.* New York: Norton, 1986. 210–31.

Riley, Terrance. "The Unpromising Future of Writing Centers." *Writing Center Journal* 15 (1994): 20–34.

Robbins, Bruce. "Oppositional Professionals: Theory and the Narratives of Professionalization." *Consequences of Theory.* Ed. Jonathan Aarac and Barbara Johnson. Baltimore: Johns Hopkins UP, 1991. 1–21.

Robertson, Linda R., Sharon Crowley, and Frank Lentricchia. "The Wyoming Conference Resolution Opposing Unfair Salaries and Working Conditions for Post-Secondary Teachers of Writing. *College English* 49 (1987): 274–80.

Rodriguez, Richard. *Hunger of Memory: The Education of Richard Rodriguez.* New York: Bantam, 1982.

Roen, Duane H., Stuart C. Brown, and Theresa Enos. *Living Rhetoric and Composition: Stories of the Discipline.* Mahwah: Erlbaum, 1999.

Rohman, E. Gordon, and Albert O. Wlecke. *Pre-Writing: The Construction and Application of Models for Concept Formation in Writing.* U.S. Office of Education Cooperative Research Project No. 2174. East Lansing: Michigan State U, 1964. ERIC ED 001 273.

Rose, Mike. *Lives on the Boundary.* New York: Penguin, 1989.

Roskelly, Hephzibah, and Kate Ronald. *Reason to Believe: Romanticism, Pragmatism, and the Teaching of Writing.* Albany: State U of New York P, 1998.

Rosner, Mary, Beth Boehm, and Debra Journet, eds. *History, Reflection, and Narrative: The Professionalization of Composition, 1963–1983.* Stamford: Ablex, 1999.

Royster, Jacqueline Jones. *Traces of a Stream: Literacy and Social Change among African American Women.* Pittsburgh: U of Pittsburgh P, 2000.

———. "When the First Voice You Hear Is Not Your Own." *CCC* 47 (1996): 29–40.

Royster, Jacqueline Jones, and Jean C. Williams. "History in the Spaces Left: African American Presence and Narratives of Composition Studies." *CCC* 50 (1999): 563–84.

Runciman, Lex, and Steven Sher, eds. *Northwest Variety: Personal Essays by Fourteen Northwest Writers.* Corvallis: Arrowood, 1987.

Schell, Eileen E. *Gypsy Academics and Mother-Teachers: Gender, Contingent Labor, and Writing Instruction.* Portsmouth: Boynton, 1998.

Schilb, John. *Between the Lines: Relating Composition Theory and Literary Theory.* Portsmouth: Boynton; Heinemann, 1996.

———. "Getting Disciplined?" *Rhetoric Review* 12 (1994): 398–405.

Schultz, Lucille M. *The Young Composers: Composition's Beginnings in Nineteenth-Century Schools.* Carbondale: Southern Illinois UP, 1999.

Schultz, Lucille M., Chester H. Laine, and Mary C. Savage. "Interaction among School and College Writing Teachers: Toward Recognizing and Remaking Old Patterns." *CCC* 39 (1988): 139–53.

Selzer, Jack. E-mail to the author. Aug. 14, 2002.

———. "Exploring Options in Composing." *CCC* 35 (1984): 276–84.

Shaughnessy, Mina P. "Basic Writing." *Teaching Composition: Ten Bibliographical Essays.* Ed. Gary Tate. Fort Worth: Texas Christian UP, 1976. 137–67.

———. *Errors and Expectations: A Guide for the Teacher of Basic Writing.* New York: Oxford UP, 1977.

Sirc, Geoffrey. *English Composition as a Happening.* Logan: Utah State UP, 2002.

———. "Never Mind the Tagmemics, Where's the Sex Pistols?" *CCC* 48 (1997): 9–29.

Sledd, James. "Return to Service." *Composition Studies* 28 (2000): 11–32.

———. "Why the Wyoming Resolution Had to Be Emasculated: A History and a Quixotism." *JAC* 11 (1991): 269–81.

Sommers, Nancy. "Revision Strategies of Student Writers and Experienced Adult Writers." *CCC* 31 (1980): 378–88.

Sosnoski, James J. *Modern Skeletons in Postmodern Closets: A Cultural Studies Alternative.* Charlottesville: UP of Virginia, 1995.

———. *Token Professionals and Master Critics: A Critique of Orthodoxy in Literary Studies.* Albany: State U of New York P, 1994.

Sternglass, Marilyn S. *Time to Know Them: A Longitudinal Study of Writing and Learning at the College Level.* Mahwah: Erlbaum, 1997.

"Students' Right to Their Own Language." *CCC* 25 (1974): 1–32.

Sturken, Marita. *Tangled Memories: The Vietnam War, the AIDS Epidemic, and the Politics of Remembering.* Berkeley: U of California P, 1997.

Sullivan, Francis J., Arabella Lyon, Dennis Lebofsky, Susan Wells, and Eli Goldblatt. "Student Needs and Strong Composition: The Dialectics of Writing Program Reform." *CCC* 48 (1997): 372–91.

Tate, Gary, ed. *Teaching Composition: Ten Bibliographic Essays.* Fort Worth: Texas Christian UP, 1976.

Taylor, Marcy, and Jennifer L. Holberg. "'Tales of Neglect and Sadism': Disciplinarity and the Figuring of the Graduate Student in Composition." *CCC* 50 (1999): 607–25.

Thaiss, Chris. E-mail to the author. June 14, 2001.

Tompkins, Jane. *A Life in School: What the Teacher Learned.* Reading: Addison, 1996.

Trimbur, John. *The Call to Write.* New York: Longman, 1998.

———. "Close Reading: Accounting for My Life Teaching Writing." *Living*

Rhetoric and Composition: Stories of the Discipline. Ed. Duane H. Roen, Stuart C. Brown, and Theresa Enos. Mahwah: Erlbaum, 1999. 129–41.

———. "Composition and the Circulation of Writing." *CCC* 52 (2000): 188–219.

———. "In the Beginning Was the Sixties: A Conversation with Richard Ohmann." *Pre/Text* 13 (1992): 134–47.

———. "Resistance as Tragic Trope." *Insurrections: Approaches to Resistance in Composition Studies.* Ed. Andrea Greenbaum. Albany: State U of New York P, 2001. 3–15.

———. "Writing Instruction and the Politics of Professionalization." *Composition in the Twenty-First Century: Crisis and Change.* Ed. Lynn Z. Bloom, Donald A. Daiker, and Edward M. White. Carbondale: Southern Illinois UP, 1996. 133–45.

Trinh T. Minh-ha. *Woman, Native, Other.* Bloomington: Indiana UP, 1989.

Troyka, Lynn Quitman. "New Plan for CCCC Program Proposals." *College English* 40 (1979): 936.

Varnum, Robin. *Fencing with Words: A History of Writing Instruction at Amherst College During the Era of Theodore Baird, 1938–1966.* Urbana, NCTE, 1996.

Villanueva, Victor, Jr. *Bootstraps: From an American Academic of Color.* Urbana: NCTE, 1993.

———, ed. *Cross-Talk in Comp Theory: A Reader.* Urbana: NCTE, 1997.

Vitanza, Victor J. "Three Countertheses: Or, A Critical In(ter)vention into Composition Theories and Pedagogies." *Contending with Words: Composition and Rhetoric in a Postmodern Age.* Ed. Patricia Harkin and John Schilb. New York: MLA, 1991. 139–72.

Wall, Susan. "'Where Your Treasure Is': Accounting for Differences in Our Talk about Teaching." *Taking Stock: The Writing Process Movement in the '90s.* Ed Lad Tobin and Thomas Newkirk. Portsmouth: Heinemann-Boynton. 239–60.

Wallace, David L., and Helen Rothschild Ewald. *Mutuality in the Rhetoric and Composition Classroom.* Carbondale: Southern Illinois UP, 2000.

Warnock, John. "The Discipline and the Profession: *It's a Doggy Dog World.*" *Visions and Re-Visions in Rhetoric and Composition.* Ed. James D. Williams. Carbondale: Southern Illinois UP, 2002. 69–86.

———. E-mail to the author. July 29, 2001.

Watkins, Evan. *Work Time: English Departments and the Circulation of Cultural Value.* Stanford: Stanford UP, 1989.

Weathers, Winston. "Grammars of Style: New Options in Composition." *Rhetoric and Composition: A Sourcebook for Teachers and Writers.* Ed. Richard Graves. Upper Montclair: Boynton, 1984. 133–47.

Welch, Nancy. *Getting Restless: Rethinking Revision in Writing Instruction.* Portsmouth: Heinemann-Boynton, 1997.

INDEX

Lisa Ede is a professor of English and the director of the Center for Writing and Learning at Oregon State University. She is the author of *Work in Progress: A Guide to Academic Writing and Revising,* now in its sixth edition, and the editor of *On Writing Research: The Braddock Award Essays, 1975–1998.* With Andrea A. Lunsford, she coauthored *Singular Texts/Plural Authors: Perspectives on Collaborative Writing* and coedited *Selected Essays of Robert J. Connors.* With Connors and Lunsford, Ede also coedited *Essays on Classical Rhetoric and Modern Discourse,* which won the 1985 MLA Mina P. Shaughnessy Award. Her other awards include the 1985 CCCC Braddock Award and the 1990 National Writing Centers Association Award.